Dedicated to
the people of Missouri

The
MISSOURI
Quick-Fact Book

Compiled by
Midwest Research Institute
and Capper Press

Capper Press
Topeka, Kansas

Published by	Capper Press
Copyright	Copyright © 1991 by Capper Press

Compiled by	Midwest Research Institute 425 Volker Boulevard, Kansas City, Missouri 64110 Capper Press 616 Jefferson, Topeka, Kansas 66607
Acknowledgment	We at Capper Press and Midwest Research Institute would like to thank the state agencies, chambers of commerce, organizations, and individuals who graciously provided so much information and assistance in the publication of this book.
Midwest Research Institute	Linda W. Thornton, *Project Director* Gary Sage, *Business Manager* Robert E. Gustafson, *Creative Director* LaDene Morton, *Researcher* James Becker, *Researcher* Rita Roche, *Proofreader*
Capper Press	Ron Joler, *Project Director* Tammy R. Dodson, *Series Editor* Diana J. Edwardson, *Production Coordinator*
Book Design by	The Amundson Group 9903 West 70th Terr., Shawnee Mission, KS 66203
The Amundson Group	Jerry Amundson, *Designer* Eric Amundson, *Production Manager* Beverly Amundson, *Production Coordinator*
Cover Photo	Courtesy of the Missouri Division of Tourism
Original Art by	Diana J. Edwardson
Softcover Edition	ISBN 0-941678-23-7 Softcover Edition
Hardcover Edition	ISBN 0-941678-24-5 Hardcover Edition
First Printing	June 1991
	Printed and bound in the United States of America

Missouri is the Gateway to the West, and a familiar symbol of the state is the spectacular Gateway Arch in St. Louis. But did you also know that Missouri has over 15,000 miles of urban highway and 104,200 miles of rural highway? Or that Walt Disney was raised on a farm near Marceline? Or that Missouri is ranked 16th among the 50 states in manufacturing employment?

With *The Missouri Quick-Fact Book*, you don't have to dig through 50 different volumes to find the facts you need and want to know – we've already done the research for you! *The Missouri Quick-Fact Book* is a compilation of key information, statistics, charts, and fun facts presented in one reference volume.

This fact book features an easy-to-read format, and the chapter title and subject area are clearly marked at the top of each page for handy reference. The sidebars allow you to thumb through the pages to scan for quick facts. Major topics are highlighted in color on each page so you can easily locate information.

The Missouri Quick-Fact Book is perfect for educators, students, librarians, business executives, tourists, residents of the state, and individuals who want the facts about Missouri in one convenient edition. The fact book includes state symbols, chronology of historical events, list of county seats, population statistics, tourist attractions, arts programs, crop and livestock data, endangered Missouri wildlife, maps, charts, and more. Whether life-long residents of the state or visitors, readers will enjoy discovering the many wonderful surprises that Missouri has to offer.

Educators will find *The Missouri Quick-Fact Book* to be a beneficial teaching supplement for history, English, geography, geology, social studies, and other classroom subjects as well as an indispensable reference book for the library. Students will find the graphs and data especially useful for researching and writing reports. And all Missourians, regardless of age or profession, will enjoy learning more about their state.

The Missouri Quick-Fact Book is the result of a team project between Capper Press and the Midwest Research Institute.

Capper Press, owned by Stauffer Communications, Inc., in Topeka, Kansas, is the book publishing division of *Capper's* magazine (formerly *Capper's Weekly*), one of the oldest and most-loved publications in America. *Capper's* has been printed for more than 110 years and reaches a subscriber base of nearly 400,000 readers throughout the Midwest and the United States.

Midwest Research Institute, headquartered in Kansas City, Missouri, is an independent, not-for-profit organization that has become one of the nation's leading research institutes. Founded in 1944 by a group of Midwestern civic, business, and technical leaders, Midwest Research Institute performs and manages research and

preface

development programs for clients in business, industry, government, and for other public and private sector groups.

In doing the research for this book, we were fortunate to have talked with people from many organizations throughout Missouri. We would like to say a heartfelt thank you to the representatives and officials at the state agencies and companies who so graciously took time out to provide us with assistance and information. The Missouri Secretary of State's Office and the Missouri Department of Economic Development deserve recognition and thanks for their valuable assistance.

Thanks also goes to the numerous chamber of commerce representatives with whom we spoke about their hometowns. With their help we were able to pass along to the readers a flavor of the delightful attractions, festivals, and historical sites across the state. Whether a small town or metropolitan area, the sense of hometown pride is strong in Missouri.

Missouri is a state of many images: bright red and orange autumn leaves, the gently rolling hills of the Ozarks, the columns at the University of Missouri-Columbia, riverboats plying the Mississippi, children eating hot dogs at a Kansas City Royals or St. Louis Cardinals game, and the picturesque Bollinger Mill that is a link to the past. Our goal in producing this fact book was to showcase the state and provide a sense of the strength and character that is so predominant in Missouri.

The Missouri Quick-Fact Book is an almanac you will enjoy referring to again and again. We're sure you'll always find some interesting tidbit of information about Missouri, and that you will often say (as we did many times in the making of this book), "I didn't know that!"

Tammy R. Dodson
Capper Press

To order additional copies of The Missouri Quick-Fact Book, please call toll-free 1-800-777-7171, Ext. 107.

table of contents

The
MISSOURI
Quick-Fact Book

CHAPTER 1
INTRODUCTION

State Symbols • County Seats
County Map • Mileage Chart
Highway Map • Trivia

MISSOURI

INTRODUCTION

Photo courtesy of The Plaza Association.

CHAPTER OPENER PHOTO: The Neptune fountain in Kansas City's Country Club Plaza is only one of the many beautiful fountains on the Plaza. The fountains welcome visitors from around the world.

M issouri got its name from a tribe of Sioux Indians called Missouris. The word "Missouri" is believed to come from the Indian term "town of the large canoes." Others believe it means "muddy waters." From the first Indians to set foot on Missouri soil to those looking for a new place to live, thousands of people have discovered the magic and beauty of the state.

Behind every Missouri vehicle is the proud nickname the state has inherited, "Show Me State." This saying was popular in poems and songs of the 1890s. During an 1899 speech in Philadelphia, Congressman Willard D. Vandiver of Cape Girardeau County made the saying famous when he used the phrase, "I'm from Missouri; you've got to show me." Since then, Missouri has shown the nation what a fine state it is. From the beautiful countryside to the strong personalities of the state, Missouri has blossomed into one of the most prosperous states in the country.

Missouri may be known for its troubled history, but the Missouri of today is a fascinating place. Bustling cities like St. Louis and Kansas City on the east and west sides of the state appropriately frame the state. Inside this framework are small towns that make up the heart of Missouri. The pulse of these intimate communities can be felt in the cities and the people across the state.

Young people grow up in Missouri with a sense of pride unique to the state. Fine universities and learning centers dot the state to educate the next generations to lead Missouri into the future. For the students of the state, excellent opportunities await, for Missouri is a leader in business and rarely does one need to look outside the state to find a career. Missouri's location, in the central part of the country, is perfect for business growth.

Missouri's people are a breed apart. Through strength and perseverance the citizens have made a state worth living in. The population continues to increase. Missouri is the second-largest state bordering the Mississippi River (after Minnesota) and is larger than any state lying east of the Mississippi. For the residents of the state, living in Missouri is special. The diverse landscape is one of the feature attractions of the state. There are caves to explore, rivers to canoe, trails to be hiked and so much more to see and do in Missouri.

Some of the images of Missouri include the fiery beauty of the fall foliage, clear cool streams, the buzzing metropolis, the peaceful backwoods trail, a spirited crowd at a local football game, the sights and sounds at area crafts shows – the list is endless. A wide range of outdoor activities await travelers and residents alike. Tourism is one of the largest industries in Missouri and there is no doubt why it is so prosperous, because in any direction there is something to see and do. Discover the friendly folks at an area festival, or explore an ancient cave and see why Missouri is known as the "Show Me State." ❏

fun facts

Show Me Slogan

Missouri is known as the "Show Me State." The slogan is attributed to Congressman William Duncan Vandiver. In a speech in Philadelphia in 1899 he said, "... frothy eloquence neither convinces me nor satisfies me. I am from Missouri. You have got to show me."

Continuing Debate

The pronunciation of the state's name has garnered debate. Natives and visitors alike cannot agree on the correct pronunciation of the state's name. Is it "Missouree" or "Missourah"?

Victorious Day

The night of the 1948 Presidential election, the election returns were coming in and the *Chicago Tribune* ran the banner headline, "Dewey Defeats Truman," Harry S Truman was staying at The Elms in Excelsior Springs. He went to bed believing he had lost the election, but awoke to find that he was the President of the United States.

Shop Till You Drop

The Country Club Plaza in Kansas City is considered to be the nation's first major shopping center planned especially for automobile traffic. Construction on the Plaza began in 1922.

Bridge Over Troubled Waters

The first bridge across the Missouri River connecting Jefferson City with the northern half of the state was opened to horse and buggy traffic in February 1896. The bridge assured Jefferson City remained the capital.

Big Bad Wolf

The Timber Wolf at Kansas City's Worlds of Fun was ranked second best roller coaster in the world in 1990. There is a 95-foot drop, hairpin turns, speeds of 53 mph, and an unusual 560-degree upward spiraling helix. Installed in 1989, the Timber Wolf has had 1,022,957 total passengers so far. The cost of the wooden coaster was $3 million.

Civil War Scars

The Battlefield at Lexington is one of the few Civil War battlefields never cultivated. The trenches and earthworks are still visible.

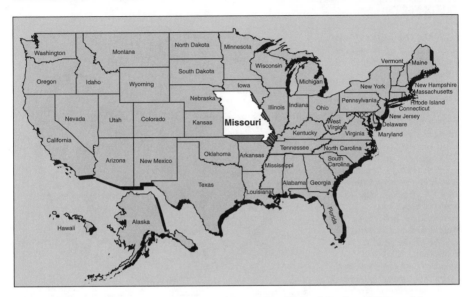

Missouri is located in the Midwestern part of the United States. Missouri is bordered by Iowa, Arkansas, Illinois, Kentucky, Tennessee, Nebraska, Kansas, and Oklahoma. Missouri is one of only two states in the nation touched by eight states.

Date admitted into the Union: August 10, 1821, as the 24th state.
Capital City: Jefferson City.
Population: 5,117,073 (1990).
Major Cities: St. Louis, Kansas City, Springfield, Independence, and Joplin.
Major Businesses and Industries: Manufacturing, tourism, agriculture, and trade.
Geographic Size: 69,674 square miles. Missouri ranks 19th in size.
Highest Point: The Taum Sauk Mountain, located in Iron County in the St. Francois Mountain area, is 1,772 feet above sea level.
Lowest Point: In southeast Missouri where the St. Francis River leaves the state it is 205 feet.
Longitude and Latitude: With the exception of the "bootheel," Missouri lies between 36° 30' and 40° 30' north latitude and mainly between the ninety-first and ninety-fifth meridians west longitude.
Time Zones: Missouri is located in the Central Time Zone.
Area Codes: The northern part of the state is in the 816 Area Code; the southwest portion is in the 314 Area Code; and the southeastern corner is in the 417 Area Code.
Nickname: "Show Me" State.
State motto: "Salus populi supreme lex esto," Latin for "let the good (or welfare) of the people be the supreme law."
State song: "Missouri Waltz."
State tree: Flowering dogwood.
State flower: The blossom of the hawthorn crataegus.
State bird: The native bluebird.

QUICK FACTS:

On the right of the Great Seal of Missouri is the United States coat-of-arms containing the bald eagle, and in its claws are arrows and olive branches signifying that the power of war and peace lies with the U.S. government.

A grizzly bear and a silver crescent moon are on the left side of the shield. The crescent symbolizes Missouri at the time of the state seal's creation. It also symbolizes the "second son," meaning Missouri was the second state formed out of the Louisiana Territory.

The shield is encircled by a belt inscribed with the state's motto. The two grizzlies symbolize the state's strength and its citizens' bravery. Below the scroll are the Roman numerals for the year 1820, the year Missouri began its functions as a state.

The helmet above the shield represents state sovereignty, and the large star atop the helmet surrounded by 23 smaller stars signifies Missouri's status as the 24th state. The cloud around the large star indicates the problems Missouri had in becoming a state.

Motto

"Salus Populi Suprema Lex Esto," translated from Latin, means "Let the good (or welfare) of the people be the supreme law."

Song

The "Missouri Waltz" was adopted by the General Assembly on June 30, 1949. The song came from a melody by John V. Eppel and was arranged by Frederic Knight Logan with lyrics written by J.R. Shannon.

The song was first published in 1914 but did not sell well initially. Sales increased substantially after Missourian Harry S Truman became president as it was reported that the "Missouri Waltz" was his favorite song.

Flag

The official flag was adopted on March 22, 1913. The flag consists of three large horizontal stripes of red, white, and blue. These were thought to represent valor, purity, vigilance, and justice. In the center white stripe is the Missouri coat-of-arms, circled by a blue band containing 24 stars.

Tree

The flowering dogwood, which is scientifically known as *Cornus Florida L.*, became the official tree on June 20, 1955. The tree sprouts tiny greenish-yellow flowers in clusters, with each flower surrounded by four white petals.

Mineral

Galena was adopted as the official mineral on July 21, 1967. Galena, which is a major source of lead ore, recognizes Missouri's status as the nation's number one producer of lead. Galena is dark gray in color. Rich deposits have been found in the Joplin-Granby area in southwest Missouri as well as Crawford, Washington, Iron, and Reynolds counties.

Insect

The honeybee was declared the official insect by Gov. John Ashcroft, who signed a bill on July 3, 1985. The scientific name is *apis mellifera*.

Illustration by Diana J. Edwardson.

QUICK FACTS:

The Great Seal of the State of Missouri was adopted by the Missouri General Assembly on Jan. 11, 1822.

The Missouri flag was designed by the late Mrs. Marie Elizabeth Watkins Oliver, wife of former State Senator R.B. Oliver.

The honeybee is common in Missouri and is often cultivated by beekeepers for honey production.

The native bluebird was named the official state bird of Missouri on March 30, 1927. The bluebird is common in Missouri from early spring until late November.

The four columns on the front portico of the Governor's Mansion were quarried in Iron County and started the tradition of each First Family leaving a gift to the Mansion.

The geographic center of Missouri is in Miller County, 20 miles southwest of Jefferson City.

state symbols

QUICK FACTS:

The white hawthorn blossom, a member of the great rose family, was named the official flower by Governor Arthur M. Hyde, who signed a bill on March 16, 1923. The scientific name, crataegus, means strength. More than 75 species of the hawthorn grow in Missouri, especially in the Ozarks.

On March 22, 1915, the 48th General Assembly set aside the third Wednesday in October each year as "Missouri Day."

Mozarkite's beauty is enhanced by cutting and polishing it into ornamental shapes for jewelry.

Missouri's climate may be described as humid continental with long summers and variable weather conditions. About 46% of the annual precipitation in the northwest occurs during the May-August crop growing months, compared with 34% in the southeast.

The oldest visible objects in Missouri are the igneous rocks (granite and porphyres) that appear in the southeastern part of the state.

Illustration by Diana J. Edwardson.

Rock

Mozarkite was adopted as the official state rock on July 21, 1967. The mozarkite appears in a variety of colors. Mozarkite is most commonly found in Benton County.

Fossil

The crinoid became the state's official fossil on June 16, 1989, after a four-year effort by a group of school students. The crinoid is a mineralization of an animal which was called the "sea lilly" because of its plant-like appearance. The crinoid that covered Missouri lived in the ocean over 250 million years ago.

Missouri Day

The third Wednesday of October each year is designated as "Missouri Day." Missouri Day was established due to the efforts of Mrs. Anna Brosius Korn, a native Missourian, and is a time for schools and Missourians to honor the state.

Illustration by Diana J. Edwardson.

State Capitol

The present capitol was completed in 1917. It is the third capitol in Jefferson City and the sixth in Missouri history.

The present capitol was constructed for $4,125,000. It is five stories high, 437 feet long, 300 feet wide in the center and 200 feet wide in the wings. The dome is 238 feet high and atop the dome is a bronze statue of Ceres, a goddess of vegetation. The height of the wings is 88 feet. It includes 500,000 square feet of floor space.

The architectural features include eight 48-foot columns on the south portico and six 40-foot columns on the north side, and its 30-foot-wide grand stairway. The bronze front doors are each 13 by 18 feet.

One of the popular attractions is a series of Thomas Hart Benton murals in the third floor House of Representatives lounge. Numerous paintings, pediments, and friezes decorate the capitol's interior.

Heroic bronze figures depicting Missouri's two great rivers, the Mississippi and the Missouri, and a 13-foot statue of Thomas Jefferson dominate the south entrance of the capitol. A bronze relief depicting the signing of the Louisiana Purchase by Livingston, Monroe, and Marbois and the Fountain of the Centaurs are the most outstanding features on the north capitol grounds.

The Governor's Mansion in Jefferson City was built in 1826. Designed by George Ingham Barnett, the Governor's Mansion is an outstanding example of Renaissance Revival architecture with Italianate and French influences. Construction took eight months and the total cost was $74,000.

The Capitol's first floor features the State Museum exhibiting memorabilia of Missouri's past. Displays depict the state's industrial and agricultural progress, including Missouri's role in the Space Age.

Old Fiddlers' contests are a popular part of many festivals in the state and Missourians of all ages enjoy the music of this versatile instrument.

county seats

County	County Seat	County	County Seat
Adair	Kirksville	Howell	West Plains
Andrew	Savannah	Iron	Ironton
Atchison	Rock Port	Jackson	Independence
Audrain	Mexico	Jasper	Carthage
Barry	Cassville	Jefferson	Hillsboro
Barton	Lamar	Johnson	Warrensburg
Bates	Butler	Knox	Edina
Benton	Warsaw	Laclede	Lebanon
Bollinger	Marble Hill	Lafayette	Lexington
Boone	Columbia	Lawrence	Mount Vernon
Buchanan	St. Joseph	Lewis	Monticello
Butler	Poplar Bluff	Lincoln	Troy
Caldwell	Kingston	Linn	Linneus
Callaway	Fulton	Livingston	Chillicothe
Camden	Camdenton	Macon	Macon
Cape Girardeau	Jackson	Madison	Fredericktown
Carroll	Carrollton	Maries	Vienna
Carter	Van Buren	Marion	Palmyra
Cass	Harrisonville	McDonald	Pineville
Cedar	Stockton	Mercer	Princeton
Chariton	Keytesville	Miller	Tuscumbia
Christian	Ozark	Mississippi	Charleston
Clark	Kahoka	Moniteau	California
Clay	Liberty	Monroe	Paris
Clinton	Plattsburg	Montgomery	Montgomery City
Cole	Jefferson City	Morgan	Versailles
Cooper	Boonville	New Madrid	New Madrid
Crawford	Steelville	Newton	Neosho
Dade	Greenfield	Nodaway	Maryville
Dallas	Buffalo	Oregon	Alton
Daviess	Gallatin	Osage	Linn
DeKalb	Maysville	Ozark	Gainesville
Dent	Salem	Pemiscot	Caruthersville
Douglas	Ava	Perry	Perryville
Dunklin	Kennett	Pettis	Sedalia
Franklin	Union	Phelps	Rolla
Gasconade	Hermann	Pike	Bowling Green
Gentry	Albany	Platte	Platte City
Greene	Springfield	Polk	Bolivar
Grundy	Trenton	Pulaski	Waynesville
Harrison	Bethany	Putnam	Unionville
Henry	Clinton	Ralls	New London
Hickory	Hermitage	Randolph	Huntsville
Holt	Oregon	Ray	Richmond
Howard	Fayette	Reynolds	Centerville

County	County Seat	County	County Seat
St. Clair	Osceola	Taney	Forsyth
St. Francois	Farmington	Texas	Houston
St. Louis	Clayton	Vernon	Nevada
Ste. Genevieve	Ste. Genevieve	Warren	Warrenton
Saline	Marshall	Washington	Potosi
Schuyler	Lancaster	Wayne	Greenville
Scotland	Memphis	Webster	Marshfield
Scott	Benton	Worth	Grant City
Shannon	Eminence	Wright	Hartville
Shelby	Shelbyville	City of St. Louis	St. Louis
Stoddard	Bloomfield		
Stone	Galena	*Source: "1989-1990 Missouri Roster,"*	
Sullivan	Milan	*Office of Secretary of State.*	

MISSOURI COUNTIES

Source: Missouri Highway and Transportation Commission.

mileage chart

	CAPE GIRARDEAU	JEFFERSON CITY	KANSAS CITY	ST. LOUIS	SPRING-FIELD
Branson	275	170	211	251	43
Camdenton	232	59	153	175	74
Cape Girardeau	X	220	350	115	255
Chillicothe	344	150	91	238	208
Columbia	225	31	126	125	162
Hannibal	217	106	201	117	237
Jefferson City	220	X	148	122	133
Joplin	321	202	157	284	70
Kansas City	350	148	X	252	167
Kirksville	304	122	158	204	253
Lebanon	218	84	176	163	55
Maryville	448	248	95	348	260
Mexico	212	48	165	111	181
Moberly	258	66	125	155	198
Poplar Bluff	78	205	360	153	194
Rolla	158	62	210	106	110
St. Joseph	408	208	55	307	219
St. Louis	115	122	252	X	215
Ste. Genevieve	61	168	298	54	232
Salem	136	89	237	123	130
Sedalia	279	61	87	186	118
Sikeston	33	248	380	135	241
Springfield	255	133	167	215	X
Van Buren	109	167	314	164	91

Example: To determine the number of miles between Kansas City and Joplin, find Joplin on the left side of the chart and read across to find the number listed under the Kansas City column. The distance is 157 miles.

Source: Missouri Highway and Transportation Commission.

MISSOURI HIGHWAYS

Source: Missouri Highway and Transportation Commission.

Highway System in Missouri

Missouri has developed an efficient highway system. Ten interstate highways with more than 1,150 miles of roadway cross the state. Interstate 70 is a vital east-west link between the metropolitan St. Louis and Kansas City areas. Interstate 44 angles through Joplin and Springfield and connects the southwest portion of the state with St. Louis. Interstate 55 winds through the state's bootheel region in the southeast section.

The state's central location in the United States allows goods to be easily transported by commercial tailers and semitrailers. Transporting raw materials and finished products by highway promotes economic development. Tourists find Missouri's highway system enables them to quickly reach their destinations.

Missouri is one of two states in the nation to record 5,000 caves.

Hannibal's population in 1830 was 30; by 1850 it was 2,020.

The 1904 World's Fair created a number of firsts for St. Louis: the first hot dog, the first ice cream cone, and the first iced tea. In the same year, the first Olympiad to be held in the United States was held in St. Louis.

The Eads Bridge over the Mississippi River, which was completed in 1874, was the first arched steel truss bridge in the world.

Maple syrup was commonly used as a cure for colds and tuberculosis in colonial Ste. Genevieve.

In 1860, sugar sold for 10¢ a pound, tobacco was 30¢, whiskey 25¢ per gallon, and city lots sold for $25 per lot.

The famous Route 66 was known as "America's Main Street" and went through St. Louis, Rolla, Joplin, and Springfield. This link from Chicago to the Santa Monica pier opened in 1929 and survived until the mid-1960s when the interstate highway system replaced it.

Photo courtesy of Anheuser-Busch Brewery.

The world-famous Budweiser Clydesdales, representatives of Anheuser-Busch for more than 50 years, make 300 appearances annually, logging more than 90,000 miles. More than 4,000 requests are received for the hitch each year.

Photo courtesy of Convention and Visitors Bureau of Greater Kansas City.
Kansas City is still one of the best cities in the nation to hear great jazz.

Jazz enthusiasts say that Kansas City jazz "uses more saxophones and always has background riffs" that make it unique. Kansas City is the home of the "12th Street Rag" by composer Scott Joplin.

The most famous trial in the Old West unfolded in Gallatin from August 20 through September 6, 1883, when Frank James faced charges of robbery and murders of conductor William Westfall and stonemason Frank McMillan during the 1881 train robbery in Gallatin.

In the early 1800s, James Yoachum settled at the west edge of what is now Lakeview with his Delaware Indian wife. During this time it is believed that James Yoachum and his family minted a now historic silver dollar that was used as currency among the hillfolk.

The University of Missouri had the first display of incandescent lighting west of the Mississippi, on Francis Quadrangle, using a generator donated by Thomas Edison.

The Branson area offers more full-length music shows than Nashville.

St. Louis' Gateway Arch has a north and south tram, each consisting of eight capsules. Each capsule holds five people and is equipped with a leveling device to keep passengers in an upright position during the four-minute ride to the top of the Arch, which is 630 feet in the air.

The name **"Ozarks"** has an obscure origin – possibly a corruption of the French expression "Aux Arkansas" meaning "to the Arkansas (Mountains)" and shortened to Aux Arks. Or, it may be a corruption of "Aux Arcs" meaning "with bows" and referring to an Indian tribe.

Perry County has the largest total of caves in Missouri: 629.

An average of nearly 2.5 million visitors come to the Branson area each year.

The Artesian Park in the southwest part of Clinton was the entertainment center of the surrounding area for many years. Artesian Park boasted a "great artesian white sulphur spring well" that spurted water high into the air.

The first fair held in the Platte Purchase area at St. Joseph began October 28, 1867, and brought in net receipts of $234.55. Net receipts of the 1868 fair jumped to $2,030.91.

The American Royal got its start when cattle breeders began boosting their personal stock by showing it near the stockyards in Kansas City and organizing in groups to promote the breeds.

Photo courtesy of the Missouri State Fair.
One of the more unusual events at the Missouri State Fair: chicken judging.

Photo courtesy of the Branson / Lakes Area Chamber of Commerce.
Close encounters are common at Exotic Animal Paradise near Springfield.

In 1979, Worlds of Fun in Kansas City gave its 100 millionth ride. In 1986, the park gave its 200 millionth ride.

Red Foley, the star of "Ozark Jubilee," was a popular performer fresh from the Grand Ole Opry in Nashville. With the popularity soaring, the show soon featured guests such as Johnny Cash, Chet Atkins, Ernest Tubb, Gene Autry, and Barbara Mandrell.

Walt Disney created Mickey Mouse in 1928. Mickey was supposed to appear in the silent cartoon entitled "Plane Crazy." However, before the cartoon could be released, sound came to motion pictures. Thus, Mickey made his screen debut in "Steamboat Willie," the world's first synchronized sound cartoon.

The Battle of Westport was the last Civil War battle west of the Mississippi River.

The first daily newspaper in the country was the *St. Louis Herald* started in 1834.

Kansas City is the only major city within 200 miles of both the geographic and population centers of the nation.

Gallatin had the first college in the state to open its doors to women, giving them equal privileges with men.

Anheuser-Busch Brewery, One Busch Place, St. Louis 63118-1852.

Branson/Lakes Area Chamber of Commerce, P.O. Box 220, Branson 65616.

Clinton Area Chamber of Commerce, 200 S. Main, Clinton 64735.

Convention and Visitors Bureau of Greater Kansas City, 1100 Main Street, Suite 2550, Kansas City, MO 64105.

Excelsior Springs Chamber of Commerce, 101 E. Broadway, Excelsior Springs 64024.

Gallatin Publishing Company, P.O. Box 37, Gallatin 64640.

Kimberling City Chamber of Commerce, N. Hwy 13, P.O. Box 495, Kimberling City 65686.

Lexington Chamber of Commerce, 1127 Main St., Lexington 64067.

"Missouri Day by Day," State Historical Society of Missouri, 1020 Lowry, Columbia 65201.

Missouri Department of Natural Resources, P.O. Box 176, Jefferson City 65102.

Missouri Highway and Transportation Commission, P.O. Box 270, Jefferson City 65102.

Missouri State Fair, Box 111, Sedalia 65301.

"The Official Manual, State of Missouri, 1989-1990," Secretary of State's Department, 208 State Capitol, Jefferson City 65102.

The Plaza Merchants Association, 4625 Wornall Rd., Kansas City, MO 64112.

Rolla Area Chamber of Commerce, 102 W. 9th, Rolla 65401.

The Ste. Genevieve Herald, P.O. Box 447, 330 Market St., Ste Genevieve 63670.

Springfield Chamber of Commerce, 320 N. Jefferson, P.O. Box 1687, Springfield 65801.

State Historical Society of Missouri, 1020 Lowry, Columbia 65201.

The Walt Disney Company, 500 South Buena Vista Street, Burbank, CA 91521.

Waynesville-St. Robert Chamber of Commerce, P.O. Box 6, Waynesville 65583.

Worlds of Fun, 4545 Worlds of Fun Ave., Kansas City, MO 64161.

CHAPTER 2

HISTORY

Missouri History • Timeline
Trails • Forts
Major Civil War Battles • Museums
Historical Attractions

Photo courtesy of St. Joseph Area Chamber of Commerce.

CHAPTER OPENER PHOTO: The Pony Express was a vital part of Missouri's history. This statue in St. Joseph commemorates those daring young riders and the mark they made on the state and the nation.

B orn out of land that was unwanted by the French and the Spanish, Missouri has become an industrial and agricultural giant today. Through years of difficulty and turmoil, the people of the state have joined to make a promising home for future generations. Just as the pioneers who settled the state had envisioned, Missouri has blossomed. The history of the state has been glamorized at times by colorful characters and unusual incidents, but throughout time Missouri has maintained a sense of dignity and honor.

Early Indian tribes in Missouri included the Osage, Missouri, Sac and Fox, Delaware, and Shawnee. When French fur traders ventured into the area, Indians began commerce with the whites. Upon encroachment by the whites, the Indians were forced out of this rich land into surrounding areas. The last major Indian episode in Missouri was the tragic removal of the Cherokee from their eastern homelands through Missouri on the Trail of Tears.

The Louis and Clark Expedition organized by Thomas Jefferson after the Louisiana Purchase was the largest undertaking of its kind in the history of the United States. Traveling up the Missouri River, the team made many camps across Missouri. On August 10, 1821, Missouri entered the Union as a slave state. During this time the state was growing tremendously. Many trails were blazed in the state's early years. The Oregon Trail opened and thousands of settlers and fortune hunters passed through Missouri. The rough and tumble Pony Express, with its young riders and their daring feats, gained a great deal of attraction for the state.

As soon as Missouri started to get a foothold on statehood the Civil War began and Missouri was ripped apart. William Quantrill raided many towns for the Union cause, then crossed into Kansas to sack Lawrence. Many residents were against slavery. Governor Claiborne F. Jackson was strongly in favor of the south and wanted to secede. However, a vote was taken and Missouri remained with the Union. Missouri played an important role in the Civil War and many battles were fought in the state.

After the Civil War, the state began to rebuild and grow. But all was not quiet. Frank and Jesse James as well as other outlaws such as the Younger brothers began robbing banks and holding up trains. Missouri's rough road to adulthood was not getting any smoother.

After the turn of the century, a progressive government lead the state into prosperous times. During World War II, Missouri bounded out of the ragged Depression years. Following the leadership of Harry Truman in the 1940s, Missouri gained recognition as a powerful and progressive state, hosting both metropolitan giants as well as smaller rural communities.

Missouri has truly deserved the slogan of "Show Me State." Through the state's scarred past has emerged a prosperous future. ❏

Riders Up | The first Pony Express rider on the inaugural run west from St. Joseph was Johnny Fry. The first eastbound rider from California was James Randall.

Monumental Gift | Thomas Jefferson's original tombstone was designed by Thomas Jefferson and given to the University of Missouri in Columbia by the family after the U.S. Congress decided it should be moved from Monticello and replaced by a grander one.

The Blue and the Gray | The National Cemetery in Springfield is the only cemetery where both Union and Confederate forces are buried side by side.

Ready, Aim, Fire | Dueling was common in Missouri Territory, and an island in the Mississippi River off St. Louis – a site often used for such confrontations – was known as "Bloody Island."

Stick 'Em Up | The Jesse James Bank and Museum in Liberty was the site of the world's first daylight bank robbery executed by the infamous James Gang in 1866.

Missouri's Madonna | For marking the National Old Trails Road across the continent, 12 duplicate Madonna of the Trail monuments were to be placed in 12 states through which the Old Trail passed. On September 17, 1928, the Honorable Harry S Truman dedicated Missouri's Madonna.

Starting Point | St. Charles was the place of rendezvous for the Lewis and Clark Expedition in 1804. William Clark and the men of the party waited from May 16-21 in St. Charles for Meriwether Lewis to join them.

Top Brass | Kansas City citizens raised $2 million in only ten days to pay for the construction of the Liberty Memorial. At the dedication in 1921, the five Allied commanders were brought together for their first and only face-to-face encounter.

Missouri History *by Steve Keppler*

(Reprinted with permission of Steve Keppler, Public Relations Manager, Missouri Division of Tourism. Originally published in the "Missouri Official State Manual" publication, 1985-86.)

Present-day Missouri is very much a product of its past. Missourians are proud of the state's heritage, both in written histories and in preserved reminders of people and events. Everywhere in Missouri, our past is still living, even as we prepare for tomorrow.

The first "Missourians" were living here as long as 25,000 years ago. For thousands of years, this land of lush prairies, rivers and abundant game was the domain of native Americans.

The first Europeans to visit Missouri may have been remnants of the Conquistadores, but probably were French explorers from Canada. Father Jacques Marquette and Louis Joliet, who descended the Mississippi from the north in 1673, supplied the first written accounts of exploration in Missouri. In 1682, the area was claimed for France by Robert Cavalier Sieu de La Salle.

Missouri was admitted to the Union as the 24th state on August 10, 1821.

As part of the Louisiana Purchase Territory, Missouri has belonged to three nations. France ceded the area to Spain in 1762. Although Spain held it for forty years, its influence was slight. The early culture of the region was determined mostly by the French.

It was the French who were responsible for the first permanent settlement of Ste. Genevieve in the mid-1730s. Numerous buildings from the 1700s still stand in the historic Mississippi River town. Ste. Genevieve stood alone in the huge upper Louisiana Territory until the establishment of St. Louis as a fur trading post in 1764. Because of its location at the confluence of the Missouri and Mississippi Rivers, St. Louis outstripped other settlements and today is one of the nation's largest cities. By secret treaty in 1802, Spain returned the Louisiana Territory to the control of France. Napoleon Bonaparte, anxious to rid himself of the vast and troublesome frontier, sold it to the United States in 1803 for a total of $15 million.

About this time President Jefferson organized the Lewis and Clark Expedition, which was the first extensive exploration of the northwestern part of the new territory. The explorers left the St. Louis/St. Charles area in 1804. Their Missouri River route includes several sites still of interest to today's "explorers." One is Fort Osage, just east of Kansas City – a reconstruction on the site of William Clark's original 1808 fort.

Missouri was organized as a territory in 1812 and was admitted to the Union as the 24th state on August 10, 1821. Missouri Governor

missouri history

Alexander McNair was at the Capitol (which still stands) in St. Charles when he heard that the territory had become a state. Missouri became the second state (after Louisiana) of the Louisiana Purchase to be admitted to the Union.

In 1820, the Missouri Compromise was passed, whereby Missouri was to be admitted as a slave state and Maine as a free state. Although admitted as a slave state, Missouri remained with the Union during the Civil War.

At the beginning of the Civil War, most Missourians wanted only to preserve the peace. Governor Claiborne Fox Jackson, however, was strongly pro-Confederacy and attempted to align Missouri with the Confederate cause. He and most of the legislature were forced to flee to southern Missouri, where they passed an ordinance of secession. By then, his government no longer was recognized by most Missourians. The provisional government set up by the Federals in Jefferson City generally was accepted as the "real" government.

The most important battle fought in Missouri was the Battle of Wilson's Creek near Springfield. Although the battle lasted only a little more than four hours, it was one of the bloodiest of the war. Today, the site is a National Battlefield, preserved by the National Park Service.

Other important battles in Missouri were fought at Carthage, Lexington, Westport, and Boonville. Missouri was the scene of 11 percent of the total engagements in the war.

Before and after the Civil War, Missouri was literally the crossroads of the nation – a jumping-off point for settlers heading westward. Some settlers, of course, chose to stay in Missouri. From the lead mining region of southeast Missouri to the German settlements along the Missouri River, a flood of immigrants made their home on the Missouri frontier.

As the frontier moved farther west, pioneers passed through Arrow Rock, Independence, Kansas City, and other towns. St. Joseph assured a niche in frontier history when the Pony Express began there in 1860; the old Pony Express Stables now are a museum.

As the 1800s gave way to the 1900s, Missouri's history became more and more entwined with international events. During World War I, Missouri provided 140,257 soldiers, one-third being volunteer. Notable leaders, such as General John J. Pershing of Laclede, commander of the American Expeditionary Forces in Europe, came from Missouri.

In World War II, Missouri contributed more than 450,000 men and women to the various armed forces. Eighty-nine top officers were from Missouri including General Omar N. Bradley and Lieutenant General James H. Doolittle.

The nation's leader during the last year of the war was Lamar-born Harry Truman. After assuming office upon the death of Franklin D. Roosevelt in 1945, President Truman was elected to a four-year term.

His was the fateful decision to use the atom bomb and hasten the Japanese surrender consummated on the deck of the battleship USS Missouri in Tokyo Bay.

World War II added an unusual page to Missouri's history as well. When Sir Winston Churchill came to Missouri in 1946 to speak at Fulton's Westminster College, his speech entered the term "iron curtain" into the world's lexicon. The centuries-old church of St. Mary Aldermanbury was brought from London and now stands in Fulton as a memorial to Churchill.

In recent years, Missouri's history has moved rapidly into the space age, with Missouri companies providing vital components for exploration of this new frontier. From the rock carvings of ancient Missourians to the mysterious depths of space, Missouri's history is a diverse – but unbroken – chain.

For those who take the time to study it, our history is more than a yellowed page in a book of memories. It's a multihued tapestry of great events and daily life ... of famous personalities and obscure citizens. It's explorers, settlers and builders. It's frontier trails, sleepy country towns and bustling cities.

It's Missouri. ❑

Photo courtesy of Missouri Division of Tourism.

This mural by Thomas Hart Benton, located in the Capitol, depicts only a small part in Missouri's colorful and complex history.

1682 The Mississippi Valley was claimed for France by LaSalle.

1720 Lead was first produced by French explorers near Fredericktown.

1735 First permanent settlement in the state (Ste. Genevieve).

1771 The Spanish ruled Missouri until 1892.

1797 In the Spanish census of 1797, there were 40 people in Florissant.

1801 Daniel and Nathan Boone trapped beaver on Ha Ha Tonka Lake.

1803 Louisiana Purchase. France, after a brief one-year rule, sold the territory to the United States for $15 million.

1804 The American flag was raised in St. Louis.

1804 Lewis and Clark Expedition in the area until 1806.

1808 *The Missouri Gazette,* first newspaper west of the Mississippi, was established in St. Louis.

1811 The cataclysmic New Madrid earthquake caused severe destruction in southeast Missouri on December 16. The quake was so strong that it was felt as far away as the Carolinas, and shocks were felt intermittently throughout 1812. Earth was swallowed up, the Mississippi River changed course, and many farmers lost their land.

1812 The area of Missouri was organized as a territory.

1820 The Missouri Compromise was passed whereby Missouri was to be admitted as a slave state and Maine as a free state.

1820 Alexander McNair was inaugurated as the first Governor of Missouri on September 19.

1820 Daniel Boone died at his home in Defiance on September 26.

1820 On November 25, Governor Alexander McNair signed a bill making St. Charles the first capital of Missouri.

1821 On August 10, Missouri was admitted to the Union as the 24th state.

1821 St. Charles became Missouri's first state capital.

1822 The "emblems and devices" of the Great Seal of the State of Missouri was established by law.

1831 The Mormons, or Latter-day Saints, first settled in Missouri at Jackson County.

1832 St. Louis University, the first university west of the Mississippi, was incorporated.

1835 The first county fair west of the Mississippi was held in Columbia.

1837 The first state capitol building in Jefferson City was destroyed by fire.

1838 More than 4,000 Cherokee Indians died during the famous Trail of Tears trek that passed through the town of Billings. The trek began in Tennessee when the government relocation project forced more than 13,000 Cherokees to walk to Oklahoma through fierce winter weather with few supplies. The deaths wiped out one-fourth of the Cherokee Nation.

1838 In August, an election was held in Gallatin. Efforts were made to prevent the Mormons from exercising their right to vote. A fight developed and the incident mushroomed into what was called the "Mormon War."

1839 The University of Missouri, the first state university west of the Mississippi River, was founded.

1843 John James Audubon, the great naturalist and artist, traveled up the Missouri River to the Yellowstone.

1852 The Missouri River's greatest disaster occurred on April 9, when the steamboat "Saluda" exploded, killing more than 200 people and leaving a number of nameless children, many suffering burns and other injuries, lying on the riverfront at Lexington.

1857 The U.S. Supreme Court's ruling against Dred Scott, a slave of U.S. Army Surgeon John Emerson of Missouri, was one of the incidents that led to the Civil War in 1861. The Court declared no Negro, free or slave, could claim United States citizenship. It also declared that Congress could not prohibit slavery in U.S. territories.

1859 The Hannibal and St. Joseph railway was completed and reached across the state.

1860 The Pony Express began at St. Joseph.

1861 The Civil War began. In total, 11% of all Civil War battles were fought in Missouri.

1861 The Battle of Wilson's Creek (called Oak Hills by the Confederates) was fought 10 miles southwest of Springfield on August 10. Named for the stream that crosses the area where the battle took place, it was a bitter struggle between Union and Confederate forces for control of Missouri in the first year of the Civil War. The Union suffered a defeat. Two Union troops wore gray, two Confederate troops wore blue, and the Missouri State Guard wore civilian clothing, causing confusion during the battle.

1861 From September 18-20, Union and Confederate forces clashed at the Battle of Lexington. With their food and water depleted, and their ammunition nearly gone, the Union soldiers under the command of Colonel James A. Mulligan asked for terms of surrender. By 2 p.m., the Union soldiers walked out of their fortification and laid down their arms.

1861 Meeting of "Rebel" Legislature at Neosho and Cassville. Missouri secession ordinance passed.

1862 Battle of Pea Ridge, Arkansas, was one of the decisive battles affecting Missouri. Confederate forces were defeated.

1862 Battle of Kirksville. Porter's Confederate force was routed by McNeil's Federal troops.

1862 Confederate soldiers drove a Union occupying force from Independence in the First Battle of Independence.

1864 Battle of Pilot Knob.

1864 Centralia massacre and Battle of Centralia on September 27.

1864 Battle of Westport. General Sterling Price's forces were defeated and driven from the state on October 23. This defeat came at one of the largest battles fought west of the Mississippi. Price's withdrawal ended organized Confederate military operations in Missouri.

1865 The Civil War ended.

1865 Slavery was abolished in Missouri by ordinance of the Constitutional Convention.

1865 "Wild Bill" Hickok shot Dave Tutt over a gambling debt on the square in Springfield. Hickok turned himself in to the sheriff, but was later found not guilty of murder after a jury trial.

1869 The first bridge across the Missouri – the Burlington Bridge at Kansas City – was completed.

1874 The Eads Bridge over the Mississippi River was dedicated at St. Louis. It was the first arched steel truss bridge in the world.

1877 The first long distance phone call west of the Mississippi River was made at the First Telephone Exchange Office at Main and Themis Streets in Cape Girardeau on December 18.

1882 Jesse James, age 34, was killed by Bob Ford on April 3 in St. Joseph. He was shot in the back while straightening a picture on the wall. Frank James surrendered to Governor Crittenden in Jefferson City.

1889 Harry S Truman was born in Lamar, Missouri.

1890 Hannibal's first electric powered street car made its initial run.

1899 The National Hereford Show was held in a tent in the Kansas City Stockyards and was later acknowledged as the first American Royal Show.

1899 The State Legislature established the Missouri State Fair as the official exposition of the Commonwealth of Missouri. Later that year Sedalia was selected as the location.

1901 The first Missouri State Fair was held Sept. 9-13 in Sedalia.

1908 The world's first school of journalism was founded at the University of Missouri.

1911 The second state capitol in Jefferson City was destroyed by fire on February 5 when a bolt of lightning struck the dome.

1912 On March 22, Governor Elliot Major signed a law giving Missouri its first and present flag based on the design of Mrs. Marie Elizabeth Oliver, the wife of a former state senator from Cape Girardeau.

1912 The original shopping center for the Country Club District in Kansas City was built in 1912 at 51st and Oak because merchants refused to deliver goods to residents so far in the country.

1913 Construction began on the state capitol in Jefferson City. It was completed in 1917.

1915 The Jaycees began in St. Louis as the Junior Citizens.

1921 The Liberty Memorial in Kansas City was dedicated.

1931 The Missouri State Highway Patrol was created by law.

1932 Springfield was the site of the largest single massacre of law enforcement officers in the history of the United States. Six officers were slain on Jan. 2 by Harry and Jennings Young.

1945 Harry S Truman, Vice President of the United States, became President on April 12. He was the first Missourian to hold the office.

1948 John Pershing died at Walter Reed Army Hospital on July 15. He is buried at Arlington National Cemetery with the highest military honors.

1951 Christian College, now called Columbia College, was organized and was the first four-year women's college west of the Mississippi River.

1952 Ronald and Nancy Reagan were in Springfield to attend the movie premiere of "The Winning Team."

1959 Lamar Hunt established and organized the American Football League.

1963 On February 12, the first stainless steel section of the Gateway Arch in St. Louis was set in place.

1963 On May 14, the Kansas City Chiefs were organized. They won their debut game against Houston, 28-7.

1965 The last stainless steel section of the Gateway Arch was fitted into place on October 28.

1967 The St. Louis Cardinals baseball team won the World Series.

1970 The Kansas City Chiefs won Super Bowl IV by defeating the Minnesota Vikings, 23-7. Len Dawson was named the game's Most Valuable Player.

1972 Harry S Truman died.

1973 Worlds of Fun in Kansas City opened with 60 rides, shows, and attractions.

1977 His Royal Highness the Price of Wales (Prince Charles) visited the Gateway Arch on October 21.

1982 The St. Louis Cardinals baseball team won the World Series.

1983 In January, dioxin contamination was discovered at Times Beach, Missouri.

1985 The Kansas City Royals played the St. Louis Cardinals in what became known as the "I-70 Series." The Kansas City Royals won the World Series championship.

1988 In March, Missouri held its first presidential primary.

1990 Debbye Turner, of Columbia, became Miss America.

1990 The U.S. Supreme Court decided the Nancy Cruzan case, which argued the right-to-die issue.

1990 Missouri recorded its 5,000th cave. Governor John Ashcroft declared 1990 as "Year of the Caves" in Missouri.

HISTORIC TRAILS
IN MISSOURI

© Facts On File, Inc. 1984

Source: State Historical Society of Missouri.

The Oregon Trail

Independence, Missouri, was the trailhead for a great adventure. In 1841, the Oregon Trail was established and was the route initially from Independence to the Pacific Northwest. Beginning in the western part of the state, the Oregon Trail stretched 2,000 miles into Oregon. The trail was originally used by fur traders, gold seekers, missionaries, and emigrants. Thousands of emigrants traveled this route in order to find a better life in the West. It continued to be the main road west until the advent of the transcontinental railroad in the 1870s.

The Santa Fe Trail

On Sept. 21, 1821, Captain William Becknell, known as the father of the Santa Fe Trail, started for Santa Fe, New Mexico, from Old Franklin, Missouri. This was the beginning of the Santa Fe Trail. The Trail itself originates in Independence, Missouri, and covers 780 miles to Santa Fe. Missourians began their trade with Mexicans in Santa Fe in the 1820s. The Santa Fe Trail became one of the longest commercial routes in the country in the pre-railroad days.

The Lewis and Clark Trail

In 1804, Meriwether Lewis and William Clark were commissioned by President Thomas Jefferson to explore and map the territory that had been obtained from France by the signing of the Louisiana Purchase Treaty in 1803. Starting east of St. Charles, the expedition followed the Missouri River west and north through St. Joseph and beyond.

Boone's Lick Road

The Boone's Lick Road was surveyed, marked, and straightened by Col. Nathan Boone, son of Daniel Boone. In 1815, the trail went from St. Charles to Old Granklin, a total of 154 miles. The first stagecoach line was established over the road from St. Louis to Old Franklin in 1819. The trail was extended to Ft. Osage, 276 miles from St. Louis, in 1821.

Butterfield Overland Mail Route

The Overland Mail was established on September 16, 1858. Mail was simultaneously transported by stage from St. Louis to San Francisco. This route followed the southern route between the two points. The western stage arrived in St. Louis on September 28, having made the trip in only two weeks.

The Pony Express

The Pony Express originated in St. Joseph by Alexander Majors of Russell, Majors & Waddell, owners of the Central Overland California Pikes Peak Express. The plan was to carry the mail over a 2,000 mile overland route between St. Joseph and Sacramento, California, in the incredible time of 10 days. The telegraph soon ended the Pony Express and on November 20, 1861, the last run was made by the Central Overland California Pikes Peak Express.

The Mormon Trail

In 1831, Joseph Smith, founder of The Church of Jesus Christ of Latter-day Saints (the Mormons) declared Independence, Missouri, to be the Mormon's Mt. Zion. By 1832, nearly 1,200 followers had settled in Independence. In October 1838, there were two major setbacks for the Mormons in Missouri, and 20 Mormons were killed and 15 wounded in these two incidents. In 1839, the Mormons were driven out of the state by Governor Lilburn W. Boggs. They established Nauvoo in Illinois after their expulsion.

Trail of Tears

In 1830, the President of the United States was given authorization to remove by force any Indian tribes east of the Mississippi River and relocate them on reservations to the west. In 1838, U.S. troops forced more than 13,000 Cherokee Indians from their homelands in North Carolina, Georgia, and Tennessee, to walk 1,200 miles to Indian Territory (Oklahoma). One-fourth of the Cherokee Nation died on this trail. In Missouri, the Trail of Tears crossed the Mississippi River into Cape Girardeau and wound north and west through Rolla, and south through Springfield and Monett into Arkansas. The route was treacherous and took place during the bitter winter months. Many Cherokee walked barefoot and with few provisions. So many people died along the route that it became known as the "Trail of Tears."

Arrow Rock Fort

George Sibley, factor and Indian agent at Fort Osage, established a trading post for the government at Arrow Rock on the Missouri River in Saline County in the fall of 1813 after Fort Osage was temporarily abandoned during the War of 1812.

Fort Benton

Built in March of 1861 on Fort Hill in the town of Patterson, it was garrisoned by the 3rd Cavalry, Missouri State Militia. Forewarned in April of a large scale Confederate cavalry raid, the troops pulled out of the fort burning what they couldn't carry. Confederate troops put out the fires and saved the remaining stores. On September 22, 1864, a strong Confederate force again attacked Federal-held Patterson and destroyed much of the town including the fort.

Fort Davidson

An important Federal-built Civil War earthwork fortification erected in 1863 was located near Ironton. It was intended to protect the Pilot Knob and Iron Mountain mineral deposits. The Confederates suffered a bloody defeat here in September 1864, with some 1,200 casualties.

Fort Howard

Constructed in 1812 after the outbreak of the War of 1812, Fort Howard was located two miles south of Winfield. Built to consolidate the area's forces, the fort was one of the largest and most important defenses erected in Missouri during the war. It required 60 to 70 men, including Captain Nathan Boone's Mounted Ranger, nearly three weeks to build.

Fort Osage *(Fort Sibley)*

Fort Osage was the first United States government outpost in Louisiana Territory. Meriwether Lewis and William Clark selected the site in 1804 during their first exploratory trip into the uncharted wilderness, marking its place on their map as "Fort Point." The fort had two purposes: to inform the Spanish, British, and the Indians that the American government would protect its newly acquired territory by military means, and to establish a friendly rapport with the region's Indians by providing them with a government-operated trading post. For almost two decades, Fort Osage was a place of congregation on the migration westward and a deterrent of foreign encroachments. Today Fort Osage is reconstructed to look as it did in1808. The Fort Osage Restoration at Old Sibley is 14 miles northeast of Independence.

Fort Zumwalt

The 45-acre Fort Zumwalt State Park, located about two miles southwest of the town of O'Fallon, contains the remains of the old fort, which originally was Jacob Zumwalt's residence, erected in 1798.

major civil war battles

Liberty, seizure of United States Arsenal......................April 20, 1861	Sibley...........................June 23, 1863
Camp Jackson.............May 10, 1861	Boonville................October 11, 1863
St. Louis ....May 11, 1861	Lamar..........................May 28, 1864
Boonville......................June 17, 1861	Laclede ....June 17, 1864
Independence ....June 17, 1861	Fayette ....July 1, 1864
Farmington ....July 4, 1861	Camden Point ....July 13, 1864
Carthage.......................July 5, 1861	Versailles ....July 13, 1864
Neosho..........................July 5, 1861	Arrow Rock.................July 20, 1864
Athens......................August 5, 1861	Shelbina ....July 26, 1864
Potosi ....August 10, 1861	Rocheport.............August 20, 1864
Springfield.............August 10, 1861	Steelville................August 31, 1864
Wilson's Creek........August 10, 1861	Tipton...................September 1, 1864
Birds Point ....August 19, 1861	Centralia...........September 7, 1864
Lexington, surrender of by Union Forces.............September 20, 1861	Doniphan ....September 19, 1864
Osceola..............September 22, 1861	Keytesville ....September 20, 1864
Charleston ....October 2, 1861	Patterson ....September 22, 1864
Belmont ....November 7, 1861	Farmington.......September 24, 1864
Warsaw, destruction of U.S. stores ....November 21, 1861	Fayette..............September 24, 1864
	Jackson ....September 24, 1864
Charleston ....December 12, 1861	Arcadia Valley ..September 24, 1864
Mount Zion Church (Boone County)............December 28, 1861	Ironton ....September 26, 1864
	Shut-In Gap......September 26, 1864
New Madrid ....March 3, 1862	Arcadia.............September 27, 1864
Clinton ....March 30, 1862	Centralia...........September 27, 1864
Doniphan.....................April 1, 1862	Fort Davidson, Pilot Knob, attack on ....September 27, 1864
Jackson.........................April 9, 1862	
Bloomfield ....May 10, 1862	Franklin...................October 1, 1864
Florida ....May 31, 1862	Union ....October 1, 1864
Lotspeich Farm.............July 9, 1862	Osage River ....October 5, 1864
Moore's Mill.................July 24, 1862	Jefferson City ....October 7, 1864
Kirksville.................August 6, 1862	Moreau Creek..........October 7, 1864
Newtonia ....August 8, 1862	Boonville...................October 9, 1864
Independence, surrender of Union Forces..................August 11, 1862	California.................October 9, 1864
	Danville ....October 14, 1864
Lone Jack...............August 14, 1862	Glasgow ....October 15, 1864
Lamar ....August 24, 1862	Paris.......................October 15, 1864
Ozark, captured by Confederate Troops ....January 7, 1863	Sedalia...................October 15, 1864
	Carrollton, surrender of by Union Forces..................October 17, 1864
Springfield.............January 8, 1863	Big Blue ....October 23, 1864
Bloomfield............January 27, 1863	Westport ....October 23, 1864
Fredericktown............April 22, 1863	Charlot....................October 25, 1864
Cape Girardeau ....April 26, 1863	Clinton ....October 25, 1864
Jackson......................April 26, 1863	Newtonia ....October 28, 1864
	Source: State Historical Society of Missouri.

museums

Appleton City

M.K.&T. Depot and Caboose. This restored depot and caboose feature railroad memorabilia and M.K.&T. artifacts.

Belton

Belton Museum. Rotating and permanent exhibits including ones about President Harry S Truman, Carry A. Nation, and Dale Carnegie.

Bethel

Bethel German Colony. Founded as a German communal colony in the 1840s, Bethel contains 30 original historic buildings, some of which are open for tours: museum, blacksmith shop, potter, printmaker, restaurants, bed and breakfast, and antique shop.

Blue Springs

Missouri Town. The village museum uses original structures and interpreters wearing period clothing to portray a way of life of this area in mid-19th century. Special events from April through December.

Bolivar

North Ward Museum. Antique furniture, a Model-T Ford, musical instruments, and other historic collectibles are on display.
The Old Jail Museum. Originally the Polk County Jail. The first floor living quarters, female and juvenile cells, and "bull pen" are still in the jail as part of the museum.

Branson

Harold Bell Wright Theater and Museum. The theater features a 30-minute film on the life of author Harold Bell Wright. The museum houses original manuscripts, antiques, and paintings.

Butler

Museum of Pioneer History. The pioneer history museum has 16 rooms of local history, a log cabin, and two other buildings featuring many exhibits including a pioneer print shop and period clothing.

Canton

The Remember When Toy Museum. Home of the world's largest Marx toy collection featuring over 10,000 antique and collectible toys from the past 60 years. Tourists are allowed to see the research and development lab where old-style toys are redesigned by a research staff.

Cape Girardeau

Cape River Heritage Museum. The museum, located in the old Fire and Police Station, features a hands-on River Room with a steamboat race, a knot-tying board, and a video depicting a trip down the Mississippi River. Special activities are offered for children.

Carthage

Powers Museum. Museum of local history and the arts, with research library and a variety of changing exhibits.

Chillicothe

Grand River Historical Museum. The museum features exhibits pertaining to life in the Grand River Basin area from 1820s to 1950s.

Clinton

Henry County Museum. The building was constructed in 1866 by Anheuser-Busch as a distributing point. Treasures of historical significance such as old documents, war relics, and memorabilia.

Columbia

State Historical Society of Missouri. The historical society contains reference and newspaper libraries, as well as collections of historical manuscripts, journals, personal letters and diaries, photograph albums, and scrapbooks. An art gallery features works done by Missouri artists.

Concordia

Lohoeffener House Museum. This Federal Gothic-style brick home depicts local German history through pictures and furnishings.

Dunklin County

The Dunklin County Museum. Thousands of items on permanent exhibition. Of special interest is the record-size alligator gar fish. The museum also houses a working collection of scale-model, mechanized steam engines and toys.

El Dorado

Wayside Inn Museum. Located in a 108-year-old hotel, the museum displays souvenirs, furniture, photos and rooms depicting the city's and the area's history since 1881.

Excelsior Springs

Excelsior Springs Historical Museum. The museum is housed in a former bank building and is a Clay County historic site.

Farmington

Missouri Mines Museum. Displayed are remnants of the lockers and showers used by the miners and millworkers. It also features exhibits on geology, mineral resources, and outstanding mineral specimens.

Fulton

Winston Churchill Memorial and Library. The reconstructed 17th century Christopher Wren Church houses a museum of Churchill and Wren memorabilia, including original oil paintings by Churchill.

Kingdom of Callaway Historical Society Museum. The 1890 home has period furniture, clothing, collection of Callaway County photos, memorabilia, and artifacts.

Gerald

Gerald Depot and Museum. The depot was built in 1910. The museum contains original pictures and railroad memorabilia.

Glasgow

Glasgow Community Museum. An 1861 Gothic Revival church houses period church furnishings and historic community treasures.

Grandview

Grandview Historical Society Depot Museum. Photographs and antiques are in the restored Kansas City Southern Depot.

Hamilton

J.C. Penney Museum. The items belonged to J.C. Penney and explain Penney's contribution to American retailing. The department store chain now includes approximately 1,700 stores across the country.

Hannibal

The Adventures of Tom Sawyer Museum. A review of the book *The Adventures of Tom Sawyer* can be found in dioramas. There are 16 miniature handcarved scenes.
Mark Twain Boyhood Home and Museum. The museum houses a collection of Twain memorabilia, Mark Twain's father's law office, Pilaster House, and Grant's Drug Store.
South River Fort and Museum. The Civil War fort was moved from its original location. Original railroad (St. Joseph Railroad) building was relocated here and now includes a gift shop and antiques.

Hermann

Historic Hermann Museum. The German School, built in 1871, houses the museum, which consists of a Heritage Room, Children's Room, and the mechanism of the 1890 Clock Tower.
Whiskey Jack's Museum. The largest known collection of memorabilia depicting one of America's most colorful eras – Prohibition.

Independence

Harry S Truman Library and Museum. Trace the life of Harry Truman. Artifacts from his childhood through his political career.

Jackson

Old Timer's Museum and Park. A large collection of antique farm machinery plus an indoor display area are at the museum. Videotapes and demonstrations are also presented.

Jefferson City

Cole County Historical Museum. The 1871 row house is furnished with period furniture and has a special display of inaugural ball gowns worn by Missouri governors' wives.

Joplin

Dorthea B. Hoover Museum. Includes rooms such as a rustic kitchen, parlour, bedroom, doll collection, and a Victorian dollhouse.
Tri-State Mineral Museum. Displays include native rock and minerals, mining machinery, and hand tools.

Kahoka

Clark County Historical Museum. An 1857 organ and the beam on which Bill Young was hung by a mob after his acquittal on mass murder charges are also on display. Features antiques, old newspapers, and photos.

Kansas City

John Wornall House Museum. The 1858 farmhouse has been restored to its Antebellum appearance.
Kansas City Museum. The museum has regional history exhibits, a natural history hall, and the only public planetarium in the metro area.
Liberty Memorial Museum. The museum is America's only major museum specializing in World War I memorabilia. Exhibits include a walk-through trench and dugout.

Kearney

Jesse James Birthplace and Museum. This restored home has original furnishings and artifacts. The museum exhibits Jesse James' personal possessions and a multi-media production.

Kirksville

Adair County Historical Society Museum. Items from Northeast Missouri State University and Kirksville College of Osteopathic Medicine, early agriculture implements, and photographs.
Andrew County Historical Society. The large doll collection features many Kewpie dolls and a 19th-century doll of French and German origin. Also displayed are Hummel figurines, and more.

Kirkwood

History House. The house has displays of area history and features programs of interest to all Kirkwood area residents.
National Museum of Transport. The transportation museum has the largest collection of locomotives in the United States, plus railway cars, automobiles, streetcars, buses, trucks, horse drawn vehicles, aircraft, and communication devices.

Lexington

Lexington Historical Museum. Pictures and items illustrate Lexington's history, including items from the Battle of Lexington and Pony Express days.

Liberty

Clay County Museum. Housed in an authentic 19th century drugstore, this museum contains a restored doctor's office, X-ray room, and waiting room.

Jesse James Bank Museum. This was the site of the first successful daylight bank robbery, with Frank, Jesse and the "James Gang" eventually being blamed for it, although no one knows for sure.

Linn Creek

Camden County Museum. Exhibits are maintained for the preservation of historical data, records, and memorabilia of the county.

Lone Jack

Civil War Museum of Jackson County. Site of the August 16, 1862, Battle of Lone Jack. Electronic map, displays, and dioramas are located in the museum. A presentation of the Civil War soldier's life is given at the site periodically during the summer.

Malden

Malden Historical Museum. Features a collection of Egyptian antiquities and five rooms of permanent exhibits with items of historical significance to the area.

Mansfield

Laura Ingalls Wilder-Rose Wilder Lane Museum and Home. The home was where Laura wrote the series of "Little House" books. The house appears as it did when she lived there and includes artifacts, pictures, and family possessions.

Maryville

The Nodaway County Historical Society Museum. The museum and Historical Society serve to promote interest in local history and to develop an appreciation for individual heritage.

Mexico

Audrain Historical and American Saddle Horse Museum at Graceland. The museum has items associated with Audrain County and the American Saddle Horse artifacts relating to prominence of that breed in the surrounding area. Graceland, the home of the Audrain Country Historical Society, is a stately Antebellum mansion built in 1857. Graceland has an extensive collection of Currier and Ives prints.

Nevada

Bushwhacker Museum. The old stone jail building was in use 1860-1960, and the cell room is in original condition.

New Madrid

New Madrid Historical Museum. Displays depicting the 1811 New Madrid earthquake and Civil War items are included in the museum.

Novinger

Coal Miner's Museum. The museum has displays of clothing, mining equipment, horse and stable wares, news clippings, photos, artifacts, and other reminders of the town's heyday.

Paris

Monroe County Courthouse and Historical Museum. The 1912 courthouse contains murals depicting 50 years of the county's history, Indian artifacts, textiles, and artwork from Gordon Snidow.

Platte

Ben Ferrel, Platte County Mini-Mansion Museum. A Victorian mini-mansion, furnished with pre-1900 Platte County family heirlooms.

Plattsburg

Clinton County Historical Society Museum. The museum features exhibits including early Chautauqua programs and banners, military uniforms, furniture, magazines, art prints, books, and toys.

Richmond

Ray County Historical Society and Museum. Features exhibits on the past including Indian artifacts and Victorian parlors.

Robidoux

State Hospital Psychiatric Museum. The museum has reproductions of treatment devices and portrayal of treatment methods spanning 400 years of psychiatric history.

Rolla

Memoryville U.S.A. The antique auto museum has an arts and crafts section and art gallery. Visitors can view restoration of antique cars.
Phelps County Museum. Housed in an 1838 log house, the museum features pioneer tools and furniture, country store, country kitchen, and collection of household utensils.

Roscoe

Roscoe Museum. The switchboard used in Roscoe before installation of modern phones, a collection of antique tools and office equipment, and other local artifacts are in the museum.

museums

St. Clair

St. Clair Historical Museum. This museum features historical exhibits and artifacts of St. Clair and the surrounding area.

St. James

Meramec Iron Works. Site of the first iron works west of the Mississippi, in operation 1826-1876. The park contains remains of iron furnace, and a historical museum.

St. Joseph

Jesse James Home. The house in which outlaw Jesse James was killed is located on the grounds of the Patee House Museum. The home features original furnishings and articles from the days of the notorious outlaw Jesse James.

Patee House Museum. This museum has everything from fire trucks to a Japanese Tea House.

Pony Express Museum. The historic stables where the Pony Express began in 1860 have been restored as a museum.

The St. Joseph Museum. The museum exhibits a 5,000 piece Native American collection representing over 300 tribes. An exhibition of North American vertebrates and invertebrates, a fur trading post exhibit, and covered wagon exhibit are also displayed.

St. Louis

Campbell House Museum. This townhouse was the home of a prominent fur trade figure in the 1820s and 1830s, and his wife. It is furnished with original pieces and family memorabilia.

Concordia Historical Institute. Holds the world's largest collection of resources relating to the history of Lutheranism in America.

Eugene Field House and Toy Museum. Built in 1845, the home now features antique toys and dolls as well as furnishings, manuscripts, and items of poet Eugene Field.

History Museum of the Missouri Historical Society. The museum has exhibits on history of St. Louis, American West, firefighting, the 1904 World's Fair, weapons, Charles A. Lindbergh, and free audio-visual programs.

Soldiers' Memorial Military Museum. Two museum rooms contain a collection of military items depicting St. Louis' patriotic and active military involvement from 1800 through the present.

Ste. Genevieve

Amoureaux House. Home and museum built in 1770, furnished in antiques. Also has an outstanding antique doll and toy display.

Ste. Genevieve Museum. Artifacts dating to the French and Spanish period and prehistoric artifacts dating to 12,000 B.C. are displayed, as well as equipment used at Saline Creek Salt Works.

Salem

Dent County Museum. The home of former congressman W.P. Elmer, built in 1896, houses artifacts of the area.

Sedalia

Pettis County Historical Society Museum. This museum includes a collection of artifacts from early Missouri. The museum is housed in the 1924 Courthouse.

Ragtime Archives Collection. Ragtime memorabilia depicting Sedalia's colorful history of ragtime music.

Springfield

Museum of Ozarks History. The restored 18-room circa 1892 Victorian mansion has exhibits of local history.

Stanton

Antique Toy Museum. Museum houses a collection of over 2,000 toys, featuring the various modes of transportation, farm tractors, and a complete set of rare cast iron doll house furniture from 1930.

Trenton

Grundy County Museum. This feed and implement store was built in 1895 and has been restored and adapted to display exhibits from the county's agricultural, railroad, and cultural heritage.

Trimble

Ma and Pa's Museum of Yesteryears. Rooms of the museum are designed to display a workroom, stable, general store, and schoolroom.

Tuscumbia

Miller County Historical Society Museum. The museum depicts the history of Miller County. The exhibits include Indian heritage and early home accessories.

Versailles

Morgan County Historical Museum. Housed in the old Martin Hotel buildings, built in 1877 and 1884. The 28 rooms are decorated with antiques using themes including a beauty shop, chapel, weaving room, war relics room, child's room, and a typical hotel guest's room.

Warsaw

Benton County Museum. Located in the 1886 Warsaw school building, the museum is filled with hundreds of items.

Weston

Herbert Bonnell Museum. Museum is a farmhouse displaying items during the late 1800s. Outbuildings contain tools from the same period.

Arrow Rock

Arrow Rock State Historic Site. A historic village including the home of artist George Caleb Bingham, and the Old Tavern where visitors can dine in 1800s atmosphere.

Athens

Battle of Athens State Historic Site. This is the site of the northernmost battle fought west of the Mississippi River during the Civil War.

Blue Springs

Missouri Town. Step back in time at this living history community, which is a re-creation of an 1855 farming community.

Boonville

Boone's Lick. Salt was made at Boone's Lick Spring as early as 1805 by Daniel and Nathan Boone, sons of famed frontiersman Daniel Boone. A wooded trail leads to the spring.

Burfordville

Bollinger Mill. A 140-foot, self-supporting Howe truss covered bridge, one of only four covered bridges left in the state, is located next to the grist mill. Corn meal is still ground there.

Cape Girardeau

Glenn House. The 1883 residence features stenciled ceilings, intricate woodwork, and decorated slate fireplaces.
Old St. Vincent's Church. The church, dedicated in 1853, is an excellent example of English Gothic architecture.

Carthage

Battle of Carthage. The four-acre tract is the site of the final confrontation in a 12-hour running battle in July 1861. The site remains just as it was when the Southern troops camped there.

Clayton

Martin Franklin Hanley House. Built in 1855, the building is typical of Greek-Revival houses built in the pre-Civil War period. All of the furnishings date from the 19th century.

Clinton

The Anheuser Busch Brewing Building. Now the Henry County Museum, this building was built in 1886 and was a shipping center for Anheuser Busch.
Crome House. This Federal style brick house was built in 1904. Many of the materials used in this house were imported. The house has both gas and electrical fixtures and a turntable in the garage.

Whitaker House. This home was built in 1892 and features a bell-cast mansard roof with a widow's walk.

Columbia

Maplewood. The farm home was built in 1877. Outbuildings to be restored are farm barns, carriage house, and tenant house.

University of Missouri-Columbia. The campus includes the Francis Quadrangle with its famous six Ionic Columns and has 18 buildings listed in the National Register of Historic Places.

Crestwood

Sappington House. This house, built in 1808, is believed to be the oldest brick house in St. Louis County.

Davisville

Dillard Mill. One of the most picturesque in Missouri, the mill was built around 1900. It has been restored and is operating again.

Defiance

Daniel Boone Home. The stone mansion was built by Boone and his son Nathan. Daniel Boone died in the house in 1820.

Excelsior Springs

Watkins Woolen Mill. A woolen mill built and equipped in 1860, it is one of the few 19th century factories in the country which still contains original machinery.

Watkins Home. The home was built in 1850, and many of the original furnishings remain. An unusual walnut staircase leading to the second floor enhances this home, built in the Greek Revival style.

Florissant

Casa Alvarez. Built in 1790, it is the only remaining home linking Florissant with Spain.

Old St. Ferdinand's Shrine. The oldest Catholic Church building between the Mississippi River and the Rocky Mountains.

Taille De Noyer Home. This 17-room mansion began as a log cabin fur trading post in 1790. It was expanded to a sprawling mansion by St. Louis millionaire John Mullanphy.

Glasgow

Lewis Library. Built in 1866, the library has original glass-fronted bookcases and wooden carrels and houses local artifacts.

Grandview

The Truman Farm Home. During the 10 years prior to his World War I duty, Truman farmed the 600 acres. It is authentically restored and includes a number of Truman family items.

historical attractions

Hannibal

Mark Twain Boyhood Home. The small, white clapboard house on Hill Street was built by John Clemens in 1844. It is the house in which Mark Twain spent his "Tom Sawyer" years.

Harrisonville

Sharp-Hopper Log Cabin. An 1835 log cabin furnished in pioneer style with a basement area of other types of memorabilia.

Hermann

Deutschheim. Two historic homes – the Pommer-Gentner House on Market Street and the Strehly House on West Second – are open for tours and reflect the town's early German traditions.

Higginsville

Confederate Memorial. The 109-acre memorial park area of the Old Confederate Soldier's Home is preserved in memory of the 40,000 Missourians who fought under the Confederate flag.

Hillsboro

Sandy Creek Covered Bridge. The 76-foot long bridge, built in 1872, was destroyed by floodwaters in 1886. It was later rebuilt.

Independence

Bingham Waggoner Estate. Constructed in 1855, this was the home of Missouri artist and politician George Caleb Bingham. Victorian and Edwardian furnishings from the 1890s remodeling are still intact.
Harry S Truman Courtroom and Office. The office and courtroom Truman used while serving as presiding judge of the County Court in the 1930s has now been restored.
1859 Marshal's Home and Jail. This Federal style, two-story brick house was built in 1859 and provided a home and office for the county marshal for 74 years.
The Vaile Mansion. The mansion, built in 1881, is one of the finest examples of Second Empire Victorian style architecture in the Midwest.

Jackson

Oliver House. The pre-Civil War Federal-style house, furnished with antiques of late 19th century, has been restored.

Jefferson City

Capitol Building. Visitors can tour the state capitol, including state museum and legislative chamber. Murals painted by Thomas Hart Benton, N.C. Wyeth, and others are on display in the Capitol.
Governor's Residence. Guests can tour the restored first floor of the home, one of the oldest governor's residences in the United States.

Lohman Building. Built in the mid-1830s, it is believed to be the oldest structure in Jefferson City.

Parsons' House. The house was built in the 1830s and during the Civil War was used as a hospital for wounded from both sides.

Vineyard Place. The beautiful home built in 1850 by Governor John C. Edwards is a fine example of southern influence upon the city.

Kahoka

Battle of Athens. Union troops defeated the pro-South Missouri State Guard in 1861 on this site, the northernmost location of a battle fought west of the Mississippi River during the Civil War.

Kansas City

Alexander Majors Home. The Antebellum home of the creator of the Pony Express was built in 1856 and is fully restored.

Thomas Hart Benton Home. The late Victorian style house was the noted artist's home from 1939 until his death in 1975. The house and the carriage house, which was converted into an art studio, contain many of his personal belongings.

Kearney

Claybrook House Historic Site. The restored pre-Civil War mansion is located opposite Jesse James' farm and is a fine example of mid-1800 rural Missouri architecture. At one time it was the home of Jesse's daughter, Mary James Barr.

Jesse James Farm Historic Site. Restored birthplace of Jesse James and home of Frank James. The farm has original furnishings and Jesse James' personal possessions.

Kimmswick

Kimmswick Historic Community. Founded in 1859, this historic town features several historic buildings and other sites.

Kirkwood

Saint Louis Cathedral. Built in 1907, the cathedral combines Byzantine and Romanesque architecture and has the largest collection of mosaics in the world.

Laclede

Gen. John J. Pershing Boyhood Home. Gen. Pershing, the highest ranking military officer in U.S. history and General of the Armies after World War I, lived here from age 6 (1866) until 1882, when he left for West Point Military Academy.

Locust Creek Covered Bridge. The Howe-truss bridge was built in 1868. It is the longest of the four surviving covered bridges in the state. It features arched entrances with ramps sloping away from both ends.

Lamar

Harry S Truman Birthplace. The only Missourian elected U.S. President was born here May 8, 1884. He was the 33rd president, serving from 1945-1953. The six-room frame structure was built between 1880 and 1882.

Lee's Summit

Longview Farm. Built in 1914 by R.A. Long, the complex included 60 look-alike buildings. Among the buildings are a huge harness horse barn, half-mile track, grandstand, and a hotel for unmarried male employees. It was one of the best saddle horse farms.

Lexington

Battle of Lexington. Here in 1861, the Missouri State Guard troops of Major Gen. Sterling Price defeated the Union troops of Col. James A. Mulligan in one of three major Civil War battles in Missouri. The Anderson House served as a field hospital for both sides. It is known as the "Battle of the Hemp Bales" because bales were used as breastworks.

Liberty

Liberty Jail Visitors Center. Place where Joseph Smith, first prophet and President of The Church of Jesus Christ of Latter-day Saints (Mormon), was incarcerated from 1838-1839.
Lightburne Hall. The 26-room mansion, built in 1852 in Greek Revival style, is furnished with early 19th century antiques.

Maryville

The Robinson/Bell/Baumli House. It was built in 1888 and features gingerbread trim, stained glass, and six marble fireplaces.

Monett

Jolly Mill. During the Civil War, the mill was occupied by both the Confederate and Union Armies.

New Franklin

Rivercene. The interior of the home, built in 1969, features cypress wood and marble mantels imported from Italy.

New Madrid

Hunter-Dawson Home. The Antebellum mansion was built in 1858 using labor provided by slaves and by craftsmen from St. Louis.

Paris

Mark Twain Birthplace. The museum encloses the two-room cabin in which Samuel Clemens was born in 1835. Many of his personal items and books are displayed, including an early handwritten manuscript of *Tom Sawyer*.

R.O. Osborn's Home or Grimes House. Built in 1889 in the Queen Anne style. Tradition is that it was one of the first homes to have a bathtub. The bathtub was copper with a wooden frame.

The Thomas Conyer House. Built in 1845, the original house has rafters of saplings, with one side only hewed flat to hold roof sheathing. The rest of the saplings still carry the original bark.

Union Covered Bridge. Built in 1870, it is the last surviving covered bridge with a "Burr-arch" truss construction.

Parkville

Mackay Hall National Historic Site. The unusual architectural site was built almost entirely by students. Park House Museum, the home of college founder George S. Park, has the college's history.

Perryville

National Shrine of Our Lady of the Miraculous Medal. The Shrine features St. Mary's of the Barrens Church, established in 1827; Countess Estelle Doheny Museum; Bishop Sheen Memorial Museum and Rare Book Room; Marian Grotto; and a gift shop.

Pilot Knob

Fort Davidson. The fort was the scene of the Battle of Pilot Knob in 1864, between the Union troops of Brig. Gen. Thomas Ewing Jr. and the Confederate troops of Major Gen. Sterling Price. Price's men attacked the fort and more than 1,000 men were killed or wounded in only 20 minutes of fighting, ending in the defeat of the Confederates.

St. Charles

First Missouri State Capitol. The buildings housed Missouri's government from 1821-1826. The first floor of the main building houses a restored residence and mercantile establishment.

St. Louis

Chatillon-DeMenil Mansion. The historic home with Greek Revival facade furnished in the style of the mid- to late 1800s includes the Carriage House Restaurant and the Carriage Trade Museum.

Jefferson Barracks Historic County Park. Historic buildings stand in this park which was in a former military reservation.

Scott Joplin House. Ragtime composer Scott Joplin and his wife lived in this four-family structure, built shortly after the Civil War. While Joplin was there in 1902, eight of his compositions were published.

Ste. Genevieve

Felix Valle Home. Built in 1818, the Valle home is an example of the American Federal style of architecture. It served as headquarters and storage for a company that controlled Indian trade.

Savannah

Bolduc House. The authentically restored French Colonial house is furnished in its original 1770 form.

Sedalia

Bothwell Lodge. The lodge once known as "Stoneyridge Farm" was built in four sections by John Bothwell. The castle-like structure was built in 1898. The estate is now a state park.

Wood Dale Farm. The log-constructed central section of the home was built about 1819, and is the oldest structure in continuous use in Pettis County.

Sibley

Fort Osage. Restored fort (1808-1827) overlooks the Missouri River and was the first U.S. outpost in the Louisiana Purchase. Today the fort has living history programs and other special events.

Smithville

Woodhenge Historic Site. Located at Little Platte Park at Smithville Lake. A full-scale working replica of the only known square prehistoric (800-1200 A.D.) Indian solar calendar.

Springfield

The Bentley House. Built in 1892, this Queen Anne style home has numerous architectural features in its 22 rooms, including a turret, half timbering, stained cut glass windows, cut stone, and brick.

The John Polk Campbell Farmstead. Constructed in approximately 1856. The farmstead has a log kitchen, log granary, two-crib barn, and a family cemetery that is currently being restored.

Stoutsville

Union Covered Bridge. This covered bridge, built in 1871, is the only surviving example of a Burr-arch truss system in Missouri.

Sycamore

Hodgson Water Mill. The mill, built by Alva Hodgson in 1894, is in the valley of spring-fed Bryant Creek.

Tipton

Maclay Home. Built in 1858 as a seminary for young ladies, the house was a permanent home after serving as a Union encampment headquarters during the Civil War.

Trenton

Grundy County Jewett Norris Library. The three-story Victorian Library was constructed in 1890 and is known for its architectural design and suspended staircase.

Wallace

Osage Village. This site was the location of a large Osage Indian village between 1700 and 1777. Included on the National Register of Historic Places, this site was the home of the Osage when first encountered by Europeans.

Washington

Busch Brewery. The brewery was established in 1854 by John B. Busch, Henry Busch, and Fred Gersie. The brewery is older than the famous Busch Brewery in St. Louis, founded by John B. Busch's younger brother, Adolphus.

Webster Groves

Christopher Hawken House. The house was built in 1857 by Christopher Hawken, son of Jacob Hawken, who manufactured the Hawken rifle in St. Louis. The Late Greek Revival style house is furnished with Victorian furnishings. Lillian Stupp's Doll collection is also on display.

Weston

McCormick Distilling Company. Tour America's oldest continuously-active distillery, founded in 1856. The grounds and springs were charted in 1804 by Lewis and Clark.

Photo courtesy of Springfield Convention and Visitors Bureau.

History comes to life at Wilson's Creek National Battlefield near Springfield.

Camdenton Area Chamber of Commerce, P.O. Box 1375, Camdenton 65020.

Cape Girardeau Convention and Visitors Bureau, P.O. Box 98, Cape Girardeau 63702-0098.

City of Joplin, P.O. Box 1355, Joplin 64802-1355.

City of Versailles, 104 N. Fisher, Versailles 65084.

Convention and Visitors Bureau of Greater Kansas City, 100 Main, Suite 2550, Kansas City, MO 64105.

Excelsior Springs Chamber of Commerce, 101 E. Broadway, Excelsior Springs 64024.

Florissant Valley Chamber of Commerce, 1060 Rue St. Catherine, Florissant 63031.

Hannibal Convention and Visitor's Bureau, P.O. Box 624, Hannibal 63401.

Harrisonville Area Chamber of Commerce, 400 E. Mechanic, Harrisonville 64701.

Hermann Chamber of Commerce, 115 E. 3rd, Hermann 65041.

Independence Chamber of Commerce, P.O. Box 147, Independence 64501.

"1988 Kansas City Chiefs Media Guide," Kansas City Chiefs Football Club, One Arrowhead Drive, Kansas City, MO 64129.

Kennett Chamber of Commerce, P.O. Box 61, Kennett 63857.

Lee's Summit Journal, P.O. Box 387, Lee's Summit 64063.

Lexington Chamber of Commerce, 1127 Main St., Lexington 64067.

Liberty Area Chamber of Commerce, 9 S. Leonard, Liberty 64068.

Missouri Division of Tourism, Truman State Office Building, P.O. Box 1055, Jefferson City 65102.

"Missouri Facts & Figures," Missouri Division of Tourism, March 1989.

"Missouri Travel Guide," Missouri Division of Tourism, 1990.

Paris Area Chamber of Commerce, P.O. Box 75, Paris 65275.

Raytown Chamber of Commerce, 5909 Raytown Trafficway, Raytown 64133.

Roberts, Robert B. **Encyclopedia of Historic Forts, The Military, Pioneer, and Trading Posts of the United States**. New York: Macmillan Publishing Company, 1988.

St. Charles Chamber of Commerce, 1816 Boonslick Rd., St. Charles 63301.

St. Joseph Chamber of Commerce, P.O. Box 1394, St. Joseph 64502.

The Ste. Genevieve Herald, P.O. Box 447, 330 Market St., Ste. Genevieve 63670.

Springfield Convention and Visitors Bureau, 3315 E. Battlefield Rd., Springfield 65804-4048.

The State Historical Society of Missouri, 1020 Lowry, Columbia 65201.

Waynesville Chamber of Commerce, P.O. Box 6, Waynesville 65583.

Wilson, Ray D. **Missouri Historic Tour Guide**. Carpentersville, IL: Crossroads Communications, Inc., 1988.

CHAPTER 3
GOVERNMENT

Federal Government • State Government • U.S. Congress State Officials • Senators Representatives • Local Government State Finances • Education

Photo courtesy of Missouri Division of Tourism.

51

Federal Government 55	Of the federal dollars spent in Missouri, about 32% is spent for defense purposes, more than any of Missouri's neighboring states.
State Government 56-65	The governor is elected to a four-year term during the same time as the presidential election and may seek re-election for a second four-year term.
U.S. Congress 66	Christopher Bond and John Danforth are the two U.S. Senators from Missouri.
State Officials/Voting 67	Qualified voters may register in person at the office of their election authority or at designated sites throughout the state.
State Senators 68	State senators are in office for terms of four years.
State Representatives 69-71	Elections for state representatives are held every two years. Missouri has 163 state representatives.
Local Government 72	Of the $5.8 billion in revenues collected by local governments in 1987, 67% was generated locally and 33% from intergovernmental sources (state and federal).
State Finances 73	Missouri is ranked 49th among all states in terms of total expenditures per person.
Education 74-79	Faculty at Missouri's four-year public colleges and universities receive an average salary of $37,006.

CHAPTER OPENER PHOTO: Beyond the grand facade of the capitol building is a flurry of activity when government officials are in session.

When the U.S. Congress organized the Missouri Territory in 1812, there were already 20,000 persons living in the area. William Clark, co-leader of the Lewis and Clark Expedition, was named governor of the new territory until 1820. Officially, though, Alexander McNair was elected as the first governor of the state of Missouri on August 28, 1820.

Settled mostly by Southerners who brought Negro slaves with them, Missouri asked to be admitted to the Union as a slave state. At the time there were an equal number of slave states and free states. Through the Missouri Compromise the state of Maine was admitted into the Union as a free state and Missouri became a slave state. Missouri achieved statehood August 10, 1821. The first state capital was located at St. Charles from June 1821 to October 1826. On October 1, 1826, Jefferson City was named the permanent capital.

From its inception in 1820, Missouri's state government has been constitutionally divided into three separate branches – the legislative, executive, and judicial departments. The Constitution of 1820, the state's first constitution, placed the judicial power in a Supreme Court, chancery courts (later abolished by the General Assembly), circuit and other courts to be established by the legislature.

The onset of the Civil War slowed Missouri's progress. The state was torn apart by pro- and anti-slavery activists. The famous Dred Scott case, in which a slave filed a lawsuit for his freedom, was heard by the Missouri Supreme Court. In 1857, the U.S. Supreme Court ruled against Scott in the case which began a chain reaction leading to the Civil War. After the Civil War, Missouri began to pick up the pieces of its shattered government and rebuild.

Today, Missouri government is a fine-tuned machine, molded to shape by such political figures as George Caleb Bingham, Blanche Kelso Bruce, and Harry S Truman. Missouri has a traditional government with federal, state, and local offices to maintain the integrity of the state's motto.

Missouri's future lies in the young generations attending public and private schools across the state. Missouri offers one of the finest educations in the country. Missouri students continue to exceed on both S.A.T. and A.C.T. exams, scoring higher than the national average. College and university enrollment has increased and with the help of highly-qualified faculty, students are assured a place in the state's future. With the training and education students are getting through Missouri schools, the state is gaining a valuable asset: a new generation of educated Missourians. Although some will stay in the state while others will venture to new lands, these students are learning what it takes to make it in the world today. The torch is being passed through skilled professionals, teaching quality students. It is these students who can say they were educated the Missouri way. ❐

Pledge Allegiance | "Cape Girardeau, Home of the Missouri State Flag" was adopted in 1975 as the city's official slogan. In 1907, two residents, Mrs. Marie Elizabeth Watkins Oliver and Miss Mary Kochtitzky, designed and made the flag that was to be adopted as the Missouri State Flag.

A Ton of Bricks | The cornerstone for the current Capitol was laid June 24, 1915. The cost for the construction, excluding the cost for the land and furnishings, was $3,600,000, or about 40¢ per cubic foot. There are 4,650,000 bricks in the Missouri Capitol.

Woman's Right | Ann Baxter was elected clerk of Jasper County in 1890, but women did not have the right to hold public office at that time. The State Supreme Court ruled in her favor, which set a new precedent for women's rights.

Number One Governor | Missouri's first governor was Major Alexander McNair. Prior to McNair, William Clark, co-leader of the Lewis and Clark expedition, acted as the Missouri Territorial Governor until 1820.

Reactor Factor | The University of Missouri at Columbia is the only state university in the United States which has a nuclear reactor that is used for education and research.

First University | St. Louis University was the first university founded west of the Mississippi River.

Cause to Swear | After the Civil War ended in 1865, Missouri adopted a new Constitution. A clause in the Constitution forced voters and public officials, mainly lawyers, teachers, and preachers, to swear they had not been southern sympathizers. Preachers were denied the right to preach from the pulpit if they did not take this oath.

British Honors | William Jewell College in Liberty has a comprehensive honors program that is modeled after the British system and includes a year of study at Oxford or Cambridge.

Federal Government Employees

In 1988, there were 67,000 Missourians employed by the federal government, and 31.3% of the total were employed in the defense sector. Of Missouri's neighbors, only Illinois employed more federal workers, and none had a greater percentage in defense.

PAID CIVILIAN EMPLOYMENT IN THE FEDERAL GOVERNMENT: 1988

	Total	Percent Defense	Rate per 100,000 population
U.S.	2,862,000	33.8	118.7
Arkansas	19,000	26.3	80.1
Illinois	104,000	21.2	90.0
Iowa	18,000	5.6	63.1
Kansas	24,000	29.2	97.6
MISSOURI	67,000	31.3	132.3
Nebraska	15,000	26.7	93.9

Federal Dollars Spent in Missouri

Of the total federal dollars spent in Missouri, about 32% is spent for defense purposes, more than in any of Missouri's neighboring states. Nearly 42% of federal assistance payments are direct payments to individuals such as pensions and Social Security.

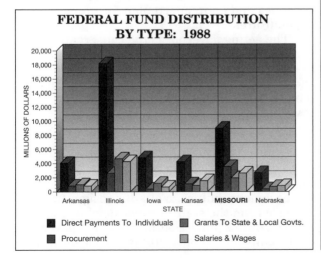

FEDERAL FUND DISTRIBUTION BY TYPE: 1988

MILLIONS OF DOLLARS

20,000
18,000
16,000
14,000
12,000
10,000
8,000
6,000
4,000
2,000
0

Arkansas   Illinois   Iowa   Kansas   **MISSOURI**   Nebraska
STATE

■ Direct Payments To Individuals   ■ Grants To State & Local Govts.
■ Procurement   ▨ Salaries & Wages

Missourians, with an adjusted gross income of more than $52.9 billion, paid more than $7.2 billion in federal taxes in 1987. That year, 2,189,000 Missourians filed tax returns.

In 1988, Missouri received nearly $2 billion in federal aid, or $378 for each Missourian. Missouri was ranked 41st nationally in the per capita amount of federal aid received.

Source: Statistical Abstract of the United States, 1990; U.S. Office of Personnel Management, Biennial Report of Employment by Geographic Area, Table 524.

There are nine congressional districts in Missouri.

The total federal fund distribution for Missouri in 1988 was $21.56 billion, which was $4,195 on a per capita basis.

Source: Statistical Abstract of the United States, 1990; U.S. Bureau of the Census, Federal Expenditures by State, Table 510.

state/executive

QUICK FACTS:

Federal Military Installations in Missouri:

Air Force
Whiteman Air Force Base, Knob Noster, MO 65305; (816) 687-1110.

Army
Ft. Leonard Wood, Waynesville, MO 65473; (314) 368-0131.

Coast Guard
2nd District, Atlantic Area, 1430 Olive St., St. Louis, MO 63103; (314) 425-4601.

The governor appoints the Board of Election Commissioners for St. Louis City, St. Louis County, Kansas City, Jackson County, and Clay County. The governor also appoints the Board of Police Commissioners for Kansas City and St. Louis City. Moreover, he appoints the Board of Probation and Parole.

The governor addresses the General Assembly on the state of government and recommends changes or other actions to be taken.

THE EXECUTIVE BRANCH OF MISSOURI STATE GOVERNMENT

Governor

The chief executive officer of the state must be at least 30 years old, a U.S. citizen for 15 years or longer and a resident of Missouri for at least 10 years before being elected governor. The governor is elected to a four-year term during the same year as a presidential election and may seek re-election to a second four-year term. No person may hold the office for more than two terms.

The governor appoints the members of all boards, commissions, the heads of all departments in state government and all vacancies in public offices unless otherwise provided by law. The board members of Missouri's state universities and colleges are appointed by the governor. The governor selects the members of the Supreme and Appellate Courts of Missouri from names submitted by the State Judicial Commissions. Most appointments require the advice and consent of the Senate.

A budget is submitted by the governor to the General Assembly within 30 days after the assembly convenes. The budget contains the governor's estimates of available state revenues and an itemized plan for proposed expenditures.

The acting governor is the conservator of peace throughout Missouri and is commander-in-chief of the state's militia. He may call out the militia to execute laws, suppress threats of danger to the state, and prevent and repel invasion.

Lieutenant Governor

Under the constitution, the lieutenant governor is ex officio president of the Missouri Senate. Upon the death, conviction, impeachment, failure to qualify, resignation, absence from the state or other disabilities, the powers, duties and emoluments of the governor devolve upon the lieutenant governor until the end of his or her term or until the disabilities of the governor are removed. By law, the lieutenant governor serves as secretary and member of the Board of Public Buildings. The lieutenant governor also serves as the state volunteer coordinator and the state's ombudsman.

Secretary of State

The secretary of state is the chief election official in Missouri. The office is also responsible for collecting, compiling, storing, and publishing a variety of state documents. The secretary of state oversees several areas in regard to state commerce – administration of the Missouri Uniform Commercial Code and registration of corporations and securities – and is the official keeper of the Great Seal of the State of Missouri.

To accommodate the responsibilities of record-keeping, registration and administration, the secretary of state's office is currently divided into three branches: Election Services, Administrative Services, and Business Services. Each branch, under the direction of a deputy secretary of state, is composed of separate divisions that perform specific functions relating to branch activities.

State Treasurer

The duties of the state treasurer, as defined by the Missouri Constitution, are: (1) to be custodian of all state funds; (2) to determine the amount of state moneys not needed for current operating expenses; and (3) to invest such moneys not needed for current operations in time deposits, bearing interest, in Missouri banking institutions selected by the state treasurer and approved by the governor and state auditor, or in short-term U.S. government obligations.

The operation of the office of state treasurer is essentially a banking operation. To disburse state funds, a warrant is prepared in the Office of Administration. The warrant, with the signature of the commissioner of

QUICK FEATURES:

Governor's Duties – The governor performs other duties assigned by the constitution, statute or custom. He issues writs of election to fill vacancies in either house of the General Assembly. The governor also has the power to grant reprieves, commutations and pardons, but this does not include the power to parole.

Missouri State Departments – The Missouri Constitution enumerates 13 specific departments (the Office of Administration and the Departments of Agriculture, Conservation, Economic Development, Elementary and Secondary Education, Higher Education, Highways and Transportation, Labor and Industrial Relations, Mental Health, Natural Resources, Public Safety, Revenue, and Social Services) and allows for the formation of up to two others (currently the Department of Corrections and Human Resources and the Department of Health). This brings the total to 15 major state departments.

QUICK FACTS:

The executive deputy secretary of state is second-in-command and is charged with implementing the policies and procedures of the secretary and supervising the day-to-day operations of certain phases of the office. The executive deputy secretary is also responsible for directing the Administrative Services Branch of the office.

The state auditor's office is Missouri's independent "watchdog" agency, charged with auditing all state agencies, boards and commissions, and the state's third- and fourth-class counties. The state auditor may also be called on to audit local units of government by citizen petition.

The state treasurer is permitted to purchase short-term U.S. government obligations, maturing and becoming payable within one year from the date of purchase. Interest received on the investment of state funds is credited either to the general revenue fund or to the fund from which the investment is made.

Photo courtesy of St. Louis Convention / Tourism Bureau.

A place of business for some, the St. Louis Courthouse is also a beautiful attraction.

administration, is presented to the state treasurer's office for processing. When the warrant is signed by the treasurer, it is converted into a negotiable check, or draft, on a designated depository of state funds.

When investing state funds, the state treasurer is required to give due consideration to the preservation of such moneys, the comparative yield and the effect upon the economy and welfare of the people of Missouri.

Attorney General

The attorney general is the attorney for the state. He represents the legal interests of Missouri and its people as a group, but cannot represent individual citizens in private legal actions.

As the state's chief legal officer, the attorney general must prosecute or defend all appeals to which the state is a party, including every felony criminal case which is appealed to the Missouri Supreme Court and courts of appeal. He is also required to institute, in the name and on behalf of the state, all civil suits and other proceedings that are necessary to protect the state's rights, interests or claims. The attorney general also may appear, interplead, answer, or defend any proceedings in which the state's interests are involved, or appear on behalf of the state in declaratory judgment proceedings when the constitutionality of a statute is challenged.

The attorney general renders official opinions to the General Assembly, the governor, secretary of state, auditor, treasurer, the heads of the various state departments and the circuit or prosecuting attorneys on questions of law relating to their duties.

In order to fulfill these and other responsibilities, the attorney general has organized his office into five divisions: litigation, criminal, trade offenses, government affairs, and human and environmental resources.

A Service Industry

Government is a service industry, and Missourians are served by a broad network of government organizations. But because of the many different names used by these groups – departments, divisions, agencies, boards, commissions, bureaus, units, sections, programs and others – it can be difficult to determine which area of government is responsible for certain services, or to sort out responsibilities or relationships within the governmental framework.

From the legislative, executive and judicial branches spring the variety of organizations which deliver services of state government. The legislative and judicial branches rely generally on committees or other small, appointed groups to perform research, develop policy, provide advocacy services or handle administrative duties. In these two branches, most services are delivered through the offices of the elected officials themselves and not by related agencies. Missouri state government has 15 major state departments.

QUICK FACTS:

Approximately 177 state agencies and programs, the state's circuit court system, and 94 third- and fourth-class counties must be audited by the state auditor regularly. Approximately 10 audits of local government entities, petitioned by local voters, are performed each year.

The attorney general may institute quo warranto proceedings to oust any corporation from doing business in Missouri if it has abused its franchise or has violated the state's laws. He also may institute quo warranto proceedings against any person unlawfully holding any office or move to oust any public official for misfeasance, nonfeasance, or malfeasance in office.

It is through the executive branch that many state services are delivered; consequently a network of government bodies has been developed to administer these needs.

Joshua Barton, an attorney from St. Louis County, became Missouri's first secretary of state in 1820.

QUICK FACTS:

Legislative power in Missouri is vested by Section 1, Article III of the 1945 Constitution in the General Assembly, composed of the Senate and the House of Representatives.

The General Assembly convenes annually on the first Wednesday after the first Monday of January. In odd-numbered years, it adjourns on June 30, with no consideration of bills after June 15. In even-numbered years adjournment is on May 15, with no consideration of bills after April 30.

The governor may convene the General Assembly in special session for a maximum of 60 calendar days at any time. Only subjects recommended by the governor in his call or a special message may be considered.

Both the Senate and House of Representatives are required to keep a daily journal (or record) of their proceedings. At the end of the session, the journals are bound by the office of secretary of state.

THE LEGISLATIVE BRANCH OF MISSOURI STATE GOVERNMENT

The Missouri General Assembly

The Senate consists of 34 members, elected for four-year terms. Senators from odd-numbered districts are elected in presidential election years. Senators from even-numbered districts are chosen in the "off year" elections. Each senator must be at least 30 years of age; a qualified voter of the state for three years; and of the district he or she represents for one year. The lieutenant governor is president and presiding officer of the Senate. In the absence of the lieutenant governor, the president pro tem, elected by the Senate members, presides.

The House of Representatives consists of 163 members, elected at each general election for two-year terms. A representative must be at least 24 years of age; a qualified voter of the state for two years; and of the district he or she represents for one year. The House of Representatives is presided over by the speaker, chosen by the members, and in the absence of the speaker, by the speaker pro tem.

Reapportionment of both houses of the Missouri General Assembly following each decennial U.S. Census is provided for by the Missouri Constitution.

Organization of the General Assembly

Following the general election in November of even-numbered years, the majority and minority members of each house caucus and separately nominate candidates for the offices to be elected by each body and organize their parties for the coming session. Nominees of the majority party are, in effect, elected. Each party names its floor leader, caucus chairman, and secretary.

Both houses of the General Assembly convene at noon on the opening day of the session. Temporary officers are named and the roll of new and carryover senators is read. Newly elected senators are then sworn in, usually by a judge of the Supreme Court. The president pro tem and other permanent officers are then elected and take an oath of office administered by the president of the Senate.

The House of Representatives is called to order by the secretary of state and the oath is administered to all members. After the swearing-in ceremony, a roll call is taken and a temporary speaker is named. He or she presides for nomination and election of permanent officers. Temporary rules, usually the rules in force for the preceding session, are adopted.

Each house determines its own rules and procedures, and rules may not be dispensed with except by unanimous consent or concurrence by a constitutional majority in the House or by a vote of at least a majority of the Senate following at least one day's notice.

How Bills Become Laws

Introduction of a Bill: Bills may be introduced by any senator or representative during the session. When introduced, a bill is assigned a number and read for the first time by its title by the Senate or House reading clerk. It then goes on the calendar for second reading and assignment to committee by the speaker of the House or the president or president pro tem of the Senate.

A public hearing before the committee to which a bill is assigned is the next step in the legislative process. Except in the case of some unusual bills, the bill is presented by its sponsor and both proponents and opponents are heard in a single hearing. When hearings are concluded, the committee meets to vote and makes its recommendations. The committee may: (1) report the bill with the recommendation that it "do pass"; (2) recommend passage with committee amendments, which are attached to the bill; (3) return the bill without recommendation; (4) substitute in lieu of the original bill a new bill to be known as a committee substitute; (5) report the bill with a recommendation that it "do not pass" or (6) make no report at all.

QUICK FEATURES:

General Provisions of a Bill – No law is passed except by bill. Bills may originate in either house. No bill (except general appropriations bills) may contain more than one subject, which is to be expressed clearly in its title. No bill can be amended in its passage through either house so as to change its original purpose. No bill can be introduced in either house after the 60th legislative day of a session in an odd-numbered year or after the 30th legislative day of a session in an even-numbered year, unless consented to by a majority of the elected members of each house. The governor may request consideration of proposed legislation by a special message. Bills are designed as Senate bills or House bills, depending on the house in which they originate.

QUICK FACTS:

Bills may be written by the legislature or drafted by the staff of the Committee on Legislative Research at the request of a senator or representative.

Supreme Court and Court of Appeals judges are selected for 12-year terms. Circuit judges serve six-year terms, and associate circuit judges serve four-year terms.

The Supreme Court has been the state's highest court since 1820. The court at that time consisted of only three members. At various times, the court sat in St. Louis, Jackson, Cape Girardeau, St. Charles, Boonville, Fayette, Hannibal, Lexington, and other cities.

In 1890, the Supreme Court was divided into two divisions in order to permit it to handle and decide more cases in a shorter time. Under the present Constitution, the court may sit en banc (all seven judges together) or in as many divisions as the court determines are needed. Today, all cases are assigned to and decided by the court en banc.

Perfection of a Bill: If a bill is reported favorably out of committee or a substitute is recommended, it is placed on the "perfection calendar" and when its turn comes up for consideration it is debated on the floor of the originating house. When all amendments have been considered, a motion is made to declare the bill perfected. If a majority of members vote to perfect, the bill is reprinted in its amended form.

Final Passage of a Bill: After perfection and reprinting, a bill goes on the calendar for third reading and final passage. When the bill is reached in the order of business any member may speak for or against its passage but no further amendments of a substantive nature can be offered. At the conclusion of debate, a recorded vote is taken. Approval of a constitutional majority of the elected members (18 in the Senate and 82 in the House) is required for final passage.

Passage of the bill is then reported to the other house where it is read a second time; referred to committee for hearing; reported by committee; perfected; and read a third time and offered for final approval. If further amendments are approved, these are reported to the originating house with a request that the changes be approved. If the originating house does not approve, a conference may be requested and members from each house are designated as a conference committee. Upon agreement by the conference committee, each reports to its own house on the committee's recommendation.

Upon final passage, a bill is ordered enrolled. It is typed in its final form, printed, and the bills are closely compared and proofed for errors.

Signing of the Bill: Bills truly agreed to and finally passed in their typed form are then signed in open session by the House speaker and Senate president or president pro tem. At the time of signing, any member may file written objections which are sent with the bill to the governor.

THE JUDICIAL BRANCH OF MISSOURI STATE GOVERNMENT

Selection of Judges

In the first 30 years of Missouri's statehood, the judges of the supreme, circuit, and chancery courts were appointed by the Governor with the advice and consent of the Senate. After much public discussion, the constitution was amended in 1849 to provide for the popular election of judges, and this system continues in effect for most Missouri courts even today. In most cases, the judges are elected by the voters in partisan elections.

Under the Missouri Court Plan, as it is often called, a vacancy on a court to which the plan applies is filled by appointment by the governor, who selects one person from a three-person panel chosen by a nonpartisan judicial commission of laymen, lawyers and judges. A judge appointed in this way must stand for retention in office at the first general election occurring after the judge has been in office for 12 months; his name is placed on a separate judicial ballot, without political party designation, and the voters must vote either for or against his retention in office. The Missouri Court Plan has served as a national model for the selection of judges and has been adopted by a number of other states.

Photo courtesy of Missouri Division of Tourism.
The Truman Library in Independence.

QUICK FEATURES:

Judges' Qualifications and Terms – Judges of the Supreme Court and the Court of Appeals must be at least 30 years of age and residents of their district. They must have been United States citizens for at least 15 years and qualified voters of Missouri for nine years preceding their selection.

Circuit Court judges also must be at least 30 years of age and residents of their circuit. They must have been United States citizens for at least 10 years and qualified voters of Missouri for at least three years before their selection.

Associate circuit judges must be at least 25 years old, qualified Missouri voters, and residents of the counties in which they serve. Every supreme, appellate, circuit, and associate circuit court judge must be licensed to practice law in Missouri.

The 1976 constitutional amendments require all judges other than municipal judges to retire by age 70.

The court holds sessions to hear oral arguments in cases in January, May, and September of each year.

The first general intermediate courts in Missouri were provided for in the 1865 Constitution and were known as district courts. There were district courts in Jefferson City, Springfield, Cape Girardeau, Macon, St. Joseph, and St. Charles. Each district was composed of three circuits. Appeals were taken from the circuit court to the district court, and then to the Supreme Court. However, the district courts were abolished in 1870 by a constitutional amendment.

The Constitution requires at least one resident associate circuit judge in each county. The statutes authorize additional associate circuit judges depending on county populations. Presently, 170 circuit judges are required by statute.

In 1988, Ann Kettering Covington became the first woman appointed to the Missouri Supreme Court.

Supreme Court

Supreme Court Jurisdiction: Originally, the Supreme Court had only the traditional powers to decide cases on appeal from the lower four courts (either the circuit courts or the Court of Appeals) and to issue and determine original remedial writs, such as habeas corpus, mandamus, and prohibition. The Constitution of 1945 also authorized the court to establish rules for practice and procedure in the courts and to make temporary transfer of judicial personnel. Maintaining and updating the rules is a continuous process requiring substantial time. Each year, the court (through its Office of State Courts Administrator) transfers several hundred court personnel on a temporary basis to assist other courts. This usually is done when a judge has been disqualified by the parties in a case or when a judge's docket has become overly crowded and he cannot handle all the cases expeditiously.

Under the amendments of 1976 and 1982, the Supreme Court has exclusive appellate jurisdiction in all cases involving: (1) the validity of a treaty or statute of the United States or of a statute or provision of the Missouri Constitution; (2) the construction of the state's revenue laws; (3) the title to any state office; (4) and in all cases where the punishment imposed is death.

In addition to its decision-making powers, the court is responsible for the supervision of all lower courts in the state. It is assisted in this task by the Office of State Courts Administrator, established in 1970. The Supreme Court also licenses all lawyers practicing in Missouri and disciplines those found guilty of violating the legal Rules of Professional Conduct.

Chief Justice: The seven judges of the Supreme Court select one of their number to be chief justice and reside over the Court. The chief justice handles many of the administrative details for the court. The position is rotated every two years.

Missouri Court of Appeals

Alarmed at the congested docket of the Supreme Court, the St. Louis Bar Association urged the 1875 Constitutional Convention to provide for another appellate court. The St. Louis Court of Appeals was created. Three judges heard appeals from St. Louis, St. Charles, Lincoln, and Warren counties. Its territorial jurisdiction was expanded to include several more counties in 1884.

That same year another constitutional amendment established the Kansas City Court of Appeals and authorized creation of another appellate court, when necessary, by the General Assembly. The Springfield Court of Appeals was organized in 1909. Missouri's current appellate structure – a single Court of Appeals consisting of three districts – was established by a 1970 constitutional amendment.

The Court of Appeals may issue and determine original remedial writs and has general appellate jurisdiction in all cases not within the exclusive jurisdiction of the Supreme Court. However, as previously mentioned, cases not within the Supreme Court's exclusive jurisdiction may be transferred when it is determined that a case involves an important issue that should be decided by the state's highest court.

Missouri Circuit Courts

Constitutional amendments approved by Missouri voters in 1976 – and subsequent enabling legislation enacted by the General Assembly in 1978 – provide that the circuit courts shall be courts of original civil and criminal jurisdiction. All trials start at this level. On January 2, 1979, former courts of limited jurisdiction became divisions of the circuit court.

Within the divisions of the Circuit Court there are three levels of jurisdiction: the circuit division, the associate circuit division, and the municipal division. Judges may hear and determine all cases within their jurisdiction.

QUICK FACTS:

Missouri's first two circuit courts were established in 1815. The 1820 Constitution provided for the creation of four circuits, each circuit consisting of from four to eight counties. In 1831, the number of circuits was increased to five, and over the years additional circuits have been created, bringing the number to 44 today.

The number of circuit judges is determined by the General Assembly. The Constitution requires at least one circuit judge in each of Missouri's 44 judicial circuits.

Municipalities with 400,000 or more people must establish municipal divisions to hear ordinance violations, or the municipality may request that those matters be heard in the associate division of the Circuit Court. Municipal judges are paid locally.

Missouri has 44 judicial districts, divided along county lines. There are three appellate districts in Missouri, located in Kansas City, St. Louis, and Springfield.

NATIONAL CONGRESSIONAL DELEGATION

United States Senate	Elected	Term Expires
Sen. Christopher S. "Kit" Bond	Nov. 1986	Jan. 1993
Sen. John C. Danforth	Nov. 1988	Jan. 1995
Term: Six years.		

United States House of Representatives		
Dist 1: Rep. William "Bill" Clay, Sr.	Nov. 1990	Jan. 1993
Dist. 2: Rep. Joan Kelly Horn	Nov. 1990	Jan. 1993
Dist. 3: Rep. Richard A. Gephardt	Nov. 1990	Jan. 1993
Dist. 4: Rep. Ike Skelton	Nov. 1990	Jan. 1993
Dist. 5: Rep. Alan Wheat	Nov. 1990	Jan. 1993
Dist. 6: Rep. Tom Coleman	Nov. 1990	Jan. 1993
Dist. 7: Rep. Melton D. "Mel" Hancock	Nov. 1990	Jan. 1993
Dist. 8: Rep. Bill Emerson	Nov. 1990	Jan. 1993
Dist. 9: Rep. Harold L. Volkmer	Nov. 1990	Jan. 1993
Term: Two years.		

MISSOURI CONGRESSIONAL DISTRICTS: 1982*

*Based on 1980 Census.
Source: Missouri Secretary of State, Elections Division.

EXECUTIVE BRANCH ELECTED OFFICIALS

	Elected	Term Expires
Governor:		
John Ashcroft	Nov. 1988	Jan. 1993
Lieutenant Governor:		
Mel Carnahan	Nov. 1988	Jan. 1993
Secretary of State:		
Roy D. Blunt	Nov. 1988	Jan. 1993
State Auditor:		
Margaret B. Kelly	Nov. 1990	Jan. 1995
State Treasurer:		
Wendell Bailey	Nov. 1988	Jan. 1993
Attorney General:		
William L. Webster	Nov. 1988	Jan. 1993

Term: Four years.

Voter Registration

To be eligible to vote in Missouri, a person must be: (1) United States citizen, (2) 18 years of age or older, (3) a resident of Missouri, and (4) registered to vote. Qualified citizens may register in person at the office of their local election authority, at designated sites throughout the state such as public libraries or school district offices, or by mail.

Voter registration and the conduct of elections is the responsibility of boards of election commissioners in the counties of Clay, Jackson, and St. Louis and the cities of Kansas City and St. Louis.

Electoral College

Missouri voters, like those throughout the nation, cast ballots to elect a slate of electors – members of the Electoral College. The Electoral College determines the outcome of the U.S. Presidential race. Missouri has 11 electoral votes, which is the sum of the number of U.S. Senators (2) plus the number of U.S. Representatives (9) from the state.

QUICK FACTS:

To contact state officials –

Governor:
State Capitol, P.O. Box 720, Jefferson City, 65101; (314) 751-3222.

Lt. Governor:
121 State Capitol, Jefferson City, 65101; (314) 751-3000.

Secretary of State:
208 State Capitol, P.O. Box 778, Jefferson City, 65102; (314) 751-2379.

State Auditor:
224 State Capitol, P.O. Box 869, Jefferson City, 65102; (314) 751-4213.

State Treasurer:
229 State Capitol, P.O. Box 210, Jefferson City, 65102; (314) 751-2411.

Attorney General:
Supreme Court Building, P.O. Box 899, Jefferson City, 65102; (314) 751-3321.

There were 2,943,025 registered voters in Missouri in 1988.

Three basic voting and tabulation systems are approved in Missouri: paper ballot, lever machines, and electronic devices (punch card or optical scan).

Missouri has two established political parties on a statewide basis: the Republican and Democratic parties.

MISSOURI (STATE) SENATE

District/Name/Hometown

1 Irene Treppler, Mattese
2 Fred Dyer, St. Charles
3 John E. Scott, St. Louis
4 John F. Bass, St. Louis
5 J. B. (Jet) Banks, St. Louis
6 Larry Rohrbach, California
7 Francis E. Flotron, St. Louis
8 Robert T. Johnson, Lee's Summit
9 Phil B. Curls, Kansas City
10 Harry Wiggins, Kansas City
11 Henry A. Panethiere, Kansas City
12 Pat Danner, Smithville
13 Wayne Goode, Normandy
14 John D. Schneider, Florissant
15 Walt Mueller, Des Peres
16 Mike Lybyer, Huggins
17 Edward E. Quick, Kansas City

District/Name/Hometown

18 Norman L. Merrell, Monticello
19 Roger B. Wilson, Columbia
20 Danny Staples, Eminence
21 James L. Mathewson, Sedalia
22 Jeremiah Nixon, Herculaneum
23 Jeff W. Schaeperkoetter, Owensville
24 Edwin L. Dirck, St. Ann
25 J. T. Howard, Dexter
26 Thomas W. McCarthy, Chesterfield
27 John Dennis, Benton
28 Steve Danner, Kirksville
29 Emory Melton, Cassville
30 Dennis Smith, Springfield
31 Harold L. Caskey, Butler
32 Marvin Singleton, Joplin
33 John T. Russell, Lebanon
34 Sidney Johnson, Gower

Term: Four years.

Even-numbered districts elected November 1990, terms expire January 1995.
Odd-numbered districts elected November 1988, terms expire January 1993.

MISSOURI SENATE DISTRICTS: 1982*

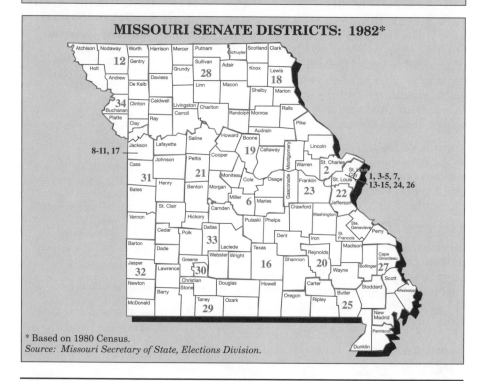

* Based on 1980 Census.
Source: Missouri Secretary of State, Elections Division.

state representatives

MISSOURI HOUSE OF REPRESENTATIVES

District/Name/Hometown

1 Stephen R. Waters, Canton
2 Kathleen Steele, Kirksville
3 Beth M. Wheeler, Trenton
4 Phil Tate, Gallatin
5 Everett Brown, Maryville
6 Timothy M. Kelley, Savannah
7 Millie Humphreys, St. Joseph
8 Edward Schellhorn, St. Joseph
9 Charles W. Shields, St. Joseph
10 Bob F. Griffin, Cameron
11 Dale Whiteside, Chillicothe
12 John J. Kauffman, Excello
13 Steven R. Carroll, Hannibal
14 Sam Leake, Laddonia
15 Joe Maxwell, Mexico
16 Philip Smith, Louisiana
17 George Dames, O'Fallon
18 Joseph R. Ortwerth, St. Peters
19 Steven E. Ehlmann, St. Charles
20 Ted House, St. Charles
21 Craig Kilby, Lake St. Louis
22 Russell Brockfeld, Warrenton
23 Gracia Y. Backer, New Bloomfield
24 Jim G. Pauley, Ashland
25 Kenneth B. Jacob, Columbia
26 Christopher S. Kelly, Columbia
27 William A. Markland, Armstrong
28 Norwood Creason, Braymer
29 Martha F. Jarman, Excelsior Springs
30 Sandra Reeves, Kansas City
31 Gary Witt, Platte City
32 Bonnie Sue Cooper, Kansas City
33 Joe Bock, Gladstone
34 Bill Skaggs, Kansas City
35 Henry C. Rizzo, Kansas City
36 Vernon Thompson, Kansas City
37 Ronnie DePasco, Kansas City
38 Jacqueline T. McGee, Kansas City

District/Name/Hometown

39 Fletcher Daniels, Kansas City
40 Karen McCarthy, Kansas City
41 Annette N. Morgan, Kansas City
42 Joseph S. Kenton, Kansas City
43 Mary Bland, Kansas City
44 Robert Sego, Raytown
45 Vernon E. Scoville III, Kansas City
46 Sandy Kauffman, Kansas City
47 Thomas Hoppe, Kansas City
48 Pat Kelley, Lee's Summit
49 Carson Ross, Blue Springs
50 James Barnes, Raytown
51 Carol Jean Mays, Independence
52 Carole Roper Park, Sugar Creek
53 W. T. Dawson, Independence
54 Don Lograsso, Blue Springs
55 Richard Franklin, Independence
56 Paula J. Carter, St. Louis
57 O. L. Shelton, St. Louis
58 Louis H. Ford, St. Louis
59 William L. Clay, Jr., St. Louis
60 Russell Goward, St. Louis
61 Elbert A. Walton, Jr., St. Louis
62 Charles Troupe, St. Louis
63 Ronnie L. White, St. Louis
64 Thomas P. Stoff, St. Louis
65 Anthony D. Ribaudo, St. Louis
66 Matt O'Neill, St. Louis
67 Patrick Dougherty, St. Louis
68 Ron Auer, St. Louis
69 Gail L. Chatfield, St. Louis
70 Edward E. Ottinger, St. Louis
71 Timothy P. Green, St. Louis
72 Laurie B. Donovan, Florissant
73 Richard Dorsey, Florissant
74 Kaye H. Steinmetz, Florissant
75 Michael Reid, Florissant
76 Judith O'Connor, Bridgeton
77 David C. Hale, St. Louis

District/Name/Hometown	District/Name/Hometown
78 Mary M. Hagan-Harrell, Ferguson	116 Thomas W. Marshall, Marshall
79 Francis R. Brady, Jennings	117 Todd Smith, Sedalia
80 Robert J. Quinn, Ferguson	118 Delbert Scott, Lowry City
81 Neil Molloy, Pasadena Park	119 Bob Schemenauer, Clinton
82 Chet Boeke, Overland	120 Gene Lang, Warrensburg
83 Patrick J. Hickey, Bridgeton	121 David A. Oetting, Concordia
84 Mark Holloway, Maryland Heights	122 Gene Olson, Harrisonville
85 W. Todd Akin, St. Louis	123 Harold G. Weil, Butler
86 John Hancock, St. Louis	124 Bubs Hohulin, Lamar
87 Sue Shear, Clayton	125 William G. Marshall, Greenfield
88 Sheila Lumpe, University City	126 T. Mark Elliott, Webb City
89 James N. Riley, Richmond Heights	127 Gary L. Burton, Joplin
90 Raymond W. (Bill) Hand, Warson Woods	128 Chuck Surface, Joplin
91 William C. Linton, Grover	129 Galen Browning, Neosho
92 James Talent, Chesterfield	130 Earle F. Staponski, Pierce City
93 Pat Secrest, Manchester	131 Nolan G. McNeill, Cassville
94 David Klarich, Manchester	132 Doyle Childers, Reeds Spring
95 Jim Murphy, Crestwood	133 Donald L. Gann, Ozark
96 Francis M. Barnes, Kirkwood	134 Doug Harpool, Springfield
97 Emma L. McClelland, Webster Groves	135 Connie Wible, Springfield
98 May Scheve, Affron	136 B. J. Marsh, Springfield
99 Bill Raisch, Affton	137 Chuck Wooten, Springfield
100 Clarence Wohlwend, St. Louis	138 Craig Hosmer, Springfield
101 Michael Yates, Clayton	139 Philip P. Wannenmacher, Springfield
102 Joseph L. Treadway, Lemay	140 Thomas M. Macdonnell, Marshfield
103 Jonathan Selsor, Kimmswick	141 Kenneth Legan, Halfway
104 Jo Ann Karll, Fenton	142 Elizabeth L. Long, Lebanon
105 William P. McKenna, Barnhart	143 James W. Mitchell, Richland
106 George Engelbach, Hillsboro	144 Jerry E. McBride, Edgar Springs
107 Norman E. Sheldon, De Soto	145 Jim Montgomery, Cabool
108 Wesley A. Miller, Washington	146 Mervin R. Case, Ava
109 Al Nilges, Bourbon	147 Jess Garnett, Brandsville
110 James V. Froelker, Gerald	148 Don Koller, Summersville
111 Merrill M. Townley, Chamois	149 Ken Fiebelman, Salem
112 Carl Vogel, Jefferson City	150 Wayne F. Crump, Potosi
113 Don Steen, Eldon	151 Robert D. Ward, Bonne Terre
114 Larry T. Whitten, Camdenton	152 Herbert C. Fallert, Ste. Genevieve
115 Paul Sombart, Boonville	153 Jim Graham, Fredericktown
	154 Joseph L. Driskill, Doniphan

state representatives

District/Name/Hometown	District/Name/Hometown
155 Mark Richardson, Poplar Bluff	161 Fred E. Copeland, New
156 Marilyn Williams, Dudley	Madrid
157 Dennis Ziegenhorn, Sikeston	162 Opal Parks, Caruthersville
158 David Schwab, Jackson	163 Larry Thomason, Kennett
159 Mary C. Kasten, Cape	*Term: Two years.*
Girardeau	*Elected November 1990; term*
160 Ollie Amick, Scott City	*expires January 1993.*

MISSOURI HOUSE OF REPRESENTATIVES
DISTRICTS: 1982*

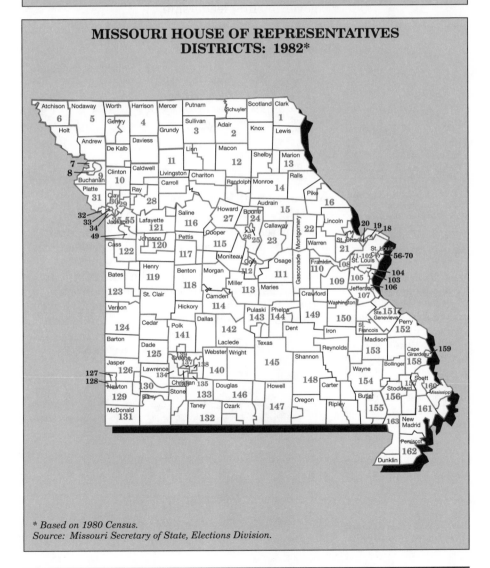

* Based on 1980 Census.
Source: Missouri Secretary of State, Elections Division.

local government

QUICK FACTS:

The Community Development Block Grant program provides fiscal assistance to communities in the form of grants or loans.

Local Jurisdictions

Missouri has a network of 3,147 local governmental jurisdictions, including county, municipal, township, school districts and various special districts (natural resource, fire protection, and housing/community development). Municipal governments and school districts provide the primary governmental leadership.

NUMBER OF LOCAL GOVERNMENTS BY TYPE
MISSOURI & SELECTED STATES: 1987

	Total	County	Municipal	Township	School Districts	Special Districts
U.S.	83,186	3,042	19,200	16,691	14,721	29,532
Arkansas	1,396	75	483	0	333	505
Illinois	6,627	102	1,279	1,434	1,029	2,783
Iowa	1,877	99	955	0	451	372
Kansas	3,803	105	627	1,360	324	1,387
MISSOURI	**3,147**	**114**	**930**	**325**	**561**	**1,217**
Nebraska	3,152	93	534	454	952	1,119

Source: Statistical Abstract of the United States, 1990; U.S. Bureau of the Census.

Missouri statutes permit villages to have only one form of government: an elected board of trustees.

Municipalities are classified according to statute on the basis of population and are limited to the form of government options of each classification.

Carrollton was incorporated in 1833 and operates under a special charter.

Source: Statistical Abstract of the United States, 1990; U.S. Bureau of the Census.

Sources of Revenue

In 1987, local governments in Missouri generated most of their revenues from local taxes and other local sources. Federal sources accounted for only about 5% of revenue to Missouri communities. Of the $5.8 billion in revenues collected by local governments in 1987, 67% was generated locally and 33% from intergovernmental sources (state and federal).

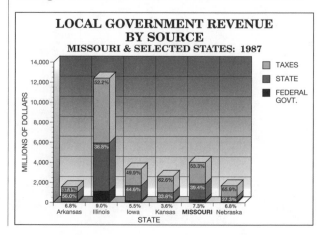

LOCAL GOVERNMENT REVENUE BY SOURCE
MISSOURI & SELECTED STATES: 1987

The State Budget

The 1991 Fiscal Year Budget for Missouri shows that most of the state's revenues are generated through taxes, primarily individual income taxes, which accounts for more than 50% of all revenue. The second largest revenue source, sales and use taxes, accounts for nearly 30% of all revenue. By far the greatest single appropriation is toward elementary and secondary education.

QUICK FACTS:

Missouri is ranked 49th among all states in terms of total expenditures per person, with approximately $2,068.

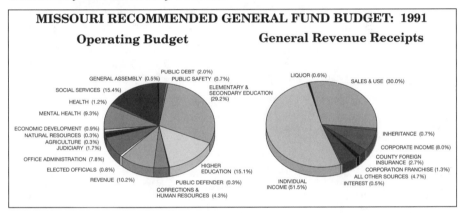

MISSOURI RECOMMENDED GENERAL FUND BUDGET: 1991

Operating Budget   **General Revenue Receipts**

Tax Collections

In 1988, Missouri's state tax collections amounted to $4.4 billion. About 52% of the tax collections were derived from sales receipts and approximately 34% came from individual income tax payments.

Source: Executive Budget; Fiscal Year 1991; State of Missouri.

The legislature has the ultimate authority over the total level of appropriations in the state budget.

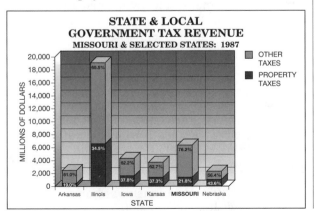

STATE & LOCAL GOVERNMENT TAX REVENUE
MISSOURI & SELECTED STATES: 1987

In 1987, nearly 47% of Missouri's nearly $10.7 billion of general revenue came from non-property taxes.

Source: Statistical Abstract of the United States, 1990; U.S. Bureau of the Census, Governmental Finances, Series GF, No. 5 Annual.

education

QUICK FACTS:

In the ten year period between 1980-81 and 1989-90, enrollment in Missouri public schools has decreased by 4.7%. Within the different grade levels, there was a 1.6% increase in grades K-8, but a 16.5% decline in grades 9-12.

The State Board of Education consists of eight members appointed by the governor and confirmed by the Senate.

In 1989, the total number of students enrolled in private schools was 102,681.

Source: 1987-1988 and 1989-1990 Report of the Public Schools of Missouri, Missouri State Board of Education.

The total number of students enrolled in vocational education institutions in 1988-1989 was 363,449.

Blanche Kelso Bruce, second Negro to hold the office of U.S. Senator, was a teacher in Hannibal.

ACTUAL FALL ENROLLMENT IN MISSOURI PUBLIC SCHOOLS: 1989-1990

Grade	Enrollment
Kindergarten	64,627
1st	68,509
2nd	63,596
3rd	63,849
4th	64,933
5th	63,099
6th	62,268
7th	62,348
8th	58,052
Ungraded	5,103
Total (K-8)	**576,384**
9th	64,372
10th	58,526
11th	54,550
12th	52,420
Total (9-12)	**229,868**
Ungraded	1,682
Total public school enrollment	**807,934**

Private School Enrollment

In the ten-year period between 1979-80 and 1989-90, enrollment in Missouri private schools has declined by slightly more than 12%. Within the different grade levels, there has been a 7.6% decrease in grades K-8, and a 24.4% decrease in grades 9-12.

Vocational Institution Enrollment

During the 1988-89 academic year, over 363,000 students were enrolled in Missouri's vocational education institutions. Most of these students (almost 217,000) were at the secondary level. The programs with the most students are industrial arts (all levels), with more than 97,000, and consumer home economics, with nearly 82,000.

Public High School Graduates

The number of public high school graduates in the 1989 school year was more than 10,000 less than in the 1975 school year. The greatest graduation rate, or rate of total students eligible to graduate, occurred in 1976, with 77.5% of all eligible students graduating.

QUICK FACTS:

Hannibal had the first free public library west of the Mississippi River. The library was dedicated on Feb. 15, 1902.

TOTAL NUMBER OF HIGH SCHOOL GRADUATES: 1979-1989

Year Graduated	Number of Graduates	% Change Previous Year	Graduation Rate *
1979	64,163	—	74.7
1980	62,265	-3.0%	73.7
1981	60,340	-3.1%	74.0
1982	59,872	-0.8%	75.4
1983	56,420	-5.8%	76.2
1984	53,388	-5.4%	77.3
1985	51,306	-3.9%	77.4
1986	49,204	-4.1%	76.6
1987	50,840	3.3%	76.1
1988	51,316	0.9%	75.5
1989	51,968	1.3%	73.5

* Percentage of freshman class that graduated.

High School Dropout Rate

During the 1988-89 school year, 15,208 students in secondary schools dropped out of Missouri's public schools. Of this total, 57.2% were males and 42.6% females. The largest number of males quit school in the 10th grade, while the largest number of females quit in the 11th grade.

Source: 1988-89 Report of the Public Schools of Missouri, Missouri State Board of Education.

The Missouri School for the Deaf (MSD) is located in Fulton, and the Missouri School for the Blind (MSB) is located in St. Louis.

MISSOURI HIGH SCHOOL DROPOUTS: 1988-1989

Grades	Male	Female	Total
9	2,272	1,452	3,724
10	2,464	1,801	4,265
11	2,349	1,968	4,317
12	1,650	1,252	2,902
Total	**8,735**	**6,473**	**15,208**

Source: 1988-1989 Report of the Public Schools of Missouri, Missouri State Board of Education.

QUICK FEATURES:

Food for Thought –
The State Fruit Experiment Station is operated by Southwest Missouri State University. The station has been the site of extensive grape experimentation since 1900, including some of the first experiments in the United States on grafting rootstocks on American grapes. The station is located on 190 acres on the outskirts of Mountain Grove, east of Springfield. Today, special emphasis is given to research on the French hybrid varieties and their wines. New fruit varieties are also tested for their adaptability to Missouri soil and climate.

Source: Missouri Board of Education.

Missouri Tigers –
The University of Missouri-Columbia is the oldest state university west of the Mississippi River and the oldest in the Louisiana Purchase Territory. The university was founded in 1839 and was shaped in accordance with Thomas Jefferson's ideals for education.

EDUCATIONAL FACILITIES IN MISSOURI

Public Schools	Number
High Schools (including vocational schools)	569
Junior High Schools	108
Middle Schools	139
Elementary Schools	1,270
Total	**2,086**

Private Schools	
Catholic	312
Lutheran	70
7th Day Adventist	6
Christian (non-denominational)	18
Other	11
Independent	44
Local institutions for neglected/delinquent students	8
Laboratory schools	4
Unclassified	1
Total	**474**

Public school enrollment (K-12) September 1989 (fall semester) 806,639

Number of public school districts 544

Number of classroom teachers in public schools (1989-90)................................51,361

Current expenditures per pupil (in average daily attendance) *$4,226

* Estimated state average (1989-90)

Number of Classroom Teachers

During the 1988-89 academic year, the state of Missouri employed 50,800 classroom teachers, or about 85% of all educational staff. Most of these were elementary teachers, and 75% of these were female.

Average Teachers' Salaries

For the 1988-89 school year, Missouri classroom teachers had an average salary of $26,006. The average female teacher's salary was more than $2,600 less than that of her male counterpart. In fact, female education staff have consistently lower salaries than males in the same positions.

MISSOURI AVERAGE AMERICAN COLLEGE TEST (ACT) SCORES: 1982-1989		
	Missouri	National
1982-83	18.5	18.3
1983-84	18.8	18.5
1984-85	18.8	18.6
1985-86	19.2	18.8
1986-87	19.2	18.7
1987-88	19.1	18.8
1988-89	19.0	18.6

MISSOURI AVERAGE SCHOLASTIC APTITUDE TEST (SAT) SCORES 1982-1989		
	Missouri	National
1982-83	976	893
1983-84	981	897
1984-85	993	906
1985-86	995	906
1986-87	992	906
1987-88	990	904
1988-89	989	903

For each academic year from 1971-72 to 1988-89, students have consistently scored above the national average on both the verbal and math portions of the S.A.T.

For each academic year from 1977-78 to 1988-89, Missouri students have consistently scored higher than the national average on various levels (English, math, social studies and natural science) of the A.C.T.

Source: 1988-1989 Report of the Public Schools of Missouri, Missouri State Board of Education.

Faculty Members' Salaries

Faculty at Missouri's four-year public colleges and universities receive an average salary of $37,006, greater than the other Missouri institutions of higher education. Professor level salaries at independent universities are higher than at other Missouri institutions, while instructor level salaries at public two-year colleges are higher than instructor level salaries elsewhere. Overall, the average faculty salary in Missouri is $35,968.

Number of Educators in the Higher Education System

As of fall 1989, public and private higher education institutions employed 26,000 people across the state. Over 36% of the total were teaching faculty and nearly 21% were school administrators and professional non-faculty personnel.

The University of Missouri-Rolla is one of only two institutions of higher education in the country offering professional training in all of the energy and minerals engineering disciplines.

Missouri State Teachers' Association has the first permanent building built for any state teachers' association in the United States.

QUICK FACTS:

Overall, enrollment in higher education institutions in Missouri has increased more than 5% between 1981 and 1989.

The school symbol at Westminster College, a school of 650 full-time undergraduates in Fulton, Missouri, is the restored 17th century English Church of St. Mary, relocated from London in the 1960s.

In 1988, Missouri institutions of higher education conferred 37,392 degrees, of which 58.5% were bachelor's degrees, and 20.3% were master's degrees.

Source: "Statistical Summary of Missouri Higher Education, 1989-1990," Missouri Coordinating Board for Higher Education.

Missouri has a total of 77 private colleges, public universities, and community colleges that offer a variety of degrees.

In 1930, William Volker, Kansas City philanthropist, gave the University of Kansas City (now UMKC) 40 acres purchased from the William Rockhill Nelson estate.

College Enrollment

Enrollment has increased over the last decade for all types of higher education institutions, with the exception of public universities and four-year colleges, which have declined in enrollment by only 0.4%. The greatest increase occurred for two-year public community colleges, which increased in enrollment by 25.8%, followed by private colleges and universities where enrollments grew 20.1%.

FALL ENROLLMENT AT MISSOURI COLLEGES AND UNIVERSITIES: 1989

Four-year institutions:
Public universities and
four-year colleges 94,135
Private Colleges and
Universities 48,533
Total: *(Four-year institutions)* 142,668

Two-year institutions:
Public Community Colleges................38,114
Private Two-Year Colleges.....................842
Total: *(Two-year institutions)* 38,956

Combined Total: (All colleges
and institutions)...............................181,624

Top Undergraduate Programs

Undergraduate programs at the University of Missouri (Columbia, Rolla), St. Louis University, Washington University, and Rockhurst College appear among the nation's most highly ranked, according to the Gourman Report. The University of Missouri at Columbia has the distinction of having the top ranked journalism program in the country. MU (Rolla) was ranked 2nd in the country for its geological engineering program. St. Louis University's highest ranking undergraduate program is in physical therapy (15th); Washington University's highest rank is in systems engineering (3rd); and Rockhurst's physical therapy program was ranked 94th.

Top Graduate Programs

Graduate programs at the University of Missouri (Columbia, Rolla, Kansas City, and St. Louis), St. Louis University, and Washington University appear among the nation's most highly ranked. Within the University of Missouri system, the Columbia campus' highest ranking graduate programs are in journalism (3rd) and mass communications/theory (10th); the Rolla campus' is in ceramic sciences and engineering (8th); the St. Louis campus' is in optometry (13th); and the Kansas City campus' is in pharmacy (31st). St. Louis University's highest ranking program is in social welfare/social work (23rd); and Washington University's is in physiology (10th).

QUICK FACTS:

Washington University appears on Gourman's list of top graduate schools, ranked 34th.

In 1870, Mary Louise Gillett was the first woman to receive a degree at the University of Missouri.

Source: Official Manual, State of Missouri, 1989-90.

FOUR-YEAR PUBLIC COLLEGES AND UNIVERSITIES IN MISSOURI

Institution	Location	Year Founded
Land-grant universities		
University of Missouri-Columbia	Columbia	1839
University of Missouri-Kansas City	Kansas City	1929
University of Missouri-Rolla	Rolla	1870
University of Missouri-St. Louis	St. Louis	1963
Lincoln University	Jefferson City	1866
Statewide liberal arts		
Northeast Missouri State University	Kirksville	1867
Comprehensive universities		
Central Missouri State University	Warrensburg	1871
Northwest Missouri State University	Maryville	1905
Southeast Missouri State University	Cape Girardeau	1873
Southwest Missouri State University	Springfield	1905
Four-year colleges		
Harris-Stowe State College	St. Louis	1857
Missouri Southern State College	Joplin	1965
Missouri Western State College	St. Joseph	1915

Chief Clerk of the Missouri House of Representatives, State Capitol, Jefferson City 65101.

The College Blue Book: Narrative Descriptions, 21st Edition. New York: Macmillan Publishing Company, 1987.

Federal Information Center, 1520 Market St., Room 2616, St. Louis 63103.

Federal Yellow Book, New York: Monitor Publishing Co., Fall 1987.

Gourman, Dr. Jack. **The Gourman Report: A Rating of Graduate Programs in American and International Colleges and Universities,** 4th Edition, National Education Standards.

Gourman, Dr. Jack. **The Gourman Report: A Rating of Undergraduate Programs in American and International Colleges and Universities,** 7th Edition, National Education Standards.

Hardy, Richard J., and Richard R. Dohm. **Missouri Government and Politics.** Columbia, Mo.: University of Missouri Press, 1985.

"Higher Education Staff Information (EE06) Short Form, Statistical Summary of Missouri Higher Education, 1988-1989," Missouri Coordinating Board for Higher Education, June 1989.

Missouri Department of Elementary and Secondary Education, 205 Jefferson St., P.O. Box 480, Jefferson City 65102.

Missouri Roster 1989-1990, Office of the Secretary of State, Jefferson City 65102.

"The Missouri State Capitol," Missouri Secretary of State, 301 W. High St., Room 152, Jefferson City 65101.

Official Manual of the State of Missouri, 1987-1988, Office of the Secretary of State, 208 State Capitol, Jefferson City 65102.

Paris Chamber of Commerce, 110 N. Main, P.O. Box 75, Paris 65275.

"Report of the Public Schools of Missouri, 1988-1989," Missouri State Board of Education.

"Report of the Public Schools of Missouri, 1987-1988," Missouri State Board of Education.

St. Louis Convention and Visitors Bureau, 10 S. Broadway #300, St. Louis 63102.

Secretary of the Missouri Senate, State Capitol, Jefferson City 65101.

Secretary of State Roy Blunt, P.O. Box 778, Jefferson City 65102.

State Information Book, INFAX Corporation, Rockville, MD, 1987.

Statistical Abstract of the United States, 1990, U.S. Department of Commerce, Bureau of the Census.

"Statistical Summary of Missouri Higher Education, 1989-1990," Missouri Coordinating Board for Higher Education, July 1990.

Supreme Court of Missouri, Supreme Court Building, P.O. Box 150, Jefferson City 65102.

U.S. Senator Christopher S. Bond, Russell Office Building, Washington, D.C. 20510.

U.S. Senator John C. Danforth, 497 Russell Building, Washington, D.C. 20510.

CHAPTER 4
PEOPLE

**Population • Vital Statistics
Employment • Housing
Famous Missourians**

Photo courtesy of the Branson/Lakes Area Chamber of Commerce.

overview

Population Characteristics
85-88

The urban population of Missouri has grown steadily since 1840, while the rural population has declined steadily since 1900.

Vital Statistics
89-92

The average life expectancy for Missourians in 1979-1981 was nearly 74 years, lower than any of its neighboring states, but almost exactly the age of the average American.

Employment
93

The unemployment rate prior to World War II in Missouri reached nearly 15% in 1940, but only 10 years later was at a low point of 3.3%.

Households and Housing
94-95

More than 50% of all Missouri's 1.9 million households are composed of two or fewer persons.

Famous Missourians
96-107

Actress and pin-up girl Betty Grable was born in St. Louis. Some of her film credits include "Pin-Up Girl" and "A Yank in the RAF."

CHAPTER OPENER PHOTO: Missouri's personality can be found on the faces of the people. The future of the state relies upon the people who want to teach what they know to the next generation as this blacksmith does at Silver Dollar City.

From the beginning, Missouri's people have shown what they are made of. "I come from a state that raises corn and cotton and cockleburs and Democrats, and frothy eloquence neither convinces nor satisfies me. I am from Missouri. You have got to show me." It is this speech by William Duncan Vandiver that has given Missouri its nickname of the "Show Me State." This speech also represents the character of the people. They are strong and determined, and confident in their abilities.

Missourians are good people who watch out for their family and friends. This is how the first Missourians were able to succeed in the early years. Through the decades of adversity and prosperity, the people of Missouri have shown their strengths and qualifications in every area of society.

As a whole Missouri has continued to grow. Population has steadily increased since 1945, and with the promise of jobs in the state, people are finding Missouri to be a good place to stay. Employment areas in the state have fluctuated. Originally the majority of the jobs were on the farms, where rural life was booming. Through the years, a swing from rural to urban life has taken place. From farming to Fortune 500 corporations, Missourians can find a wide range of employment opportunities.

The broad landscape of the state allows for many types of people and cultures to merge. Ethnic riches are scattered across the state. Amish, German, French, and English communities add to the mystique of Missouri. The northern region of the state is home to many large farms. The family farm is still a vital part of the state's economy. The delicate relationship between rural and urban living is balanced in the central part of the state. For the people who live in this region, the best of both worlds is available. Some of the most relaxing parts of the state are in the south. Time seems to stand still in the Ozarks. People take their time and seem to have less worries. The opposite occurs in the largest cities which border the state on the east and west. There, life constantly buzzes with excitement.

Missourians have had many influential people to refer to in the past. With leaders such as Harry S Truman, Mark Twain, and General John J. Pershing, today's generation has a better state in which to live. Missourians can be proud of the celebrities, artists, politicians, scientists, educators, and other outstanding citizens who have emerged from the state. It is from these innovators that the young people of Missouri learn and follow.

The future is bright for the citizens of Missouri. Missourians have emerged from a time of unrest to a state of prosperity. The people of Missouri are what make the state an excellent place to live or visit. The strength and courage of the pioneers who settled the state can still be found in the faces of Missouri's people. ❐

M.V.P. | Len Dawson was named Most Valuable Player in 1970 at Super Bowl IV when the Kansas City Chiefs beat the Minnesota Vikings 23-7.

Unsinkable Molly | Margaret Tobin Brown was born in 1867 in Hannibal. She later became known as "The Unsinkable Molly Brown" after the sinking of the Titanic in 1912.

Teacher, Teacher | In 1873, John J. Pershing accepted a teaching position at Prairie Mound School, located near Laclede, for $30 to $35 a month.

Bad Gamble | On July 21, 1865, "Wild Bill" Hickok shot Dave Tutt over a gambling debt on the square in Springfield. Wild Bill Hickok turned himself in to the sheriff, but was later found not guilty of murder after a jury trial.

Tea Time | Virginia McDonald opened the McDonald Tea Room in Gallatin, Missouri, in 1931. It was ranked by the late Duncan Hines as "one of the ten best places to eat in America." In 1962 she was honored by the Duncan Hines Institute for 25 years of food preparation achievement.

Disney's Land | Walt Disney, who was raised on a farm near Marceline, Mo., became interested in drawing and sold his first sketches to neighbors when he was only seven years old.

Fallen Angel | Once, hiding from the law in Texas, Cole Younger assumed such a cloak of solid citizenry he became a member of a church choir and worked for the government as a Census taker.

Little Kit | Kit Carson lived in Missouri from infancy until age 17.

Doctor's Orders | Dr. Margaret Ruck de Schell Schmidt, the first licensed woman doctor in Missouri, practiced medicine in Hannibal in the 1860s.

Theater Major | George C. Scott started his stage career at the University of Missouri.

Population Density

Most counties in Missouri (90) have a low population density of less than 50 persons per square mile. Only eight counties have a total population exceeding 100,000. In 1990, St. Louis County had the largest population (993,529), and Worth County had the smallest population (2,440). Population densities in these two counties ranged from 1,963 persons per square mile to 9 persons per square mile, respectively.

QUICK FACTS:

Missouri has a total of 68,945 square miles and an average population density of 73.5 persons per square mile.

Source: "Statistical Abstract for Missouri, 1990," University of Missouri - Columbia.

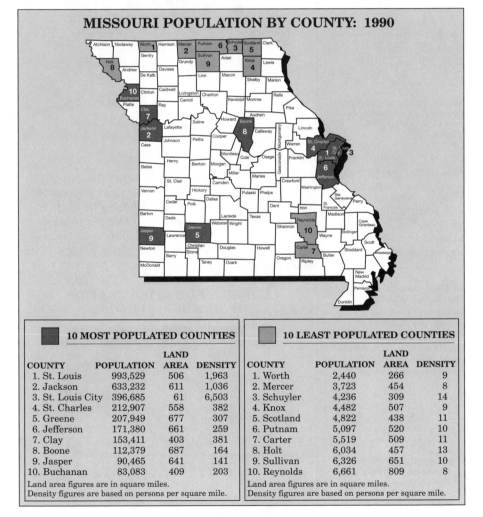

MISSOURI POPULATION BY COUNTY: 1990

10 MOST POPULATED COUNTIES

COUNTY	POPULATION	LAND AREA	DENSITY
1. St. Louis	993,529	506	1,963
2. Jackson	633,232	611	1,036
3. St. Louis City	396,685	61	6,503
4. St. Charles	212,907	558	382
5. Greene	207,949	677	307
6. Jefferson	171,380	661	259
7. Clay	153,411	403	381
8. Boone	112,379	687	164
9. Jasper	90,465	641	141
10. Buchanan	83,083	409	203

Land area figures are in square miles.
Density figures are based on persons per square mile.

10 LEAST POPULATED COUNTIES

COUNTY	POPULATION	LAND AREA	DENSITY
1. Worth	2,440	266	9
2. Mercer	3,723	454	8
3. Schuyler	4,236	309	14
4. Knox	4,482	507	9
5. Scotland	4,822	438	11
6. Putnam	5,097	520	10
7. Carter	5,519	509	11
8. Holt	6,034	457	13
9. Sullivan	6,326	651	10
10. Reynolds	6,661	809	8

Land area figures are in square miles.
Density figures are based on persons per square mile.

QUICK FACTS:

Missouri has a metropolitan/suburban focus. More than 65% of the state's population resides in six metropolitan areas.

Between 1865-1870, Kansas City's population surged from 6,000 to 30,000. According to the preliminary 1990 Census figures, the population for Kansas City, Mo., is 435,146.

Source: Missouri Vital Statistics, 1989. 1990 Data from U.S. Bureau of the Census.

In 1911, the Missouri population was 3,317,000, while the 1990 population figure was 5,117,073.

Missouri is the 15th most populated state.

In 1880, nearly 75% of the population in Missouri lived in rural areas. By 1990, the rural population had declined to 33.8% while the urban population had increased to 66.2%.

Source: 1980 Census of Population, Number of Inhabitants, Table 1, U.S. Department of Commerce, Bureau of the Census. "Statistical Abstract for Missouri, 1990," University of Missouri - Columbia.

Population Trends

Between 1945-1990, Missouri has recorded significant population growth, increasing 45%. This period is the longest sustained period of population growth in the state's history.

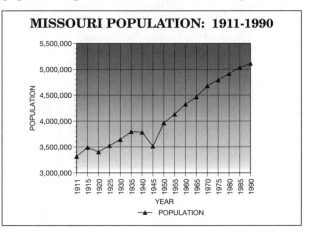

Urban and Rural Population Trends

The urban population of Missouri has grown steadily since 1840, while the rural population has declined steadily since 1900. The shift in the rural to urban majority of the population occurred sometime between 1920 and 1930, where for the first time more Missourians lived in urban areas than rural.

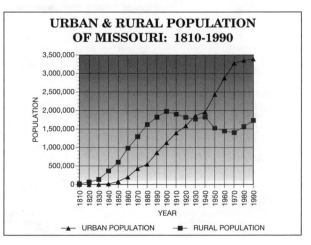

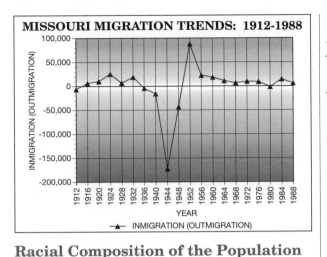

MISSOURI MIGRATION TRENDS: 1912-1988

Source: "Missouri Vital Statistics, 1989," Missouri Department of Health, State Center for Health Statistics.

QUICK FACTS:

During the 1912-1988 period, the state has recorded net outmigrations of population in more than 48% of the 77-year span.

Racial Composition of the Population

The racial composition of Missouri is more diverse than at the beginning of the century. However, the state is still predominantly white. Today, more than 89% of the population is white, compared to nearly 95% in 1900. Since the turn of the century, the white population has increased about 2.2 million, while non-white groups increased approximately 447,000.

Rosie O'Neill, originator of the Kewpie doll, was raised in the Missouri Ozarks region.

	MISSOURI POPULATION BY RACE: 1900-1990					
Year	Total	White	Black	American Indian, Eskimo, & Aleut	Asian or Pacific Islander*	Other Races
1900	3,106,665	2,944,843	161,234	130	458	–
1910	3,293,335	3,134,932	157,452	313	634	4
1920	3,404,055	3,325,044	178,241	171	547	52
1930	3,629,367	3,403,876	223,840	578	1,049	24
1940	3,784,664	3,539,187	244,386	330	408	353
1950	3,954,653	3,655,593	297,088	547	1,046	379
1960	4,319,813	3,922,967	390,853	1,723	3,146	1,124
1970	4,676,501	4,177,495	480,172	5,405	7,207	6,222
1980	4,916,686	4,345,521	514,276	12,129	10,958	33,802
1990	5,786,393	5,177,073	548,208	19,835	41,277	NA

* Prior to 1990, Asian or Pacific Islander were classified under racial classifications (i.e. Japanese, Filipino, etc.). Some categories previously included in Other Races are now included here.

Age and Sex Characteristics

Missouri, like in most states, has an aging population and more males (51.2%) live in the state than females (48.8%). In 1910, about one-half of the population was under age 25. Today, only about 36% of the population is under 25.

Source: 1980 Census, General Population Characteristics, Table 17, Preliminary Reports for 1990.

population

QUICK FACTS:

Twenty Missouri communities have populations of more than 25,000. Only four cities have a population of more than 100,000 (St. Louis, Kansas City, Springfield, and Independence).

Source: 1990 Census of Population, U.S. Department of Commerce, Bureau of the Census.

More than one-third of the U.S. population resides within 600 miles of Kansas City; more than 55 million people are within a day's drive.

Rose Wilder Lane was the highest paid woman author in the country in the 1920s.

Small town living is an important lifestyle in Missouri. There are 152 incorporated communities in the state with less than 25,000 inhabitants.

Cole Younger is buried in Lee's Summit, where his tombstone may still be seen. He died of old age, at 72. He had been wounded 24 times during his career as an outlaw.

Source: 1990 Census of Population, U.S. Department of Commerce, Bureau of the Census.

10 MOST POPULATED COMMUNITIES*: (1990 ESTIMATES)

Community	Population
Kansas City	435,146
St. Louis	396,685
Springfield	140,494
Independence	112,301
St. Joseph	71,852
Columbia	69,101
St. Charles	54,555
Florissant	51,206
Lee's Summit	46,418
St. Peters	45,779

* Incorporated cities.

U.S. Population Center

In 1980, the center of the U.S. population moved into Missouri, one-quarter mile outside the town of DeSoto. The 1985 Census estimates placed the current center about 10 miles northwest of Potosi, Missouri. The westward movement of the U.S. population center has accelerated since 1940. If the current rate of movement continues, the center of population should remain within Missouri during the next two decades.

10 LEAST POPULATED COMMUNITIES*: (1990 ESTIMATES)

Community	Population
Potosi	2,570
Monroe City	2,630
Fayette	2,730
Vandalia	2,730
Hermann	2,750
Holts Summit	2,790
Riverside	2,910
Windsor	2,930
Bethany	2,960
Bowling Green	2,960

* Incorporated towns.

Ancestral Background

Most Missourians come from an ancestral background of German, or German combined with other groups.

POPULATION OF SELECTED ANCESTRY GOUPS IN MISSOURI: 1980	
Ancestry Group	**Population**
English	527,041
French	51,174
German	633,291
Irish	242,610
Italian	52,849
Polish	28,447
German & other groups	942,141
Irish & other groups	886,539
English & other groups	669,734
French & other groups	288,894

Religious Affiliations

The majority of Missourians who have a religious affiliation are Protestant. However, the largest single religious denomination is Roman Catholic, followed by Southern Baptist groups and United Methodists.

QUICK FACTS:

Daniel M. Boone, son of the famous pioneer, and Major Elias Bancroft were commissioned to plan and lay out Jefferson City. The town was incorporated in 1825.

There are no American Indian reservations in Missouri.

Source: 1980 Census, General Social and Economic Characteristics, Table 105.

Source: "Churches and Church Memberships in the United States, 1980," Glenmary Research Center, Atlanta, Ga.

SELECTED COMMON CHURCHES AND CHURCH MEMBERSHIPS IN MISSOURI: 1980		
Church Name	**Number of Churches**	**Number of Adherents ***
African Methodist Episcopal Zion Church	8	5,134
American Baptist Churches in the U.S.A.	17	13,564
American Lutheran Church, The	29	6,485
Assemblies of God	494	77,158
Catholic Church	573	800,228
Christian Church (Disciples of Christ)	415	116,875
Christian Churches and Churches of Christ	369	58,029
Church of Jesus Christ of Latter-day Saints, The	68	18,908
Churches of Christ	543	49,444
Episcopal Church, The	103	35,939
Conservative Judaism	5	3,220
Reform Judaism	14	17,964
Lutheran Church in America	35	13,099
Lutheran Church - Missouri Synod, The	295	144,829
Southern Baptist Church	1,813	700,053
United Church of Christ	185	73,533
United Methodist Church	1,103	270,469
United Presbyterian Church in the U.S.A., The	307	56,176

* Adherents: All members, including full members, their children, and the estimated number of other regular participants who are not considered as communicant, confirmed or full members.

vital statistics

QUICK FACTS:

The birth rate in Missouri in 1945 was 19.3 births per thousand.

Birth and Death Rates

The birth rate in Missouri has remained stable at between 15 to 16 births per 1,000 population for the last decade, compared to a high of 24.2 births per thousand in 1957. The death rate was also comparatively low in 1989 at 10 deaths per thousand, compared to a high of 12.2 deaths per thousand in 1945.

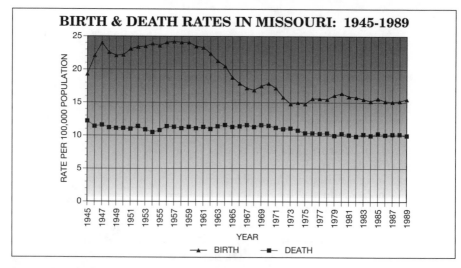

BIRTH & DEATH RATES IN MISSOURI: 1945-1989

Source: "Missouri Vital Statistics, 1989," Missouri Department of Health.

Scott Joplin, the king of ragtime music, studied composition and harmony during extensive musical training at the George R. Smith College in Sedalia. He lived and worked in Sedalia and became known for composing "The Ragtime Dance" and "The Maple Leaf Rag."

Average Life Expectancy

The average life expectancy for Missourians in 1979-1981 was nearly 74 years, lower than any of its neighboring states except Arkansas and Illinois, but almost exactly the age of the average American. The average life expectancy is 77.72 years for Missouri females and 69.92 years for Missouri males. While women on average have a longer life than men in all areas, Missouri females have a lower life expectancy than females in any neighboring state, except Illinois.

Only 60 years ago, the average life expectancy for an American was 57.1 years, more than 17 years less than it was in 1988. Females have a greater life expectancy than males in all categories, and whites have a greater life expectancy than all other races.

Overall Crime Rate

Missouri has a higher overall crime level than many of its neighboring states, with the exception of Illinois and Kansas, and has the second highest crime rate for robbery, burglary, aggravated assault, and motor vehicle theft among all comparative states. Missouri is below the national average for all violent and property crime rates.

Leading Causes of Death

Heart disease and cancer are the leading causes of death in Missouri, and together account for more than 58% of all deaths. Motor vehicle accidents of all types account for nearly 38% of all accidental deaths in Missouri.

QUICK FACTS:

In 1988, Missouri recorded 4,845 crimes per 100,000 population, while the national average was 5,664 per 100,000 population.

The leading cause of death in Missouri in 1989 was heart disease.

Source: "Missouri Vital Statistics, 1989," Missouri Department of Health.

LEADING CAUSES OF DEATH IN MISSOURI: 1989

Cause of Death*	Deaths	Percent
Diseases of the Heart	17,633	35.1%
Malignant Neoplasms	11,614	23.1%
Cerebrovascular Diseases	3,458	7.0%
Accidental Deaths	2,017	4.4%
Chronic Pulmonary Disease	2,204	4.0%
Pneumonia and Influenza	1,824	3.6%
Diabetes Mellitus	1,073	2.1%
Suicides	669	1.3%
Nephritis and Nephrosis	520	1.0%
Homicide and Legal Intervention	448	1.0%
Atherosclerosis	436	0.9%
Liver Disease & Cirrhosis	411	0.8%
All Other Causes	7,862	15.7%
TOTAL	**50,169**	**100.0%**

Cause of Accidental Death	Deaths	Percent
Motor Vehicle Collision with Another Vehicle	479	22.7%
Motor Vehicle Collision with Fixed Objects	337	16.0%
Falls	274	13.0%
Motor Vehicle Noncollision	140	6.6%
Fires	118	5.6%
Motor Vehicle Injury to Pedestrian	107	5.1%
Drowning	83	3.9%
Poisonings	74	3.5%
Other Motor Vehicle	67	3.2%
Non-Agriculture Work Related	56	2.7%
Firearms	34	1.6%
Suffocation	29	1.4%
Agriculture Work	24	1.1%
Water Transport	7	0.3%
Air Transport	5	0.2%
All Other Causes	276	13.1%
TOTAL	**2,110**	**100.0%**

* Cause of death figures are for Missouri residents only. Causes of accidental death figures include non-resident population.

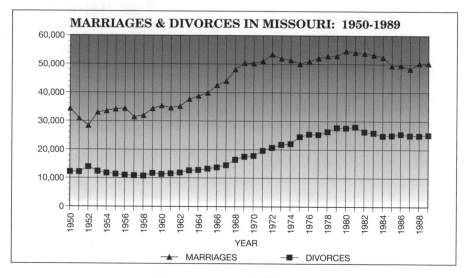

MARRIAGES & DIVORCES IN MISSOURI: 1950-1989

Source: "Missouri Vital Statistics, 1989," Missouri Department of Health.

The number of divorces in 1987 (24,984) is more than double the 1950 figure (12,177), but is nearly 11% less than the high in 1981 (27,975).

The median age when marriage occurs in Missouri is 26-27 years for the groom and 24-25 years for the bride. The total number of marriages in Missouri in 1989 was 50,331.

Marriage and Divorce Rates

The number of marriages in Missouri has increased almost 46% since 1950, but declined 11% since the high point in 1980. While the overall marriage rate in Missouri has been declining almost steadily since 1980, the lowest rate since 1950 occurred in 1952. Similarly, the Missouri divorce rate in 1989 of 4.9 divorces per thousand represents a decline over the rate of 5.7 divorces per thousand seen in 1979 and 1981.

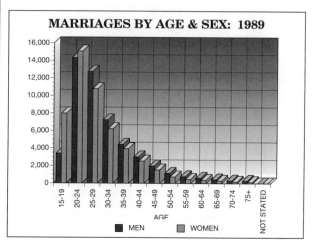

MARRIAGES BY AGE & SEX: 1989

Source: "Missouri Vital Statistics, 1989," Missouri Department of Health.

employment

MISSOURI

Unemployment Rates

The unemployment rate prior to World War II in Missouri reached nearly 15% in 1940, but only 10 years later was at a low point of 3.3%. In recent years (1980-1988) Missouri's unemployment rate fluctuated between 6.2% and 7%, but by November 1988, the rate was low at 5.7%.

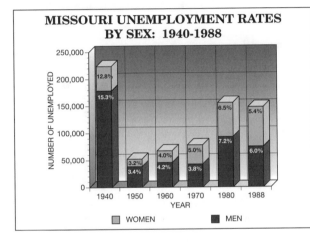

MISSOURI UNEMPLOYMENT RATES BY SEX: 1940-1988

NUMBER OF UNEMPLOYED

- 1940: 12.8% / 15.3%
- 1950: 3.2% / 3.4%
- 1960: 4.0% / 4.2%
- 1970: 5.0% / 3.8%
- 1980: 6.5% / 7.2%
- 1988: 5.4% / 6.0%

YEAR

☐ WOMEN   ■ MEN

Effective Buying Income

The increase of the effective buying income of the average Missourian has slightly exceeded that of the average American, increasing nearly 300% since 1970.

QUICK FACTS:

The Columbia, Mo., SMSA has shown the greatest increase in buying income – more than 315% increase since 1970.

Missouri's maximum weekly unemployment benefits ranked 6th-lowest in the United States in 1988.

The number of females in the work force over age 14 was 1,141,000 in 1988. The number of employed males over age 14 was 2,445,000.

Source: Statistical Abstract of the United States, 1990, U.S. Department of Commerce.

Source: Sales & Marketing Management Magazine: "Survey of Buying Power," annual years 1971, 1976, 1981, 1986; "Survey of Buying Power: Data Service 1989."

PER CAPITA AND MEDIAN HOUSEHOLD INCOME: 1970-1989

State	Per Capita Income (Effective Buying Income*)					Median Household Income (Effective Buying Income*)				
	1970	1975	1980	1985	1989	1970	1975	1980	1985	1989
U.S.	$3,308	$5,003	$7,940	$11,627	$13,158	$10,565	$12,824	$19,146	$23,680	$25,976
MISSOURI	$3,096	4,639	7,508	11,059	12,381	9,406	11,305	17,530	22,415	24,484
Columbia	3,185	4,627	7,096	12,225	13,294	10,566	11,788	16,285	24,037	25,372
Joplin	2,577	3,652	5,597	9,588	10,287	7,309	8,338	12,434	18,764	19,453
Kansas City	3,726	5,786	9,489	13,243	14,401	10,984	14,328	22,530	27,736	29,370
St. Joseph	3,090	4,434	7,153	10,775	11,824	9,036	10,740	16,886	21,679	22,964
St. Louis	3,452	5,101	8,457	12,311	13,952	11,100	13,975	21,222	26,667	29,453
Springfield	3,046	4,401	7,018	10,757	11,624	9,081	10,591	16,139	20,972	22,125

* Effective Buying Income: A term used by *Sales and Marketing Management* magazine which is defined as total income less taxes, penalties, social insurance, and payments to military and government personnel overseas.

households/housing

QUICK FACTS:

Less than 30% of Missouri's householders are under 35 years of age, while more than 23% of all householders are over age 65. About 13.6% of all women are widowed, compared to 2.6% of the men.

On October 18, 1925, Marcie Burks, who claimed to have originated the Charleston dance, gave a demonstration for guests at the Elms Hotel in Excelsior Springs.

Source: Census of the Population, General Population Characteristics, "Summary of General Characteristics," U.S. Department of Commerce, Bureau of the Census.

In 1950, the total number of households in Missouri was 1,243,602. By 1980 that number had increased to 1,793,399.

The median size of houses in Missouri, both urban and rural, is 5.1 rooms.

In 1989, the estimated number of households in Missouri with six persons was 61,993, or 3.2% of the total.

Source: "Survey of Buying Power, Data Service," Sales and Marketing Management, 1989.

Urban & Rural Households

Since 1950, the total number of households in Missouri has grown more than 44%. While urban and rural farm households have grown approximately 57% and 92% respectively, the number of households living in rural nonfarm areas have declined more than 61%. The average size of the Missouri household has declined since 1950, from 3.18 persons to 2.67 persons in 1980.

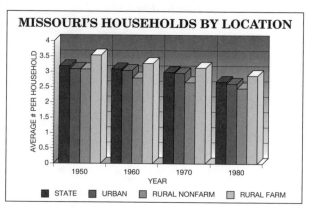

MISSOURI'S HOUSEHOLDS BY LOCATION

Household Size

The majority of Missourians live in comparatively small family groups. More than 50% of all Missouri's 1.9 million households are composed of two or fewer persons. One-person households make up 23.8% of this total.

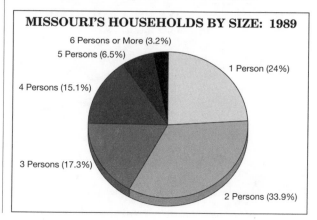

MISSOURI'S HOUSEHOLDS BY SIZE: 1989

6 Persons or More (3.2%)
5 Persons (6.5%)
4 Persons (15.1%)
1 Person (24%)
3 Persons (17.3%)
2 Persons (33.9%)

households/housing

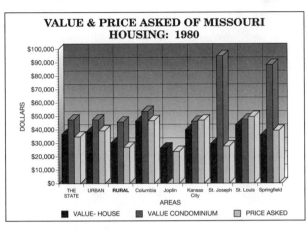

VALUE & PRICE ASKED OF MISSOURI HOUSING: 1980

DOLLARS

$100,000
$90,000
$80,000
$70,000
$60,000
$50,000
$40,000
$30,000
$20,000
$10,000
$0

THE STATE · URBAN · **RURAL** · Columbia · Joplin · Kansas City · St. Joseph · St. Louis · Springfield

AREAS

■ VALUE- HOUSE   ■ VALUE CONDOMINIUM   ▨ PRICE ASKED

Value of Households

In 1980, the average value of occupied housing units in Missouri was about $36,700, compared to $47,400 for condominium units. The values for urban housing were approximately 27% higher in urban areas than in rural areas, while condominiums were valued about 3.7% higher in urban areas than in rural areas.

QUICK FACTS:

The state average for housing rent was $135 in 1980. The average rent asked for vacant rental housing units in Columbia was $173.

Source: 1980 Census of Housing, General Housing Characteristics, U.S. Department of Commerce, Bureau of the Census.

Missouri's household median income is $24,484 and the mean household buying income is $33,138.

A young lady enjoys a magical day in Missouri.   *Photo courtesy of Worlds of Fun.*

The Early Days

William Anderson – Buried in Richmond. The pro-southern guerrilla leader during the Civil War earned the nickname "Bloody Bill."

Daniel Boone – (1734-1820). Defiance. Pioneer and scout who explored much of the state. Boone came to Missouri in 1799 as governor of the Spanish-ruled territory.

Margaret Tobin Brown – Hannibal. She was born in Hannibal in 1867 and later became known as "The Unsinkable Molly Brown" after the sinking of the Titanic in 1912.

Ben Holladay – Weston. Holladay became known as the "Stage Coach King" as he started frontier stagecoach companies. He also founded the McCormick Distilling Co. in Weston.

Calamity Jane – Born in Princeton. She was born Martha Jane Canary and later was a Pony Express rider and scout for Gen. George A. Custer's 7th Cavalry.

Jesse James – (1847-1882). This famous outlaw was born in Kearney on Sept. 5, 1847. Kearney is the site of the family home where Jesse and his brother, Frank, were raised. Also at Kearney is Jesse's grave.

John H. Parker – Pettis County. Known as "Gatling Gun Parker," he invented the Gatling Gun.

Younger Brothers – Brothers Cole, John, James, and Robert were outlaws who pulled off a series of bank robberies in the late 1800s.

Jesse James

Photo courtesy of State Historical Society of Missouri.

Politics & Government

Blanche Kelso Bruce – Hannibal. The second Negro to hold the office of U.S. Senator was a one-time teacher in Hannibal.

Senator Stuart Symington – (1901-1988). St. Louis. In 1947 he was named the nation's first Secretary of the Air Force. He served in the U.S. Senate from 1952-1976.

Elizabeth "Bess" Wallace Truman – Independence. She was born Feb. 13, 1885, the daughter of an Independence businessman. After a courtship of almost a decade, she married Harry S Truman on June 28, 1919, and was the nation's First Lady during her husband's Presidency.

Harry S Truman – (1884-1972). Independence. Truman served as the 33rd President of the United States from 1945-1953. Truman's birthplace is Lamar.

James Milton Turner – Born a slave in St. Louis County in 1840, he was the first black American to receive a diplomatic post and in 1871 was appointed minister resident and counsel general to Liberia.

Literature & Playwrights

Sally Benson – Born in St. Louis, Sept. 3, 1900. Author who wrote the novel *Meet Me in St. Louis* and in 1946 she received an Academy Award nomination for her screenplay "Anna and the King of Siam."

Samuel Clemens (Mark Twain) – (1835-1910). Born in Florida, Mo., and grew up in Hannibal. His stories about Tom Sawyer and friends reflected his love for his hometown of Hannibal, where he lived from 1839-1853.

Homer Croy – Maryville. Author who was also a screen writer for movies starring Will Rogers.

Janet Dailey – Branson. Popular romance novelist who wrote *Rivals* and *Masquerade*.

T.S. Eliot – St. Louis. Poet/playwright who received the Nobel Prize for Literature in 1948.

Eugene Field – (1850-1895). St. Louis. Field, who was born in St. Louis in 1850, was a children's poet whose works included "Little Boy Blue."

Aurand Harris – Jamesport. Harris is the most-produced children's playwright in the United States. His works include "Punch and Judy" and "Androcles and the Lion."

Photo courtesy of The Harry S Truman Library. Photo by Leo Stern.

Harry S Truman

Photo courtesy of State Historical Society of Missouri.
Samuel Clemens (Mark Twain)

Robert A. Heinlein – Science fiction writer who was born in Butler and grew up in Kansas City.

James Langston Hughes – (1902-1967). Joplin. He was an author, anthologist, songwriter, columnist, founder of theaters and jazz innovator. He used African heritage themes throughout his work and received many awards, including the Spingarn Medal in 1959.

Rose Wilder Lane – Mansfield. She lived in Mansfield from 1894 to the mid-1930s. Rose Wilder Lane wrote biographies for Herbert Hoover, Charley Chaplin and others. Her most well-known books include *Let the Hurricanes Roar* and *Free Land*.

John Selby – Gallatin. Author who wrote 10 novels, including *Island in the Corn, Sam,* and *Starbuck.*

Laura Ingalls Wilder – (1867-1957). Mansfield. The author lived in Mansfield when she began her writing career in 1932. She moved to Missouri with her husband and daughter in 1894. All of her "Little House" books were written at Rocky Ridge Farm in Mansfield, where she lived until her death in 1957.

Photo courtesy of Laura Ingalls Wilder Museum.

Laura Ingalls Wilder

Harold Bell Wright. Wright wrote several popular books about the Ozarks, including the best seller *Shepherd of the Hills* in 1907. He held pastorates in several Missouri churches.

Education

Susan Elizabeth Blow – (1843-1916). St. Louis. She opened the first successful public kindergarten in 1873 in the Des Peres School in Carondelet, now St. Louis, and later opened training classes for kindergarten teachers.

Ste. Rose Philippine Duchesne – (1769-1852). St. Louis. In 1818, she established a school which became the first free school west of the Mississippi. She established more than 40 schools for white, black, and Indian children in Missouri and other states and foreign countries. She was cannonized July 3, 1989.

Clifton C. Edom – Forsyth (1907-1991). This photojournalism pioneer was credited for starting the photojournalism department at the University of Missouri at Columbia.

Phoebe Apperson Hearst – (1842-1919). Born in Franklin County and married in Steelville. Mrs. Hearst was a co-founder of the PTA.

Music

Chuck Berry – St. Louis. The singer, entertainer, and actor was born in St. Louis and attended Summer High School.

Jack Fascinato – Hannibal. He was an arranger and accompanist for Tennessee Ernie Ford. He was a school orchestra director in Hannibal in the 1930s.

Jan Howard – West Plains. Country music singer who sang with Bill Anderson.

Scott Joplin – (1868-1917). Sedalia. The pianist and composer developed the style of music known as "Ragtime." His well-known works include "The Maple Leaf Rag" and "The Entertainer." Joplin spent much of his life in Missouri.

Speck Rhoades – West Plains. Performer who appeared as the fiddle player in the plaid suit on "The Porter Wagoner" television show. Speck was well-known for his two black front teeth.

Porter Wagoner – West Plains. He lived in West Plains and worked as a meat cutter and worked in the shoe factory. Wagoner later became a popular country music entertainer who has appeared on the "Grand Ole Opry" and television shows.

Egbert Anson Van Alstyne – Hannibal. He attended schools in Hannibal and lived in the Saverton area in his youth. The composer's works include "In the Shade of the Old Apple Tree" and many World War I songs.

The Arts

Thomas Hart Benton – (1899-1975). Neosho. Benton was born in Neosho and lived in Kansas City from 1939 until his death in 1975. His fluid style was colorful and at times controversial and it vividly depicted American life and legend. Characteristically, his works contain figure and perspective distortion. Two of his murals are displayed in the Missouri State Capitol in Jefferson City.

George Caleb Bingham – (1811-1879). Well-known for his portraits and paintings of life on the Missouri frontier. He was also elected to the Missouri Legislature and served as state treasurer and adjutant general.

Photo courtesy of State Historical Society of Missouri.

Thomas Hart Benton

Photo courtesy of The Walt Disney Company.
Walt Disney and Mickey Mouse

Walt Disney – (1901-1966). He grew up in Marceline and Kansas City, Missouri. Disney was well-known for his animation and created such classical animated films as "Snow White and the Seven Dwarfs," "Pinocchio," and "Cinderella." Disney created the first animated cartoon with sound, "Steamboat Willie," which introduced the lovable character Mickey Mouse. Disney also established the amusement park Disneyland in Anaheim, Calif.

Gordon Snidow – Paris. Internationally-acclaimed artist whose works can be found in the Monroe County courthouse in Paris, Missouri.

Motion Pictures & Television

Robert Altman – Born in Kansas City, Feb. 20, 1925, and attended University of Missouri. Altman directed many motion pictures, including "M*A*S*H" and wrote, produced, and directed movies and episodes of the television series "Combat."

Arthur Artling – Born in Missouri. Cinematographer who, in 1927, was the operative cameraman on "Gone With the Wind."

Burt Bacharach – Born in Kansas City, May 12, 1928. Composer/conductor/arranger whose works include music for the movie "Butch Cassidy and the Sundance Kid."

Josephine Baker – (1906-1975). Born in St. Louis on June 3, 1906, she was the daughter of a washwoman. Baker later became Broadway and Paris music hall star of French films. She was decorated by the French Government.

Bob Barker – Educated at Drury College in Springfield and attended naval aviation preparatory school at William Jewell College in Liberty in the last days of World War II. He is best known as the game show host of "Truth or Consequences" and "The Price is Right."

Tom Berenger – The actor attended the University of Missouri at Columbia. His credits include the motion pictures "Looking for Mr. Goodbar," "Rustler's Rhapsody," "Someone To Watch Over Me," "Shoot To Kill," "The Big Chill," and "Platoon." Some off-Broadway plays include "The Rose Tattoo" and "Streetcar Named Desire."

Linda Blair – Born in St. Louis on Jan. 22, 1959. The actress' motion picture credits include "The Exorcist."

Linda Bloodworth-Thomason – Born in Poplar Bluff. Creator and writer of the television series "Designing Women" and "Evening Shade."

Edgar Buchanan – (1903-1979). Born in Humansville. The actor was known for his role as Uncle Joe in the television series "Petticoat Junction."

Bert Convy – Born in St. Louis on July 23, 1934. The actor was also the television game show host of "Tattletales" and "Win, Lose, or Draw."

Bob Cummings – Born in Joplin, June 10, 1908. Actor who appeared in numerous plays and "The Bob Cummings Show" on television.

Photo courtesy of The Missouri Film Commission.
Linda Bloodworth-Thomason

Jane Darwell – Born in Palmyra. The actress was best-known for her role as Ma Joad in John Steinbeck's "The Grapes of Wrath," for which she won the Academy Award for Best Supporting Actress in 1940.

Jim Davis – Born in Dearborn and attended William Jewell College. The actor appeared in many roles but was best-known as J.R. Ewing's father on the television series "Dallas."

Ellen Drew – Born in Kansas City in 1915. Actress who played vivacious leads in many films in the 1950s.

Jeff East – Born in Kansas City. Actor who starred in "Huckleberry Finn," and as the young Clark Kent in "Superman."

Cliff Edwards – Born in Hannibal. The actor and musician appeared in many films and was the voice for Jiminy Cricket.

Jill Eikenberry – St. Joseph. The actress appears as Anne Kelsey on the television series "L.A. Law."

Redd Foxx – Born in St. Louis, Dec. 9, 1922. The actor starred in the television series "Sanford and Son."

James Franciscus – Born in Clayton on Jan. 31, 1934. The actor's motion picture credits include "The Greek Tycoon" and "Marooned."

Mary Frann – Born in St. Louis. Real name is Frances Luecke. She won an America's Junior Miss contest. She worked as a weathercaster at KSDK-TV in St. Louis. The actress co-starred in the television series "The Bob Newhart Show."

John Goodman – St. Louis. Goodman attended Southwest Missouri State University in Springfield. His film credits include "Raising Arizona" and "The Big Chill." He also co-stars in the television series "Roseanne."

Betty Grable – (1916-1973). The actress whose film credits include "Pin-Up Girl" and "A Yank in the RAF" was born in St. Louis.

Kathryn Grayson – Attended St. Louis schools. Actress who starred in "Showboat" and "Kiss Me Kate."

Robert Guillaume – Born in St. Louis and attended high school and college there. He has appeared in several television shows including "All in the Family," "Soap," and "Benson" and appeared on Broadway.

Moses Gunn – Born in St. Louis on Oct. 2, 1929. The actor appeared on stage and numerous television shows and motion pictures, including "Shaft" and "The Iceman Cometh."

Jean Harlow – (1911-1937). Born in Kansas City on March 3, 1911. The film actress' credits include "Red Dust," "Platinum Blonde," and "Dinner at Eight."

Paul Henning – Born in Independence, Sept. 16, 1911. He attended Kansas City School of Law, 1932. In 1937-38 he wrote "Fibber McGee and Molly." He created, wrote, and produced the television series "Beverly Hillbillies" and "Petticoat Junction" and was the executive producer of the "Green Acres" series.

John Huston – Born in Nevada in 1906. The award-winning film director's works included "Treasure of Sierra Madre," "The Maltese Falcon" and "The African Queen."

Photo courtesy of The Topeka Capital-Journal.

Don Johnson

Don Johnson – Born in Flatt Creek, Dec. 15, 1949. The actor appeared in the television series "Miami Vice."

Kevin Kline – Born in St. Louis, Oct. 24, 1947. The actor's credits include the movies "Sophie's Choice" and "The Big Chill." He received the 1989 Academy Award for Best Supporting Actor for his role in "A Fish Called Wanda."

Marsha Mason – Born in St. Louis, April 3, 1942. Attended Webster University in St. Louis. She starred in Broadway plays and in motion pictures, including "The Goodbye Girl" and "Chapter Two."

Mary Margaret McBride – Paris. Author and radio and television personality.

Edie McClurg – Born in Kansas City. The actress co-starred in the television series "Valerie's Family/The Hogans."

Steve McQueen – (1930-1980). Born in Slater on March 24, 1930. The popular actor starred in "Papillon" and "The Hunter." He resided in Slater during his early teen-age years.

Agnes Moorehead – Attended high school in St. Louis. The actress was known for her role in the television series "Bewitched."

Harriett Nelson – Educated in Kansas City. Married to Ozzie Nelson and starred in the series "Adventures of Ozzie & Harriett."

Jack Oakie – Born in Sedalia. Actor who starred in Charlie Chaplin's "The Great Dictator."

Lynne Overman – Born in Maryville in 1887. Actor who appeared in "Little Miss Marker."

Geraldine Page – (1924-1987). Born in Kirksville. The actress received three Academy Award nominations, and won the Academy Award for Best Actress in 1985 for her role in "The Trip to Bountiful."

Marlin Perkins – (1905-1986). Perkins was born in Carthage and later attended the University of Missouri at Columbia. He hosted the television show "Wild Kingdom."

Vincent Price – Born in St. Louis, May 27, 1911. He attended high school in St. Louis. The actor is known for his ghoulish roles, including "House of Usher" and "Scavenger Hunt."

Sally Rand – Born near Cross Timbers in Hickory County, 1903. The silent film actress was famous for her exotic fan dancing.

Ginger Rogers – Born in Independence, July 16, 1911, as Virginia Katherine McMath. The popular actress starred in "Stage Door" and won an Academy Award for "Kitty Foyle" in 1940.

Martha Ellen Scott – Jamesport. Broadway and motion picture and television actress who appeared in the films "Ben Hur" and "The Ten Commandments."

Kathleen Turner – Born in Springfield, June 19, 1954. The motion picture actress has starred in movies including "Romancing the Stone," "Jewel of the Nile," "Prizzi's Honor," "Body Heat," and "Peggy Sue Got Married."

Photo courtesy of The Topeka Capital-Journal.
Kathleen Turner

Dick Van Dyke – Born in West Plains, Dec. 18, 1925. The actor starred in the long-running series "The Dick Van Dyke Show."

Dennis Weaver – Born in Joplin, June 4, 1925. The motion picture and television actor is known for his role as Chester in "Gunsmoke" and also appeared in "McCloud."

Dianne Wiest – Born in Kansas City. She co-starred in the movie "Hannah and Her Sisters" and "Parenthood."

Shelley Winters – Born Shirley Schrift in St. Louis, Aug. 18, 1922, and attended Wayne University. The actress appeared in the movies "Mambo" and "The Poseidon Adventure."

Jane Wyman – Born Sarah Jane Fulks on Jan. 4, 1914, in St. Joseph. The actress appeared as Angela Channing on the series "Falcon Crest." She was the first wife of Ronald Reagan.

Sports

Jake Beckley – Hannibal. Known as "Old Eagle Eye," he played baseball for three major league teams and was inducted into the National Baseball Hall of Fame.

Yogi Berra – St. Louis. Lawrence Peter Berra was a Hall of Fame hitter. He was sometimes called the "Yankee Skipper."

Bill Jordon – West Plains. Manager of the Pittsburgh Pirates and Houston Astros. He lived in West Plains and attended high school.

Elwin "Preacher" Roe – West Plains. Pitcher for the Brooklyn Dodgers.

Leon and Michael Spinks – St. Louis. These boxers went through the St. Louis Golden Gloves program before earning national titles.

The Media

Claude Binyon – Attended University of Missouri. Newspaper reporter who wrote the famous 1929 *Variety* headline about the stock market crash, "Wall Street Lays an Egg."

Walter Cronkite – Born in St. Joseph in 1916. The well-respected journalist served as news anchorman for "The CBS Evening News" and has narrated several documentaries.

Dave Garroway – (1913-1982). He attended high school in St. Louis. The television journalist served as the first host of "The Today Show."

Joe Jones – West Plains. Journalist.

Henry LaCossitt – This journalist spent his boyhood in Hannibal and later served as editor of *Collier's* magazine.

Elijah Parish Lovejoy – St. Louis. Editor of the *St. Louis Observer* who promoted the black abolition movement. He later published the *Alton* (Ill.) *Observer*. He was killed while trying to stop a mob from destroying a new press.

William Rockhill Nelson – Kansas City. Founder of the *Kansas City Star* in 1880. He founded the Western Gallery of Art in Kansas City and left his fortune to the public.

famous missourians

Joseph Pulitzer – (1847-1911). St. Louis. The journalist and businessman who established the *St. Louis Post-Dispatch* and later purchased the *New York World*. He founded the first journalism graduate school at Columbia in 1903 and later established the Pulitzer Prizes, which have been awarded annually since 1917.

The Sciences & Social Sciences

George Washington Carver – (1864-1943). Diamond. He was born a slave near Diamond, Missouri, and later became one of the country's greatest research scientists.

Dr. Thomas A. Dooley – St. Louis. He helped refugees fleeing from North Vietnam while serving with the U.S. Navy and established hospitals in Laos and other countries.

Photo courtesy of The State Historical Society of Missouri. Engraving from portrait by John S. Sargent.

Joseph Pulitzer

Clarence Gideon – Hannibal. Gideon served time in prison for thievery. He could not afford legal counsel, and began a series of letters to authorities pointing out the unfairness of the situation for poor people in the legal system. His efforts led to a decision by the U.S. Supreme Court in 1963 giving indigents the right to legal counsel. He was an inspiration for the book *Gideon's Trumpet* by Anthony Lewis.

Icie Macy Hoobler – Gallatin. Hoobler was a pioneer in nutrition and human health and was among the first to recognize the role of nutrition in human reproduction and growth.

Edwin Powell Hubble – Born in Marshfield in 1889. This astronomer was known for his contributions in the study of the universe. Hubble established Hubble's Law, which found that the more distant a galaxy was away from earth, the greater was its speed of recession.

Major Albert Bond Lambert – St. Louis. He was a pioneer balloonist and aviator and established the first Army balloon school in St. Louis in 1917. Lambert Field is named for him.

Margaret Ruck de Schell Schmidt – The first licensed doctor in Missouri. She practiced medicine in Hannibal in the 1860s.

Joseph Smith – (1805-1844). Independence. Founder of the Latter-day Saints movement who settled with his followers in Independence in 1831. He declared Independence to be the Mormon's Mt. Zion after the Mormons had settled in Kirtland, Ohio, from New York.

Business & Industry

Henry and Richard Bloch – Kansas City, Missouri. Two brothers who founded H&R Block, Inc., which is the nation's largest firm dealing with the preparation of federal, state, and local income tax returns. The company's headquarters are located in Kansas City.

Adolphus Busch – (1839-1913). St. Louis. Co-founder of the Anheuser-Busch Company. He launched the industry's first fleet of refrigerated freight cars and built the Adolphus Hotel in Dallas.

August Anheuser Busch, Jr. – (1899-1989). St. Louis. The businessman headed the Anheuser-Busch brewery. He bought the St. Louis Cardinals baseball team in 1953.

Dale Carnegie – Born in Maryville and lived in Belton. Famous lecturer who wrote the widely read book *How to Win Friends and Influence People*.

William H. Danforth – St. Louis. Founder of the Ralston Purina Company who pioneered the commercial feed industry. He was a farm boy in the southeast Missouri swamp country and later graduated from Washington University in St. Louis in 1892.

Herbert Gibson – Howe County. Founder of the Gibson chain stores.

Joyce Clyde Hall – Kansas City. Entrepreneur who founded the Kansas City-based Hallmark Cards, Inc. Hall arrived in Kansas City in 1910 and began operating his postcard wholesaling business out of his room at the YMCA. The company was known as Hall Brothers until 1954 when the name was changed to Hallmark Cards.

Donald Joyce Hall– Kansas City. Son of Joyce C. Hall. He serves as Chairman of Hallmark Cards, Inc., and owns a majority of Hallmark stock. He is listed on the *Forbes 500* list.

John Quentin Hammons – Springfield. He started the Holiday Inns motel franchise with partner Roy Winegardner in 1959.

Ewing Marion Kauffman – Kansas City. The businessman launched Marion Laboratories, a pharmaceutical company which developed the first calcium pill from crushed oyster shell. Kauffman also owns the Kansas City Royals baseball team.

William P. Lear – Born in Hannibal in 1902. He was the inventor of the first automobile radio, the first automatic pilot for airplanes, and he invented and produced the Lear Jet.

James S. McDonnell, Jr. – St. Louis. He founded McDonnell Aircraft Corporation in 1939.

Jesse Clyde Nichols – (1880-1950). Kansas City. The real estate entrepreneur founded the Country Club Plaza – the nation's first shopping center – and also developed the Mission Hills area.

James Cash Penney – Hamilton. He was the founder of the J.C. Penney Company. He worked for a mercantile store in Hamilton. At the time of his retirement in 1946 he headed 1,612 stores.

Russell Stover – Kansas City. He established Russell Stover Candies, Inc., the nation's largest boxed-candy producer, in 1923.

The Military

Omar N. Bradley – (1893-1981). Born near Clark. Bradley commanded the largest American force ever united under one man's leadership. Bradley also became the first Chairman of the Joint Chiefs of Staff after World War II. As a five-star general, Bradley served 69 years on active duty, which was longer than any other soldier in U.S. history.

Admiral Robert E. Coontz – Born in Hannibal. He became Commander of the United States Fleet in 1923.

Rufus E. Longan – Pettis County. Brigadier-General commanding in World War I.

John J. Pershing – (1860-1948). Born near LaClede. Pershing was the only American named General of the Armies, a rank that carries a six-star status.

Photo courtesy of The State Historical Society of Missouri.

John J. Pershing

Sterling Price – Keytesville. Price assumed command of the pro-Southern state militia when the Civil War started. He led the effort to have Missouri secede from the Union and later commanded Southern forces in their 1864 trek through Missouri.

Gen. Maxwell D. Taylor – Keytesville. Graduate of West Point who served in World War II and Korean War. From 1955 to 1959 he served as Army Chief of Staff.

Miss America

Debbye Turner – Miss America 1990. She was the first Miss Missouri contestant to win the national title in the pageant's 68-year-history.

Bartlett, John. **Familiar Quotations.** Little, Brown and Company, 1980.

Excelsior Springs Chamber of Commerce, 101 E. Broadway, Excelsior Springs 64024.

Gallatin Publishing Co., P.O. Box 37, Gallatin 64640.

Kansas City Chiefs 1988 Media Guide, One Arrowhead Drive, Kansas City, MO 64129.

Laura Ingalls Wilder-Rose Wilder Lane Museum and Home, Rt. 1 Box 24, Mansfield 65704.

"Missouri Corporate Planner," Missouri Department of Economic Development, Jefferson City 65102.

Missouri Department of Health, State Center for Vital Statistics, 1730 E. Elm, P.O. Box 570, Jefferson City 65102.

Paris Area Chamber of Commerce, P.O. Box 75, Paris 65275.

St. Charles Chamber of Commerce, 1816 Boonslick Rd., St. Charles 63301.

Sedalia Area Chamber of Commerce, 113 E. 4th St., Sedalia 65301.

"Show Me Stars," The Missouri Film Commission, Department of Economic Development, P.O. Box 118, Jefferson City 65102.

Springfield Convention and Visitors Bureau, 3315 E. Battlefield Rd., Springfield 65804-4048.

State Historical Society of Missouri, 1020 Lowry, Columbia 65201.

Statistical Abstract of Missouri, 1987; B&PA Research Center, College of Business and Public Administration, University of Missouri, Columbia; Office of Administration, Department of Education.

The Topeka Capital-Journal, 616 Jefferson, Topeka, KS 66607.

The Walt Disney Company, 500 South Buena Vista St., Burbank, CA 91521.

West Plains Chamber of Commerce, 220 W. Main, West Plains 65775.

Worlds of Fun, 4545 Worlds of Fun Ave., Kansas City, MO 64161.

CHAPTER 5
CULTURE

The Arts • Art Museums
Lambert's Cafe • Festivals
Missouri State Fair
Show Me Stardom

MISSOURI

CULTURE

Photo courtesy of Branson / Lakes Area Chamber of Commerce.

CHAPTER OPENER PHOTO: Sharing techniques and ideas is vital in maintaining culture in Missouri. Through education, youngsters can continue the traditions that are so important to fellow craftsmen in the state.

M issouri has been blessed with talented people who either have the creative abilities to produce various arts or people who have the business skills to promote the arts in the state. A diverse ethnic population in the state adds to the richness of Missouri's character. Across the state, communities celebrate ethnic heritage through festivals and the arts. Missouri has such a wide variety of culture and art that residents rarely need to venture outside the state to satisfy their personal tastes.

The arts are valuable assets to Missouri and its people. With the help of organizations, educators, and people who simply love the arts, Missouri can offer its residents some of the best cultural programs in the country. Organizations across the state enable visitors to experience everything from local talent to professional artisans. Through educational programs, Missouri's culture is guaranteed for future generations. Schools and businesses are getting involved with students and adults alike in showcasing Missouri culture.

Every town in Missouri has its own way of celebrating its culture. Most do so by holding annual events and festivals. This is perhaps one of the best ways to truly get in touch with Missouri culture. Booths line streets and parks inviting people to enjoy local traditions. It is a perfect means for youngsters to discover the ways of their ancestors and perhaps even take up an art of their own. If nothing else, area festivals and events are excellent opportunities for a community to come together and show off a little.

The Missouri State Fair has the cultural flavor that everyone can enjoy. The fair is held annually in August and attracts thousands of visitors. Local citizens and visitors from other states flock through the front gates to enjoy the wide variety of cultural delicacies that only a fair can offer. From produce and livestock shows to nationally known celebrities, the fair has something for everyone. The Missouri State Fair is becoming one of the largest in the country.

Not only are the arts important to individuals, they are equally important to the state economically. Tourism dollars are kept in the state for further growth of the arts. Missouri has an abundance of cultural opportunities to offer newcomers. One large industry that has benefited from Missouri's culture is the film and motion picture industry. The range of landscapes in Missouri has drawn movie makers to the state who want to shoot on location.

Never at a loss is local talent. Almost every community in Missouri has some cultural activity. From the flashy music shows in the big cities to the small town talent show, Missouri has an array of arts and cultures that will amaze visitors.

Opera, ballet, jazz, painting, theater, wood carving, furniture making and more – Missouri has a cultural delight for all who want to experience it. ❐

Paris Portrait | A reproduction of the Norman Rockwell painting "The Country Editor" can be seen in the office of the *Monroe County Appeal* in Paris. Rockwell came to Paris and used the Appeal's editor, the late Jack Blanton, and other employees as his models for the series of paintings which includes "The Country Editor."

All That Jazz | The Jazz Film Collection at the University of Missouri-Kansas City has a collection of nearly 3,000 films and is the only jazz archive in the United States.

Jubilant Premier | In 1954, "Ozarks Jubilee" was first telecast on network television to an audience of 15 to 18 million viewers.

First Lady | Vinnie Ream was the first woman commissioned by Congress to do a sculpture. Ream lived in Columbia and attended Christian College. She also did the life-size statue of Abraham Lincoln that is in the Missouri Capitol Rotunda.

A Bright Idea | The Country Club Plaza in Kansas City is famous for the beautiful lights that decorate its buildings throughout the holidays. Every year on Thanksgiving night since 1925, the Plaza holds its lighting ceremony. The occasion calls for over 3,000 man hours and 90 days to install, 156,000 bulbs, and 47 miles of wiring.

The City of Country | During the 1950s, Springfield was regarded as the city of country music with such shows as "Jubilee U.S.A." and the "Tennessee Ernie Ford Show." Both were produced locally.

Sedalia Muralist | Eric James Bransby, 20th century American artist, painted the Sedalia Murals in the Municipal Building. His bid beat 21 other artists from the surrounding four-state area. The murals tell the story of Sedalia's history.

Busch Whacked | The first event held in Busch Stadium in St. Louis was on May 12, 1966, when the Cardinals defeated the Atlanta Braves 4-3.

Arrow Rock

Lyceum Theatre. Missouri's oldest professional summer repertory theater, featuring 3 musicals, a drama, a comedy and a classic playing on a rotating repertory schedule. *For information call (816) 837-3311.*

Boonville

Thespian Hall. Oldest theater west of the Allegheny Mountains. Also open for tours Monday-Friday, June 1-August 30. *For more information call (816) 882-7977.*

Columbia

Columbia Art League. The main gallery has changing exhibitions of regional and national artists. *For more information call (314) 443-8838.*

Maplewood Barn Community Theater. Each summer open-air performances of well-known plays are produced with the rustic Maplewood Barn serving as backdrop. *For more information call (314) 875-1231.*

Missouri Cultural Heritage Center. In many categories of art and culture, the center gives programs in music, dance, storytelling, functional art, and ethnic traditions. *For more information call (314) 882-6296.*

Missouri Symphony Society. Summer music festival combines the presentation of high-quality professional concert series with a student program. Also, a "Pops" orchestra performs locally, as well as on tours. *For information call (314) 875-0600.*

University Concert Series. Concerts of fine orchestras, opera, solo artists, chamber music theater, ballet, etc. *For more information call (314) 882-3875.*

University of Missouri Department of Theater. During the academic year, award-winning productions are directed, designed and performed by professors and students. Featuring dramas, a musical extravaganza, and innovative shows. Program also includes a professional summer repertory theater. *For more information call (314) 882-2021.*

QUICK FACTS:

The first music show opened in Branson over 30 years ago.

St. Louis was the setting for the playwright Tennessee Williams' work "The Glass Menagerie."

In December 1925, the Country Club Plaza had five buildings. That year, the merchants voted to decorate the area with miniature Christmas trees placed along the sidewalks. As a special gesture the late Charles Pitrat, then head of maintenance, installed several strings of colored lights over the doorway of the Mill Creek Building; thus began the lighting tradition on the Plaza.

In France, New Year's is a bigger greeting card-sending holiday than Christmas. In Canada, people celebrate Thanksgiving in October without the traditional American symbols of Pilgrims and Indians. In Brazil and Australia, where December 25 is in the middle of the summer, Christmas cards featuring wintery scenes are out of place.

QUICK FACTS:

Cliff Edwards, actor and musician known as Ukelele Ike, was born in Hannibal. He went to Hollywood and appeared in many films and was the voice of Jiminy Cricket.

In the Amish community at Jamesport, a new Amish buggy costs up to $3,000. A large handmade Amish quilt can cost from $400 to $500.

Lee Mace's Ozark Opry at Osage Beach has the distinction of being the first family music theater of its type in the United States.

Laclede's Landing in St. Louis is a nine-square block area that is a nightlife center.

Since 1969, more than 33 million fans have attended Royals baseball games in Kansas City. The team has won six Western Division pennants, two American League championships, and the 1985 World Series title.

To celebrate the centennial of Thomas Hart Benton's birth, the Nelson-Atkins Gallery organized a show of his works.

Florissant

Florissant Fine Arts Council. Ongoing art displays are found in the lobby of the Florissant Theater. The council also brings many entertainment productions to the community throughout the year. *For more information call (314) 921-5678.*

Hamilton

Community Arts Theater. Country music shows, comedies, local musicals, and children's theater shows. *For more information call (816) 583-2168.*

Hannibal

Mark Twain Outdoor Theatre. Presenting a two-hour pageant of Mark Twain's characters from Tom Sawyer, Huckleberry Finn, and Life on the Mississippi. This outdoor spectacular uses life-size buildings and its own showboat. *For information call (314) 221-2945.*

Joplin

Spiva Art Center. The art center features exhibits, art classes, workshops and lectures – an educational, cultural and social center. *For more information call (417) 623-0183.*

Kansas City

American Heartland Theatre. Productions include comedies, musicals, and mysteries featuring current Broadway hits. *For more information call (816) 233-7003.*
The Coterie Children's Theatre. The 7-show season offers a range of productions from classics of children's literature to original material. The theater is wheelchair accessible and interpreted performances are offered for the hearing impaired. *For more information call (816) 474-6552.*
Early Music Consort. This group specializes in instrumental and vocal music of the Renaissance, Baroque, and Classical eras. Work is performed on authentic replicas of instruments from these periods. *For more information call (816) 523-0905.*

Folly Theatre. A historic, restored theater built in 1900 is the setting. Presents live legitimate shows and variety attraction. *For information call (816) 842-5500.*

The Friends of Chamber Music. This group presents an international chamber music series including soloists, ensembles, quartets, chamber orchestras of world-class calibre, and a piano recital series. *For information call (816) 444-4429.*

Kaleidoscope. Creative art experience for children ages 5-12 sponsored by Hallmark Cards. *For information call (816) 274-8300.*

Kansas City Symphony. Symphony orchestra with major series, international soloists, Pops series, etc. William McGlaughlin, music director and conductor. *For information call (816) 471-0400.*

Kansas City Young Audiences. Provides a wide variety of arts programming to schools and community organizations. *For more information call (816) 531-4022.*

Lyric Opera of Kansas City. Classic opera performed in English. *For information call (816) 471-7344.*

The Midland Theater. "Midwest's Most Elegant Historical Landmark" now hosts the best of Broadway's national touring shows. Top notch musicals, comedies, Las Vegas headliners, and dramas call the Midland their Kansas City home. *For information call (816) 421-7500.*

Missouri Repertory Theatre. This live professional theater company presents productions ranging from the great classics to world premiere plays. *For information call (816) 267-2700.*

Quality Hill Playhouse. The first new theater in the Downtown loop in more than 30 years hosts smaller audiences with intimate plays and musicals. *For more information call (816) 421-1700.*

Starlight Theatre. Live Broadway musicals and live concerts with famous entertainers, all in 7,800 seat amphitheater in Swope Park. *For more information call (816) 363-STAR.*

QUICK FEATURES:

Symbol of Quality – Hallmark Cards, Incorporated was founded in January 1910 by Joyce C. Hall (1891-1982). The company's name was Hall Brothers, Inc. until 1954. The firm manufactures greeting cards and other social expression products under the brand names of Hallmark, Ambassador, Springbok, Crayola, Liquitex, and Heartline. The gold crown with the word "Hallmark" under it has become the company's symbol and is synonymous with quality and excellence in the minds of the American public. More than 11 million greeting cards stamped with the famous gold crown are produced daily. Each is an attempt by Hallmark to carry on the quality tradition of 14th-century English guilds. Members of these guilds fashioned their goods in long rooms called halls. Each hall vied with the others to turn out superior work, and each stamped its work with a mark called a "hall mark." A hallmark is used today to note the work of a master craftsman.

QUICK FACTS:

Kansas City is the third largest theater town in the Midwest. The city has more than 20 equity and community theaters and 75 theater departments at high schools and colleges.

Several music performers have made videos in Missouri, including Phil Collins' "Tonight, Tonight," and REO Speedwagon's "Concert–Kemper." The Kentucky Headhunters made a country music video in Mexico, Missouri.

Rose Wilder Lane persuaded her mother, Laura Ingalls Wilder, to start writing. The results were the Little House on the Prairie series. Rose Wilder Lane edited the series.

Thomas Hart Benton, perhaps Missouri's most well-known artist, was a controversial character and it was said of him that he may be the first American artist whose personality and historical importance outdistance his art.

State Ballet of Missouri. Kansas City's only year-round professional performing ballet organization, featuring a corps of dancers of exceptional talent and virtuosity. *For more information call (816) 931-2232.*

Unicorn Theatre. An equity theater that produces high quality, contemporary and off-Broadway scripts. *For more information call (816) 531-PLAY.*

Kirksville

Traveller's Community Theater. Established in 1973. Volunteer theater troupe presents three varied productions yearly. *For more information call (816) 665-9721.*

Liberty

William Jewell College Fine Arts Program. Program sponsors dance, music, and theater events by national and international artists. *For information call (816) 781-8250.*

Lockwood

Theatre of Performing Arts. The Theatre is a renovated opera house built in 1908 in which nearly 100 cloggers take their lessons weekly. Monthly shows ranging from drama to barbershop singing to ballet are available. *For more information call (417) 232-4258.*

Nevada

Little Alley Theatre. Musicals, comedies, drama, chorales presented by the Community Council of the Performing Arts. *For information call (417) 667-7299.*

Rolla

Ozark Actors Theatre. A professional summer stock theater, presenting three varied productions each summer. *For more information call (314) 364-9523.*

St. Joseph

Performing Arts Association. Presenting more than 20 events of theater, music, dance, and motion pictures each season. *For more information call (816) 233-0231.*

Robidoux Resident Theatre. A resident theater company of the historic Missouri Theater, this volunteer company, under professional direction, presents a four-play mainstage season, a studio season in the small 100-seat theater, and more. *For more information call (816) 271-4628.*

St. Joseph Symphony. Features concerts, special performances, and guest artists performing quality pieces. *For more information call (816) 233-7701.*

St. Louis

Dance St. Louis. Presents national and international professional dance companies, both classical and modern dance. *For more information call (314) 968-4341.*

Edison Theatre. In its main stage OVATIONS! series, the Edison presents professional touring companies and artists in the disciplines of dance, music, and theater in a series of 10-12 events per season, along with the new "Ovations! for young people" series of four matinees. *For more information call (314) 889-6543.*

Fox Theatre. Restored 1929 movie palace, with state-of-the-art sound and lighting, features Broadway shows; rock, pop, country and jazz artists; and classic films. *For information call (314) 652-5000.*

Laumeier Sculpture Park. It has a 96-acre contemporary sculpture park and art gallery; picnic shelter and sites; hiking trails. Free summer outdoor concerts on Sundays. *For information call (314) 821-1209.*

Metro Theater Circus. Each production features an original score performed on a wide variety of instruments, distinctive movement, and striking visual design. *For more information call (314) 727-3552.*

Missouri Arts Council. The purpose of the Missouri Arts Council is to stimulate and encourage the growth, development, and appreciation of the arts in Missouri through financial and technical assistance to arts organizations. Some of the programs offered by

QUICK FACTS:

A number of nationally broadcast commercials have been filmed in Missouri including: Porsche, Amtrak, Anheuser-Busch, IBM, Armour Foods, Southern Comfort Whiskey, Sports Illustrated, Hallmark, Wal-Mart, and Wendy's, to name a few.

The Springfield Art Museum began in 1928 when a group of Springfield women formed an art club. The nucleus of the fledgling institution's collection were two small oil paintings purchased by the club members themselves.

The Royal Theatre was built in Versailles, Missouri, in the early 1930s as a movie theatre. During the 1930s the Miss Lake of the Ozarks Beauty Contest was held at the Royal, and it was occasionally used by school children for musical numbers before and after movies were shown.

At the Mark Twain Outdoor Theater in Hannibal a body of water and a 50-foot replica of a Mississippi Riverboat lies between the audience and the stage to create realism.

QUICK FACTS:

In 1923, the word "Hallmark" appeared by itself for the first time and in 1954 became the official name of the company.

During Fiscal Year 1989, the Missouri Film Commission received a total of 485 inquiries about potential Missouri film locations and provided assistance to 134 film and video projects that spent an estimated $16.2 million in the state.

Branson has become a gathering place for Nashville stars. Several have opened theaters in this area including Roy Clark and Boxcar Willie.

The historic Hall of Waters at Excelsior Springs is modeled in Art Deco style.

The Church of St. Mary the Virgin on the campus of Westminster College in Fulton is a 12th century London church remodeled by the famous architect Sir Christopher Wren in 1677. A number of other churches in London were designed by Wren.

the Missouri Arts Council include: **Missouri Touring Program:** Each year the Council selects a number of quality visual and performing arts organizations and individuals to tour the state demonstrating their art. **Artists-In-Education:** This program offers Missouri students and adults the exciting opportunity to participate in the process of creating art by integrating professional artists into the daily life of a school or community. **Traditional Arts Apprenticeship Program:** This program provides opportunities for qualified apprentices to learn style, technique, and repertoire from recognized folk art masters in all art areas. **Show Me The Arts:** A variety of technical assistance workshops are offered so Missouri's artists can learn new skills. **Missouri Arts Awards:** These awards recognize individuals, art educators, businesses, and other organizations for their contributions to the arts industry in Missouri. *For more information about any of these programs contact the Missouri Arts Council at (314) 444-6845.*

Mid America Dance Co. Modern dance company known for its bright, witty and theatrical style. Programs are all under professional direction. *For information call (314) 367-3620.*

Opera Theatre of Saint Louis. The season generally consists of four operas presented in repertory. All productions will be sung in English and accompanied by the St. Louis Symphony. *For more information call (314) 961-0171.*

The Repertory Theatre of St. Louis. A fully-professional, not-for-profit live theatrical organization. Enjoy the mainstage season of six full-length plays and the Studio Theatre season of three new plays. *For information call (314) 968-4925.*

St. Louis Artists' Guild. Monthly juried exhibitions of multi-media art by artists in Missouri and surrounding states, invitational exhibitions, workshops, and art classes. *For more information call (314) 961-1246.*

St. Louis Black Repertory. The company, founded in 1976, offers each year six main stage productions, an extensive training program, and a year-round touring program. *For more information call (314) 231-3706.*

St. Louis Symphony Orchestra. Named recently by *Time* magazine as one of the top two orchestras in the country and offers over 240 concerts yearly. The music ranges from classical to "Pops" concerts. Eight series are presented during the year. *For more information call (314) 535-2500.*

St. Louis Young Audiences. Programs are in music, dance, storytelling, multi-media, opera, and theatre categories. Each program is designed to introduce an art form, develop the audiences' appreciation of the cultural heritage and their own creative potential. *For more information call (314) 367-1400.*

The Muny. Broadway hits, musical revivals, drama, and top entertainers year-round at indoor and outdoor facilities. *For more information call (314) 361-1900.*

Sedalia

Sedalia Community Theater. Acted, produced, directed and staffed entirely by local volunteers. It presents three productions a year – a comedy, a drama, and a musical. *For more information call (816) 827-3103.*

Sedalia Visual Arts Association. A group of artists and art supporters sponsors monthly exhibits and workshops. *For more information call (816) 826-3103.*

Springfield

Southwest Missouri State University Performing Arts. Programs include Tent Theater, a repertory theater that performs three productions each summer. Regular productions of the theater and dance department are held throughout the school year. A performing arts season during the school year features visiting artists on a national scale. *For more information call (417) 836-5648.*

QUICK FACTS:

Recent made-for-TV movies shot in Missouri include PBS's "Across Five Aprils," NBC's "Cross of Fire," and Disney's "Back to Hannibal" that premiered on the Disney Channel in October 1990.

The St. Louis Blues hockey team has played in 12 Stanley Cup Finals.

In 1968 the Kansas City Royals got their name when the club asked the public to submit a name for the new American League franchise. Some other suggestions included Mules, Steers, Bluebirds, Cowpokes, Studs, and Blues.

Cape Girardeau is called the "City of Roses." Some of Cape Girardeau's roses came from cuttings going back to the founding of America and were brought over from England.

The film "Escape from New York" was shot on location in St. Louis, where the streets were converted into burned-out urban landscapes.

QUICK FEATURES:

Notable Novelist – Gallatin has provided an exceptional contribution to the arts: novelist John A. Selby. He was born in Gallatin in 1897. After attending Park College and the University of Missouri, he joined the *Kansas City Star* as a journalist and music critic. After 11 years there he was forced to resign because of ill health. The next three years he and his wife lived in France while he recuperated. They returned to New York where he accepted a position as music and arts critic with The Associated Press. During this time Selby was writing books. He was the author of ten novels and lectured at Columbia University where he taught courses in short-story writing. Later he joined Rinehart and Company as editor-in-chief, a position he held until his retirement in 1965. Mr. Selby returned to live in Gallatin for several months in 1972, but returned to Sicily where he lived until his death in 1980. One of his most successful books was *Island in the Corn*, a novel *Sam*, and two other best sellers *Starbuck* and *Time Was*.

Springfield Little Theatre. Missouri's largest community theater; seven musicals and plays per season in restored Landers Theater, built in 1909. *For more information call (417) 866-1334.*

Springfield Symphony. Presenting a 5-concert classical series, a 3-concert pop series, and a 3-concert chamber music series as well as educational concerts for students and holiday community concerts. *For more information call (417) 864-6683.*

Tarkio

Mule Barn Theatre. The original Mule Barn was destroyed by fire in the winter of 1989. Plays are currently performed in the new theater. *Contact the box office for further information (816) 736-4185.*

University City

Center of Contemporary Arts. A visual and performing arts center offering classes and performances in dance, music, and drama. A Gallery of Contemporary Art is on the premises. *For more information call (314) 725-6555.*

Versailles

Royal Theatre Co. Housed in the old Royal Theatre, the theatre is used for live plays, musical performances, solo recitals, brass bands, religious programs, talent shows, community auctions, puppet shows and scouting ceremonies. *For information call (314) 378-9930.*

Warrensburg

Central Missouri Repertory. Three live productions performed by a professional theater company. *For information call (816) 429-4020.*

West Plains

West Plains Arts Council. Events include speakers, music, plays, and dance. They also plan such activities as window decorating contests and a fine arts scholarship.

Bolivar

Ella Carothers Dunnegan Gallery of Art.
The works of artists known worldwide and a growing number of Missouri artists are on display.

Cape Girardeau

Southeast Missouri State University Museum. Exhibits include the Beckwith pottery collection; the Blum collection of Southwestern Indian arts featuring Navaho rugs, pottery, Kachina dolls and Indian paintings; and the Houck collection of life-size statuary and reliefs produced by August Gerber of Cologne, Germany, for the 1904 World's Fair in St. Louis, as well as many other items.

Columbia

Museum of Art & Archaeology – University of Missouri. Missouri's third largest art museum features art from ancient to contemporary. Located on the University of Missouri campus, the building houses a unique combination of art and archaeology.

Kansas City

The Children's Museum of Kansas City. Children, ages 4-12, interact with exhibits designed to foster creative thinking, imagination and self confidence. Besides hands-on art, children can see various exhibits. **Nelson-Atkins Museum of Art.** One of the top general-collection museums in the United States. Its special exhibit is the Oriental collection. The Henry Moore Sculpture Garden on the south lawn showcases the largest collection of Moore Bronzes in the United States. Bookstore and gourmet restaurant available.

Poplar Bluff

Margaret Harwell Art Museum. Featuring new exhibitions of state and regional importance every month. Both traditional and contemporary art directions are included. Permanent and traveling exhibits offered.

QUICK FACTS:

Hallmark and Ambassador share the world's largest creative staff – numbering about 700 persons. These artists, designers, stylists, writers, editors, and photographers generate more than 17,500 greeting card designs and 7,500 related designs annually.

The Nelson-Atkins Museum of Art ranks as one of the eighth largest art museums in the United States.

Spinning wheels were not allowed in the Ste. Genevieve district during colonial days. They were prohibited by the French who wanted settlers to continue trade with them, offering textiles as one of the things they would trade for furs and lead.

Three kinds of marble were used on the Seville Light on the Country Club Plaza in Kansas City. These are Tuscan Travertine marble quarried in Rapolano, Italy; a reddish Travertine marble quarried in Pakistan; and white Ravaccione marble quarried in the Carrara, Italy, district.

QUICK FACTS:

The St. Louis Cathedral has one of the finest collections of mosaics in the world, with 100 pieces of stone and glass making up the artworks that line the cathedral's interior.

Paintings by the world's great masters such as Monet, Degas, Gauguin, Van Gogh, and Rembrandt hang in the Nelson-Atkins museum beside contemporary works of such notables as Andy Warhol and Wilhelm de Kooning.

Ronald and Nancy Reagan were in Springfield to attend the movie premiere of "The Winning Team" in 1952.

Edbert Anson Van Alstyne, born 1882, was the composer of the song, "In the Shade of the Old Apple Tree," and many other World War I songs. He attended the Hannibal schools and lived in the Saverton area in his youth.

In 1976, the city of St. Louis was awarded a National Hockey League franchise and the team was named the "St. Louis Blues."

St. Joseph

Albrecht Art Museum. Monthly traveling exhibits and a permanent collection, which focuses on American art. Its collection includes paintings by George Bellows, Thomas Hart Benton, and George Caleb Bingham.

St. Louis

Craft Alliance Gallery. Contemporary art from craft media such as clay, wood, fiber, and glass. Wearable art, functional ceramics, sculpture, and more.

St. Louis Art Museum. Among the top 10 museums in the United States. The museum's permanent collection includes Asian and Ancient Art, Arts of Africa, decorative arts, Early European Art, prints, photographs, 19th and 20th Century Art. Also special exhibits.

Washington University Gallery of Art. Featuring an outstanding collection of European and American art of the 19th and 20th centuries.

Springfield

Springfield Art Museum. Exhibitions range from traditional to contemporary art. A wonderful collection of over 200 watercolors. There is also a collection of outdoor sculptures.

Photo courtesy of the Nelson-Atkins Museum of Art.
The Nelson-Atkins Museum of Art in Kansas City.

lambert's cafe

Home of the Throwed Rolls

There are a number of unique eateries across the state of Missouri. However, when was the last time you ever had a roll thrown at you? The only way to truly appreciate such a cultural tradition is by going to Sikeston, Mo., and eating at Lambert's Cafe. The following is an excerpt from Lambert's own 1990 brochure:

People who visit Lambert's for the first time are invariably amazed at the generous portions served on each order. These generous servings, along with our "THROWED ROLLS," have inspired many questions.

People have asked many times – "How did you start throwing rolls?" Well, to make a long story short – necessity. In 1976, while still in our old building, I would try to pass out our hot rolls in the traditional manner. You know, real nice like, by saying, "Would you care for a hot roll?" This was really awkward and uncomfortable to me, so on an extremely busy day, when getting through the lunch hour crowd was impossible, a customer said, "Just throw the ★★★★ thing!" I did, and everybody else joined in. We started throwing rolls May 26, 1976, and have continued ever since.

In 1989 Lambert's averaged baking 520 dozen rolls per day, for a grand total of 2,246,400 individual rolls.

In 1989 we averaged baking 520 dozen rolls per day, for a grand total of 2,246,400 individual rolls. Our rolls are five inches in diameter and if we laid all the rolls that we baked in one year side by side, we would have 177.27 miles of rolls. In the past 21 months we have baked enough rolls to reach 300 miles.

On Lambert's homemade rolls last year, hungry people spread 107,250 servings of jelly and 21,600 - 44 oz. cans of sorghum molasses.

We use approximately 252 gallons of slaw a week, or 13,107 gallons a year and 2,091 gallons of mayonnaise.

Last year we cooked 110,619 lbs. of choice round beef. It took a herd of 221 USDA choice steers to serve our customers!

Last year our cooks cracked and cooked 335,400 eggs and 211,650 lbs. of chicken were cooked.

We served our customers 1,927,800 little butter patties.

The atmosphere is truly out of the ordinary at Lambert's. Scores of floating balloons fill the air and an extensive collection of mule pictures decorate the walls. The pictures are by both professional and amateur artists. Lambert's Words of Wisdom: "Before you become a collector, become a picture frame maker!" *For more information call (314) 471-4261.* ❒

March

Annual Barbershop Chorus and Quartet Show – Springfield.
Music abounds at this annual event at Landers Theater.

Annual Old Time Fiddlers Contest – Boonville. This springtime
contest is pure entertainment with some of the best fiddlers playing
for prizes.

Easter Pageant – Sunrise Beach. Held Easter morning. A large
cast of players tells the story of Easter in a natural outdoor setting.

Easter Parade – Kansas City. The only official Easter parade in the
United States. Anyone may join the Promenade of Easter Finery, with
trophies being awarded for the most outstanding lady, gentleman, and
child in the parade.

Mid-America Jazz Festival – St. Louis. Performing musicians
include: Jim Cullum Jazz Band, Jay McShan, Scott Hamilton, Ralph
Sutten, and Barbara Sutten-Curtis and others.

Spring Fling – Kimberling City. Celebrate the arrival of spring with
parades, a trout fishing pond, a balloon lift, entertainment, coloring
contest, and sidewalk sales.

Spring Rendezvous – Independence. Old-style refreshments and
demonstrations of pioneer era crafts such as candlemaking, wood
carving, lace making, quilting, and much more.

Wurstfest – Hermann. Third weekend in March. A sausage making
competition for professionals and amateurs.

April

**Annual El Kadir Tri-State Wild Turkey Day and Calling Contest
– Kirksville.** Try your luck at the turkey shoot and calling contest, or
walk through the various displays.

Annual Easter Egg Hunt – Osceola. Children and adults turn out
for this annual event on the courthouse lawn.

Dogwood Azalea Festival – Charleston. This annual festival has
crafts, entertainment, a candlelight walk on Saturday night, and ice
cream social.

Dogwood Festival – Camdenton. The Ozarks' proud display of
blooming dogwood trees. Events include the Dogwood Festival Parade
and the crowning of the Dogwood Festival Queen.

May

Apple Blossom Parade and Festival – St. Joseph. This parade was
originally a celebration for area apple growers and now averages 200
units including floats, bands, and antique autos.

Designers Showcase – Springfield. Presented by the Springfield
Symphony Guild. Fifteen interior designers will transform an area
home into a showcase piece.

Eminence Ozark Days – Eminence. Crafts, demonstrations, and
food galore.

Emmett Kelly Clown Festival – Houston. The spirit of the clown comes out in this festival featuring Emmett Kelly, Jr., arts and crafts, a petting zoo, clown contests, carnival, and much more.

Maifest – Hermann. German tradition, history, and fun are found beside the Missouri River. Features a parade, historic home and winery tours, entertainment, crafts, German food, dance, and costumes.

May Days Festival – Jamesport. Highlighted by a flea market with over 100 booths, a craft show, and a large consignment auction. Also features antique machinery and entertainment.

Mississippi River Art Festival – Hannibal. Three days of contemporary art exhibits, music, dancing, and fine food all set on the banks of the Mississippi River.

Storytelling Festival – St. Louis. Features 10 nationally recognized storytellers and 35 local storytellers with a special performance for the hearing impaired as well as interpretation for the deaf.

Valley of Flowers Festival – Florissant. An annual springtime event that includes Maypole dancing, parade, tours of historic homes, contests, and a beer garden.

June

Belton Community Days – Belton. A Midwest community celebration with games, arts and crafts, food, entertainment, pet show, and a Miss Belton contest.

Boonville Heritage Days – Boonville. A celebration of area heritage.

Carthage Heritage Festival Pow Wow – Carthage. Native American pow wow, traditional dancing, food, and exhibits. There is also a fur traders area with games and booths.

Fescue Funfest Festival – Clinton. Located at Courthouse Square. The activities include arts and crafts, fine arts show, plus numerous other performers and events.

Founder's Day Festival – Union. Family and children's games, craft show, swim carnival, 10K run, food and drink stands, and a dance.

Great River Road Tour – Paris. Lake Village. American Motorcyclist Association. Four days of events.

Kingdom Days – Callaway. Activities include an ice cream social, dance, quilt show, parade, and a balloon fly over. Downtown businesses decorate their store windows with memorabilia and themes that reflect the heritage and history of Callaway County.

Pony Express-Jesse James Day Festival – St. Joseph. Celebrate the Old West with booths of antiques, crafts, and concession stands.

Riverfest – Cape Girardeau. Activities include arts and crafts, entertainment, barbecue contest, and a tall tale contest.

Scott Joplin Ragtime Festival – Sedalia. Four days of celebrating America's first original music – Ragtime. The festival is kicked off with a period dance, live concerts, historic symposium, and dance lessons.

Summerfest – Springfield. A four day celebration at the end of June and first of July centered around Firefall, Springfield's famous Independence Day Celebration. Balloon races, concerts, fireworks, music, and live entertainment provided by the Springfield Symphony.
Warsaw Jubilee Days – Warsaw. Features a parade, carnival, country music show, fiddlers' contest, queen contest, and craft booths.

July

Bastille Celebration – Ste. Genevieve. Dinner and entertainment highlight the festivities.
Blessing of the Fleet – Portage Des Sioux. Considered the biggest marine event on the Mississippi River. Hundreds of boats are decorated to an annual theme. They will travel eight miles downstream to be blessed in front of Our Lady of the Rivers Shrine.
Cedar Stone Country Bluegrass Festival – Eminence. July 4th weekend. Music lights up the day at this 4th of July festival.
Fourth of July – Doniphan. A Miss Current River Queen Contest and traditional fireworks are part of the festivities.

Photo courtesy of Hannibal Visitors and Convention Bureau.

The Frog Jumping Contest held during National Tom Sawyer Days is an event for all ages.

Monroe County Fair – Paris. Fairgrounds. Activities include a pickup pull, tractor pull, and carnival.
National Tom Sawyer Days – Hannibal. Activities include the National Fence Painting Championship, a frog jumping competition, Tomboy Sawyer competition, and more.
Old Fashioned 4th of July – Monett. The entire park goes back in time where visitors will find antique cars, old-fashioned barbecue, political speeches, picnics, and fireworks.

Old Threshers Celebration – Paris. Events include threshing demonstration, draft horse pull, early day gas engines and tractors, wheat flour grinding, flea market and antiques displays, country cloggers performances, fiddlers, and crafts displays. Also on display is a fine collection of antique threshers and other farm equipment.

Osage Indian Heritage Days – Gravois Mill. Representatives of the Osage people attend and highlights include Indian Fry Bread and colorful costume displays. The Chief of the Osage Nations, with Assistant Chief, and members of the Tribal Council sit with the Gravois Arm Chamber of Commerce in planning the festival.

Ozark Empire Fair – Springfield. More than 10,000 exhibits highlight the second largest annual fair in Missouri. Some of the most popular entertainment around comes to Springfield. Live music, livestock competition, exhibits, carnival rides, and special foods.

Ste. Genevieve County Fair – Ste. Genevieve. Held on the fairgrounds on North Main Street.

August

Annual White River Valley Arts & Crafts Fair – Forsyth. Area craftsmen and artists display their wares.

Bootheel Rodeo – Sikeston. The largest rodeo in the state. The wide variety of events draws nationally-known cowboys and cowgirls. Entertainment features famous country music stars.

Candlelight Tour of Fort Osage – Sibley. The special look at the old fort is by pre-registration and only a limited number may participate. This after-hours tour allows visitors a look at fort life, see soldiers discussing impending war with England as they relax in their barracks, or watch a young soldier's wife ready her children for bed. A unique experience of 1855 by candlelight.

Children's Day at Missouri Town 1855 – Blue Springs. Explore the child's world of 1855 through stories, games, contests, and treats loved by children of an earlier era. Great for today's children.

Erntfest – Freistatt. Authentic German festival on the third weekend in August. The entire town comes out to celebrate the harvest, German style.

Fall Festival – Orient. A parade, Queen contest, Little Mr. and Miss contest, baby contest, entertainment, barbecue, and children's games.

Great Stone Hill Grape Stomp – Hermann. Second Saturday in August. Sponsored by the Stone Hill Winery.

Jour de Fete – Ste. Genevieve. The area's largest craft fair. Experience the French and German heritage and shop over 400 stands featuring authentic arts and crafts. Watch artists and craftsmen at work, including weavers, spinners, carvers, blacksmiths, jewelers, and potters.

Kahoka Festival of Bluegrass Music – Kahoka. Third weekend in August. This festival features top Bluegrass bands from all over the United States. Also has area clogging events, individual workshops, and many impromptu jam sessions.

Missouri State Championship Barbecue Cook Off – St. Joseph. The fund-raising cook off features commercial and amateur chefs from a four-state area.

festivals

Photo courtesy of the Missouri State Fair.

Fiddlers of all ages enjoy the contests at the Missouri State Fair.

Missouri State Fair – Sedalia. One of America's largest fairs with a wide range of exhibits, including livestock, agriculture, horticulture, and crafts. Other features are entertainment from famous personalities, horse shows, and more.

Missouri River Festival of the Arts – Boonville. Features evening performances of dance, opera, symphony, and children's programs.

Old Tyme Fair Week Parade – Palmyra. Kicks off the Palmyra Fall Festival and Marion County Junior Fair.

Republic Carnival – Republic. Food stands, games, an auction, bluegrass bands, carnival rides, and crafts.

Salt River Folklife Festival – Florida. This festival features the crafts, foods, living skills, music, and dance found in the area during the 19th century.

Santa-Cali-Gon Days – Independence. Labor Day weekend celebration with one of the largest arts and crafts displays in the Midwest. A carnival and entertainment all four days.

VP Fair – St. Louis. This large celebration features top name entertainment, St. Louis' biggest annual parade, international foods, world-class fireworks every night, air and water shows, and exhibits.

Wilson's Creek Moonlight Tour – Springfield. This mid-August night tour is held during a full moon and is lighted only by moonlight and lanterns to help re-enact the 1862 battle.

September

Apple Butter Makin' Days – Mt. Vernon. Made today just like our ancestors. Some of the huge copper kettles make as much as 60 gallons of apple butter. Other activities include a terrapin race, pet parade, nail driving contest, and log sawing contest.

Blue Springs Fall Fun Festival – Blue Springs. A festival of fun for families and friends. This outdoor street festival has a large assortment of crafts, games, displays, food, and beer garden. There will be three stages of continuous free entertainment.

Board of Boards Festival – Oak Grove. Crafts, games, car show, entertainment, and contests.

Buddy-Bass Tournament – Mark Twain Lake. The annual tournament is held at Black Jack Marina, Mark Twain Lake.

Clark County Mule Festival – Kahoka. Third weekend in September. There is nothing more humorous than watching a rider try to put a stubborn mule through a variety of relays and races. Visitors can enjoy crafts, quilt contest, exotic animals, and more.

Crappie Tournament – Lake of the Ozarks. Sponsored by the Lake of the Ozarks West Chamber of Commerce. Tournament allows contestants to fish by boat or from their favorite dock.

Floral Hall House Tour – Mark Twain Lakes Area. The annual autumn tour celebrates historical landmarks and includes a quilt and Civil War doll show display.

Hillbilly Fair – Laurie. Events include a parade, beer garden, crafts, fiddlin' contest, carnival, mountainman encampment, dancing, cloggers, and contests.

Liberty Fall Festival – Liberty. This annual festival has craft and food booths, a parade, entertainment, a talent show, car show, a little Mr. & Miss Liberty contest, and a children's area which has a carnival and petting zoo.

Pioneer Days – Monett. Fourth weekend in September. This celebration grew from the roots set forth by the pioneers. The activities include an annual Buckskin Rendezvous where an encampment of trappers have arts and crafts displayed and also a carnival.

Raytown Round-Up Days – Raytown. Features a parade, country store, auction, rides, special drawings for prizes, live entertainment, crafts, games, and food.

Steam Engine and Threshers Show – Boonville. Many working displays of live steam and threshing.

Volksmarch – Hermann. Third weekend in September. Celebrations of German heritage.

Wild West Days – Springfield. This annual mid-September festival commemorates the famous shootout between Wild Bill Hickok and Davis Tutt on Park Central Square. Live music, an abundance of food and beverages, and local crafts are available.

World Sheep Fest – Bethel. Labor Day weekend. Attracting thousands each year, this three-day celebration promotes the sheep industry and showcases rare breeds and exotic animals.

October

Annual Maple Leaf Festival – Carthage. The festival includes a parade, four-state marching band competition, statewide car show, historic homes tour, crafts, entertainment and more.

Celebration of the Anniversary of the French Revolution – Ste. Genevieve. Highlights include a French Market with colonial crafts and French Marines, plus a special Lantern Tour on Saturday evening allows visitors to stroll through the streets of Ste. Genevieve.

Chili Cook Off – Washington. If the entertainment won't warm up this fall event, the chili will. There is a chili cook off, a jalapeno eating contest, costume contest, and live entertainment.

Country Colorfest – Louisiana. Third weekend in October. An annual community-wide, two-day festival featuring arts, crafts, music, food, parade, and other activities.

Current River Days – Van Buren. First weekend in October. Old fashioned games, artists and craftsmen, exhibits and demonstration, a Saturday night street dance, tube and canoe races, and other contests.

Eldon Turkey Festival – Eldon. Activities include live turkey races, 5K Turkey Trot run/walk, turkey egg toss, wild turkey hunting exhibits, entertainment, and exhibits by local turkey growers/processors.

Fall Festival – Ferguson. The festival, held annually on Halloween weekend, is a last fling for fall. Activities include a costume parade and a twilight walk for youngsters to receive trick or treat items.

Heritage Days – Warsaw. Features demonstrations in spinning, weaving, log hewing, candlemaking, and ropemaking. Displays range from Civil War relics to steam engines. Music, square dancing and clogging will entertain as visitors sample a variety of food.

Hound Dog Festival – Aurora. The festival is held the first weekend in October. Some activities include a carnival, bed race, crafts, area school band competition, quilt show, and a large antique car show.

Lee's Summit Octoberfest – Lee's Summit. A true Bavarian celebration. There is a carnival, a German band, a beer garden, and authentic German foods.

Maple Leaf Festival – Carthage. Activities include the Belle Starr Chili Cook-off and Firemen's Saloon, parade, food, arts and crafts.

Mountainman Rendezvous – Bagnell Dam. Mid-October. Authentic mountainmen living in teepees and cooking with primitive cookware highlight this event. Powder shoots and hatchet-throwing contests are among the activities.

Octoberfest – Hermann. Every weekend in October. Large event in Old World-German style tradition. Sample the wine and enjoy a variety of ethnic foods.

Old Tyme Apple Festival – Versailles. Features a parade, arts and crafts, beard growing contest, an Old World Theater presentation, and samples of this year's apple crop and fresh apple cider.

Prairie View Festival – St. Joseph. This festival is a living history of craft demonstrators in 19th century costumes, accompanied by period performing musicians.

Robidoux Festival – St. Joseph. Held the first weekend in October, this festival provides booths displaying the skills, arts and crafts of persons in the entire area.

St. Francois River Rendezvous – Farmington. Second weekend in October. Features a black powder shoot, storytelling, special foods, and competition dancing at a pow wow.

The Versailles Olde Tyme Apple Festival – Versailles. Held the first Saturday in October, this festival celebrates the harvest. Features a 2-mile and 10-kilometer run, an old-time costume contest, beard growing contest, old-time apple cider making demonstrations, folk music, German food, and more.

November

American Royal Livestock, Horse Show, and Rodeo – Kansas City. One of America's largest agricultural exhibitions since 1899. Activities include seven horse shows, various other livestock shows, professional rodeo, a barbecue festival, a parade, and concerts.

Photo courtesy of The American Royal.

This energetic Hackney Pony steps out at the American Royal Horse Show.

Autumn Historic Folklife Festival – Hannibal. First weekend in November. Hannibal's historic district is the setting for this festival that features artisans demonstrating the crafts of the mid-1800s, storytellers, and freshly made apple cider.

Christmas Festival – Osage Beach. A Christmas parade and bridge lighting with Santa on Skis, ribbon of lights, and open house in stores from Bagnell Dam to Route KK.

The Country Club Plaza Lighting – Kansas City. This famous event takes place annually at 8 p.m. on Thanksgiving night. The 49 miles of Christmas lights outlining the 14-block district has been a tradition since 1925. Some 156,000 bulbs are used in the display.

French Colonial Days – Ste. Genevieve. Traditional crafts and demonstrations.

Tree Lighting Festival – Ferguson. Last Sunday in November. A giant tree in Caboose Park is lit up with Christmas caroling and cheer all around.

The Way to Salvation Display – Carthage. Opens Thanksgiving Day and continues through January 1st. This display is made up of electro-art sculptures with thousands of tiny bulbs and is set in a realistic background. Visitors can follow Biblical storylines from Adam and Eve ending with the newborn Baby Jesus.

December

Christmas Open House: "Windows on the Past" – Blue Springs. At Missouri Town 1855 experience a cozy weekend of holiday cheer, hearth cooking, caroling, storytelling, and age-old traditions. Bundle up and stroll through the snow-covered village with glimpses of Christmas past.

Christmas in Bethel – Bethel. This festival is one of the most charming winter events in the Midwest. There are visits from the German Black Santa and St. Nicholas, cold German drinking custard, a Christmas tree ornament show and sale, candlelight processions, caroling and the "lighting of Bethel."

Christmas Parade – Monett. The entire town is hopping with a parade down Main Street for children and adults. Santa will appear for the kids (and kids at heart).

Christmas Walk – Ste. Genevieve. Mr. and Mrs. Santa Claus will appear, carolers, tree lighting ceremony and much more. The historic downtown district at Christmas is unforgettable.

"City of Lights" – Sikeston. The town comes to life with large lighted displays throughout the community. Approximately two million lights are used in this "yuletide" extravaganza.

For more information about these or other festivals not listed, contact local Chambers of Commerce or Visitors Bureaus, or the Missouri Division of Tourism, P.O. Box 1055, Jefferson City, Mo. 65102; (314) 751-4133.

Meet Me At The Fun

In 1899, the first steps were taken to establish the Missouri State Fair. The first Fair was held September 9-13, 1901, at Sedalia. Many of the original buildings still stand on the Fairgrounds. The main attraction that year was an exhibition of an automobile on the track performing "thrilling exhibitions and fancy track work."

In 1903 two brick barns were constructed to house the exhibition horses. Tragedy struck that year, however, when a fire started in the cattle barn and spread to the fire department building and the temporary grandstand; all was destroyed. In 1906 a building program was launched and five permanent fireproof cattle and horse barns, four brick and steel tile-roof buildings for agricultural, horticultural, dairy, and poultry exhibits, a steel grandstand 410 feet long, and a large machinery building were erected.

One of the most popular events at the Fair is horse racing. In 1909 this tradition was started when the famous Dan Patch and Minor Heir raced at the Missouri State Fair. Livestock shows and racing have been important factors at the Fair, and today Missouri has one of the best horse shows in the country.

The Fair was a showcase for the finest livestock, agriculture, and produce in the state.

Attendance at the Fair in 1924 was a record-breaking 229,103. It was believed this number was so high because that was the first year in 24 years that no rain fell on any day of the Fair. Each year the Fair seemed to get bigger and better and by 1925, when the Fair celebrated its silver anniversary, Missouri was producing better agriculture as well as producing more fine saddle horses than Kentucky, more fine mules than any other state or country in the world, the finest herds of beef and dairy cattle, the finest hogs, sheep, and the best apples in all fruit-producing sections of the country. The Fair was a showcase for the finest livestock, agriculture, and produce in the state. Even today these standards of excellence are maintained.

The State Fairgrounds covers 276 acres of ground with 60 permanent buildings and a dual racing track with one mile and one-half mile tracks. From the glittering lights of the Midway to the rich agricultural products grown in the state, the Missouri State Fair has become one of the best fairs in the country. Each year there is world class entertainment making the Fair brighter than ever. The Fair is held each August in Sedalia. The Missouri State Fair has a slogan that fits the atmosphere: "Meet Me At The Fun." *For more information contact: Missouri State Fair, P.O. Box 111, Sedalia, Mo. 65301. Phone: (816) 826-0570.* ❏

show me stardom

Missouri Film Commission Promotes the Show-Me State

The Missouri Film Commission was created in 1983 to attract film, television, video, and cable productions to Missouri and to promote the film and video production industry in Missouri.

During the first nine months of 1990, the Missouri Film Commission had brought 185 film projects and $30 million into the state's economy. In 1988, the Commission attracted 215 projects that brought in $30.5 million.

Recent films lensed in Missouri have been "White Palace," starring Susan Sarandon and James Spader, and "Mr. and Mrs. Bridge," starring Paul Newman and Joanne Woodward. The Disney Channel aired "Back to Hannibal: The Return of Tom Sawyer and Huckleberry Finn," which was filmed on location in St. Charles, Missouri.

Feature Films and National Television Movies

Across Five Aprils (PBS film)
Adam at 6 A.M. (1970)
American Flyer (1984)
Article 99 (1990)
Back to Hannibal: The Return of Tom Sawyer &
    Huckleberry Finn (1990; Disney channel movie)
Beneath The Laughter (1983; PBS movie)
Blue DeVille (1986; NBC movie)
Bucktown (1974)
The Children Nobody Wanted (1981; TV movie)
The Chisholms (1979; TV movie)
Combat High (1986; NBC movie)
Concrete Cowboys (1979)
Cross of Fire (1989; NBC mini-series)
The Day After (1983; ABC mini-series)
Delirium (1979)
The Dreamer (1978)
Detour (1989)
Escape From New York (1980)
Eye on the Sparrow (1987; NBC movie)
Eyes of Fire (1984)
Except For Me and Thee (TV movie)
Fox Fire Light (1981)
The Great Southwest Bank Robbery (1958)
Hail, Hail, Rock 'n' Roll: The Chuck Berry Story (1986)
The Hoodlum Priest (1961)
Honky (1972)
Huckleberry Finn (1974)

In Cold Blood (1967)
Jesse James (1939)
Kansas (1987)
Life on the Mississippi (1979; mini-series)
Lucas Tanner (1974; TV movie)
Manhunter (1986)
Miss Missouri (1990)
Mr. and Mrs. Bridge (1990)
National Lampoon's Vacation (1983)
Old Explorers (1988)
Paper Lion (1968)
Paper Moon (1973)
Planes, Trains, & Automobiles (1987)
Pleasure of Doing Business (1978)
Prime Cut (1972)
Shepherd of the Hills (1940)
Shepherd of the Hills (1964)
Shoot It: Black – Shoot It: Blue (1974)
Sometimes They Come Back (1990; TV movie)
Stingray (1978)
Thomas Hart Benton (PBS film)
Tom Sawyer (1973)
White Palace (1990)

National Television Series

The Beverly Hillbillies (1962-1971; series)
America By Design (1986; PBS series)
Spirit of Place (1988; PBS Series)
Unsolved Mysteries (series)
Current Affair (series)
Phil Collins (music video)
Lassie (series)
Imagining America (PBS series)

The Missouri Film Commission offers services such as scouting in which they will research any type of location background and arrange the necessary clearances. They also provide pre-production services with detailed information such as film regulations, weather data, crew, talent, transportation and more. The Missouri Film Commission will also act as liaison and production coordinator.

In all, the state has benefited greatly by the efforts of the Missouri Film Commission and the film-making future looks bright for Missouri and its residents. ❏

The American Royal, 1701 American Royal Court, Kansas City, MO 64102.

Blue Springs Chamber of Commerce, P.O. Box 44, Blue Springs 64015.

Boonville Chamber of Commerce, P.O. Box 8, Boonville 65233.

Branson/Lakes Area Chamber of Commerce, P.O. Box 220, Branson 65616.

Cape Girardeau Convention & Visitors Bureau, P.O. Box 98, Cape Girardeau 63702-0098.

Carthage Chamber of Commerce, 107 East Third, Carthage 64836.

Chamber of Commerce of Greater Kansas City, 600 Boatmen's Bank Center, 920 Main St., Kansas City, MO 64105.

Charleston Chamber of Commerce, P.O. Box 407, Charleston 63834.

Chillicothe Area Chamber of Commerce, P.O. Box 407, Chillicothe 64601.

City of Joplin, P.O. Box 1355, Joplin 64802-1355.

City of Versailles, 104 N. Fisher, Versailles 65084.

Clinton Area Chamber of Commerce, 200 S. Main, Clinton 64735.

Columbia Convention and Visitors Bureau, P.O. Box N, Columbia 65205.

Convention and Visitors Bureau of Greater Kansas City, 1100 Main, Suite 2550, Kansas City, MO 64105.

Eminence Area Chamber of Commerce, P.O. Box 415, Eminence 65466.

Farmington Chamber of Commerce, P.O. Box 191, Farmington 63640.

Ferguson Chamber of Commerce, #2 S. Florissant Rd., Ferguson 63135.

Forsyth Chamber of Commerce, P.O. Box 777, Forsyth 65653.

Hannibal Visitors Bureau, P.O. Box 624, Hannibal 63401.

Houston Chamber of Commerce, 103 N. Grand, Houston 65483.

Independence Chamber of Commerce, P.O. Box 147, Independence 64051.

Joplin Chamber of Commerce, P.O. Box 1178, Joplin 64802.

Kahoka Chamber of Commerce, P.O. Box 112, Kahoka 63445.

Kirksville Area Chamber of Commerce, P.O. Box 251, Kirksville 63501.

Lake of the Ozarks Association, P.O. Box 98, Lake Ozark 65049.

Lee's Summit Chamber of Commerce, 610 S. 291 Highway, Lee's Summit 64063.

Lexington Chamber of Commerce, 1127 Main St., Lexington 64067.

Liberty Area Chamber of Commerce, 9 S. Leonard, Liberty 64068.

Louisiana Chamber of Commerce, 209 Georgia St., Louisiana 63353.

Maplewood Chamber of Commerce, 7900 Manchester Ave., Maplewood 63143.

Missouri Division of Tourism, Truman State Office Building, P.O. Box 1055, Jefferson City 65102.

Missouri Film Commission, P.O. Box 118, Jefferson City 65102.

The Missouri State Fair, Box 111, Sedalia 65301.

Monett Chamber of Commerce, P.O. Box 47, Monett 65708.

Paris Area Chamber of Commerce, P.O. Box 75, Paris 65275.

The Plaza Merchant's Association, 4625 Wornall Rd., Kansas City, MO 64112.

Raytown Area Chamber of Commerce, 5909 Raytown Trafficway, Raytown 64133.

Republic Chamber of Commerce, P.O. Box 5, Republic 65738.

Rolla Area Chamber of Commerce, 102 W. 9th, Rolla 65401.

St. Joseph Area Chamber of Commerce, P.O. Box 1394, St. Joseph 64502.

St. Louis Convention & Visitors Bureau, 10 S. Broadway #300, St. Louis 63102.

Ste. Genevieve Tourist Information Office, 66 S. Main, Ste. Genevieve 63670.

Sedalia Area Chamber of Commerce, 113 E. 4th St., Sedalia 65301.

Sikeston Area Chamber of Commerce, P.O. Box 99, Sikeston 63801.

Springfield Convention & Visitors Bureau, 3315 E. Battlefield Rd., Springfield 65804-4048.

Union Area Chamber of Commerce, P. O, Box 168, Union 63084.

Warsaw Area Chamber of Commerce, P.O. Box 264, Warsaw 65355.

CHAPTER 6
BUSINESS

**Major Corporations • Labor Force
Manufacturing • Retail • Services
Transportation • Utilities
Construction • Finance**

Photo courtesy of the Convention and Visitors Bureau of Greater Kansas City.

CHAPTER OPENER PHOTO: The impressive skyline of Kansas City. These skyscrapers are home to some of the most prestigious businesses in the country. Originating as a cattle town, Kansas City is now a major hub of business activity.

F rom hats, shoes, and jeans to telecommunications and aerospace engineering, Missouri offers a diverse business climate.

Missouri's early businesses were limited to river and train traffic. Today, Missouri has unlimited ways to promote business growth.

Twenty-two corporations headquartered in Missouri are listed on the Forbes 500 list of largest companies in the United States. H&R Block, United Telecommunications, and Hallmark Cards, Inc., in Kansas City and Ralston Purina, Monsanto, Anheuser-Busch, and Southwestern Bell in St. Louis are just some of the corporations that have a substantial impact on the state's economy, both in terms of providing jobs and overall productivity.

By far the largest employer in the state is the McDonnell Douglas Corporation. The company is headquartered in St. Louis and employs nearly 35,000 people. McDonnell Douglas designed and built the space capsule that carried the first men into space in the 1960s.

The entrepreneurial spirit lives on in Missouri. Smaller companies have earned national recognition for their products. Did you know that Faultless Starch, Stetson hats, Florsheim shoes, Lee jeans, and La-Z-Boy chairs are all manufactured in Missouri?

Businesses in the state have attracted international attention. The Missouri Department of Economic Development has been working to create new overseas markets for Missouri-produced goods and services. The "Export Missouri" program matches potential Missouri suppliers with sales leads in Europe and Asia. The program enables Missouri companies to enter foreign markets without having to spend large amounts of money to initiate marketing efforts.

The metropolitan areas offer a full range of banking, legal, and consulting services that are essential for corporations. The state's central location enables companies to rapidly ship their products to markets throughout the United States and abroad via air, rail, transport, or waterways.

Some of the most advanced telecommunications companies in the world have headquarters in Missouri. The nearly 400 companies in this industry employ about 40,000 people and the combined payroll exceeds $820 million and generates $1.1 billion in additional income. Missouri also has an impressive fiber optic network, with more than 200,000 fiber miles currently in use.

More than two million workers make up the rapidly growing work force in the state. Although Missouri is not a right-to-work state, it is a "willing-to-work" state. Missourians are hard-working, dedicated people. The labor supply is excellent in Missouri. Wages are competitive when compared with other industrialized states.

Many companies located in Missouri are among the largest and most prestigious in their fields. The state's varied business climate continues to attract new industries and ensures Missouri remains competitive in today's business world. ❑

Circus, Circus — In the late 1800s and early 1900s, Lancaster was the headquarters of "Diamond Billy" Hall, a world-famous animal trader and circus promoter of the period. Known as the "Horse King," he shipped and traded horses, mules, elephants, and other exotic animals all over the world.

Top Hat — The Stetson Hat Co. in St. Joseph is the only Stetson hat manufacturer in the United States. The straw and felt hats are manufactured at St. Joseph and shipped to outlets across the country.

Taxing Times — In 1990, electronic filing went nationwide for the Internal Revenue Service. By the end of April 1990, H&R Block, Inc., and its franchises transmitted 2,998,000 tax returns, 71.6% of all returns filed electronically in the U.S. during the 1990 filing season.

Show Fizz — C.L. Grigg, who was a soft drink salesman and owner of a general store in Missouri, introduced the Bib-Label Lithiated Lemon-Lime Soda in St. Louis in 1929. In 1931 he changed the name of the drink to 7-Up.

Flour Power — Crystal Flour, milled around the turn of the century at Warrensburg, won several awards including the Premium Flour Award at the World's Fair in St. Louis in 1880.

Chicken Out — In 1964, Leong's Tea House in Springfield opened and began featuring the first Cashew Chicken entree. The dish is so popular that there are 6,000 to 8,000 orders prepared daily among 40 locations throughout the city.

Pouring It On — The Atlas Portland Cement Company opened in 1903 and is still producing cement under another ownership. In its early days, it furnished cement for the Panama Canal and the Empire State Building.

The Bottom Line — The Procter & Gamble plant in Cape Girardeau produces Pampers and Luvs disposable diapers.

Major Corporations in the State

Twenty-two major corporations headquartered in Missouri are listed on the Forbes 500 list of largest companies in the United States. These firms represent 13 different industry groups and indicate the significance and diversity of industry in Missouri.

QUICK FACTS:

Kansas City is ranked first nationally in Foreign Trade Zone space.

Source: Forbes, May 1, 1989.

FORBES 500 COMPANIES IN MISSOURI (1): 1988

Firm Name	Location	Industry (2)	Forbes 500 ranking		
			Assets	Sales	Market Value
Anheuser-Busch	St. Louis	Beverages-Alcoholic	188	84	44
Boatmen's Bancshares	St. Louis	Banks-N. Central	111	494	473
Brown Group	St. Louis	Retailing-Apparel	–	424	–
Commerce Bancshares	Kansas City	Banks-N. Central	281	–	–
Emerson Electric	St. Louis	Electrical Equipment	296	117	52
Farm & Home Financial	Nevada	Banks-Thrift Institutions	456	–	–
General Dynamics	St. Louis	Aerospace & Defense	250	72	366
H&R Block	Kansas City	Finance-Services	–	–	319
Interco	St. Louis	Home Furnishings	–	433	–
K.C. Power & Light	Kansas City	Electric Utilities	–	–	–
Marion Merrell Dow	Kansas City	Health-Drugs	–	–	90
May Department Stores	St. Louis	Retail-Department Stores	211	81	91
McDonnell Douglas	St. Louis	Aerospace & Defense	117	36	284
Mercantile Bancorp.	St. Louis	Banks-North Central	235	–	–
Monsanto	St. Louis	Chemicals-Diversified	194	92	72
Ralston Purina	St. Louis	Food Processors	344	119	122
Sigma-Aldrich	St. Louis	Chemicals-Specialized	–	–	396
Southwestern Bell	St. Louis	Telecommunications	84	91	27
Union Electric	St. Louis	Electric Utilities	283	397	218
United Missouri Bancshares	Kansas City	Banks-N. Central	374	–	–
United Telecommunications	Kansas City	Telecommunications	174	106	61
Wetterau	Hazelwood	Food-Wholesalers	–	170	–

(–) did not make 500 list for that category.
(1) The Forbes 500 is an annual publication of Forbes Magazine. The Forbes 500s are a multidimensional look at bigness in corporate America as measured by sales, assets, profits, and market value. To qualify for a Forbes 500 listing a company must be publicly traded, U.S. based and one of the 500 largest firms by sales, profits, assets, and market value. Fiscal year-end results are used for companies with fiscal years ending in November, December, January, and, where available, February. For all other firms, sales profits and cash flow are based on latest 12-month results. Market value is the total capitalization of all classes of common stock and is based on the stock price and the number of shares outstanding as of Dec. 31, 1988. Operating revenues are used for sales. For banks this includes income plus other operating income.
(2) Industry classifications assigned by Forbes Magazine, and indicating primary, but not necessarily only, business of the firm.

QUICK FACTS:

St. Louis' McDonnell Douglas Corp. designed and built the space capsule that carried the first men into space in the 1960s.

Currently, there are approximately 2.1 million people employed in Missouri. This is nearly twice as many as in 1940. As of 1980, 43% of the employed were female, as compared to only 24% in 1940.

Source: U.S. Bureau of the Census.

From 1981-1987, Missouri's per capita income rose an average 6.1% while the U.S. income rose an average of 5.9%.

In 1940, Missouri's manufacturing was first, and trade and service industries second and third in terms of their total employment in Missouri. In 1990, those positions have reversed, with trade occupying the top spot, and service and manufacturing employment in second and third places. From 1940-1990, mining has recorded the most significant decline in its share of employees.

Source: U.S. Bureau of the Census.

MISSOURI EMPLOYMENT BY SEX: 1940-1980

Distribution of Employment

Since 1940, the distribution of employment among various job categories in Missouri has seen many changes. A greater share of professional, clerical and service workers make up the work force today, while the share of farmers, farm laborers, and private household workers has decreased significantly.

MISSOURI EMPLOYMENT BY INDUSTRY: 1940-1980

missouri meerschaum

The Corn Cob Pipe Capital of the World

Washington, Missouri, is known as the "Corn Cob Pipe Capital of the World." The Missouri Meerschaum Company, located in Washington, was started in 1869 and has been making corn cob pipes at the same location ever since then.

Missouri Meerschaum has made millions of corn cob pipes through the years, and their products have attracted the attention of many famous people. The company made all the corn cob pipes for General Douglas MacArthur until his death. General MacArthur preferred a pipe with a 4 1/2" tall bowl and a long stem. Upon getting a new pipe, the General always burned two little circles around the stem. The company sells a pipe like the one General MacArthur used, complete with burn marks on it.

Other famous people who used the corn cob pipes were General John J. Pershing, President Gerald Ford, President Dwight D. Eisenhower, and Carl Sandburg. The company also supplied corn cob pipes for the motion picture "Popeye." The corn cob pipes had to be specially balanced so that they would spin properly.

When the industry began, cobs from an open-pollinated corn were used. Today's pipes are made from a special white hybrid corn developed by the University of Missouri. The variety produces big, thick, tough corn cobs. Several farmers in the Washington area grow the cob corn with seed provided by the company. The farmers are paid a contract price per acre and they keep the corn after it is shelled. Only old, out-of-production shellers dating

Photo courtesy of The Missouri Meerschaum Company.

The original Missouri Meerschaum Company building at Front and Cedar Streets in Washington, Mo., circa 1887.

from the 1930s can be used to do the shelling because the new shellers break up the cobs. The cobs are stored in the upper two levels of the factory for a year or two until they are properly curled and dried.

The company produces 18 different styles of corn cob pipes. Most styles also have a variety of bowl shapes and come with either a bent or straight stem. About 7,000 pipes are produced, packed, and shipped per day to nearly every state as well as foreign countries.

For more information contact: The Missouri Meerschaum Co., P.O. Box 226, Washington, Mo. 63090. Phone: (314) 239-2109. ❑

QUICK FACTS:

Four companies in Springfield make over 25% of all the stretch luxury limousines in the country.

The Bass Pro Shop, with its headquarters in Springfield, is one of the largest outdoor products specialty stores in the country. Millions of sportsmen in every state and foreign countries receive the catalogs.

St. Louis is the nation's third largest rail center.

Source: 1982 & 1987 Census of Manufacturers, Geographic Area Series, U.S. Bureau of the Census.

Climate for Manufacturing

One measure of the strength of a state's manufacturing climate is "value added," or in general terms, the difference between the value of the raw material and the value of the finished product. Value added per employee is also a measure of the productivity of the individual. In 1987, Missouri was fifth among its neighboring states in value added per employee to its manufacturing.

Products Manufactured

The production of transportation equipment is by far Missouri's major manufacturing activity in terms of value added by manufacture. Six other industry groups providing important manufacturing activity in the state include: food products, chemicals, electrical and electronic equipment, fabricated metal products, printing and publishing, and non-electrical machinery. The diverse industrial base assures economic stability.

IMPORTANT PRODUCTS MANUFACTURED IN MISSOURI
1982 & 1987

Industry	Value Added by Manufacturer (million $)	
	1982	1987
Transportation Equipment	4,367.2	6,257.2
Food & Kindred Products	2,501.2	3,218.8
Chemicals & Allied Products	2,202.0	3,445.2
Electronic & Electric Equipment	1,679.2	1,736.0
Fabricated Metal Products	1,507.1	2,221.3
Printing & Publishing	1,181.8	2,031.8
Machinery, except Electrical	1,100.4	1,293.9
Paper & Allied Products	680.3	910.5
Primary Metal Industries	495.8	669.2
Rubber & Misc. Plastics Products	475.1	804.3
Apparel & Other Textile Products	452.0	554.5
Stone, Clay, & Glass Products	420.8	728.6
Leather & Leather Products	409.3	367.6
Furniture & Fixtures	248.9	407.5
Instruments & Related Products	212.1	647.8
Lumber & Wool Products	153.1	286.9
Misc. Manufacturing Industries	143.1	203.9
Petroleum & Coal Products	81.4	(D)
Textile Mill Products	28.2	(D)
ALL INDUSTRIES	**18,339.0**	**25,916.7**

(D) - Withheld to avoid disclosure

Concentrations of Manufacturing

St. Louis County, St. Louis City, and Jackson County (Kansas City) dominate the state in the number of manufacturing employees. Other concentrations occur in Greene County (Springfield), Clay County (Kansas City), St. Charles County (St. Louis), and Jasper County (Joplin). Missouri ranked 16th among 50 states in manufacturing employment in 1988.

TOP 10 COUNTIES IN MANUFACTURING: 1988

RANKING	COUNTY	EMPLOYEES
1.	St. Louis	488,814
2.	Jackson	323,703
3.	St. Louis City	286,102
4.	Greene	93,933
5.	Clay	55,790
6.	St. Charles	53,058
7.	Jasper	40,467
8.	Boone	36,772
9.	Buchanan	32,384
10.	Cape Girardeau	27,572

QUICK FEATURES:

A Square Meal – William H. Danforth, founder of the Ralston Purina Co. in St. Louis, packaged livestock and poultry feed in sacks marked vividly with a uniform red and white checkerboard pattern. He remembered the children of a family in his boyhood who were always clothed from the same bolt of checkered gingham. The checkerboard shirt or dress quickly identified each member of the family. Today, the Purina Checkerboard is one of the most famous trademarks in American business. The company is the world's largest producer of dry dog plus dry and moist cat foods, which are marketed under the Purina brand name.

To Be Ore Not To Be – Pea Ridge Iron Ore Co. operates a large iron ore mine, mill, and pellet plant in Washington County south of Sullivan. It is the only operating underground iron ore plant in the United States.

Source: 1988 County Business Patterns, U.S. Department of Commerce, Bureau of the Census.

QUICK FACTS:

The Ozark Mountain Tea Company started in Old Appleton, Mo., in 1980. An old family recipe inspired their Winter Solstice Tea.

Source: 1991 Missouri Directory of Manufacturers.

Largest Manufacturing Companies

More than 100 manufacturing firms in Missouri have more than 500 employees. All of the top ten largest employers are located in metropolitan St. Louis and Kansas City areas, and the majority of employees in this group are involved with production of transportation equipment (aircraft, automobiles, trucks).

TOP 25 MANUFACTURING FIRMS BY EMPLOYMENT: 1991

Rank	Firm	City	Employment
1.	Allied Signal Aerospace	Kansas City	7,050
2.	Hallmark Cards	Kansas City	6,700
3.	Buick Oldsmobile Cadillac	Wentzville	4,800
4.	Monsanto Company	St. Louis	4,406
5.	Ford Motor Company	Claycomo	4,245
6.	Anheuser Busch	St. Louis	4,100
7.	Marion Merrell Dow	Kansas City	4,000
8.	Chrysler Motors	Fenton	3,817
9.	Ralston Purina	St. Louis	3,300
10.	Ford Motor Company	Hazelwood	2,721
11.	Orbco	Moberly	2,500
12.	McDonnell Douglas Astronautic	St. Charles	2,414
13.	Chrysler Motors	Fenton	2,275
14.	Olin/Lake City Army Ammunition	Independence	2,200
15.	Zenith Electronics	Springfield	2,100
16.	Hussmann Corporation	Bridgeton	2,005
•17.	Brown Group Inc.	Clayton	1,700
•17.	Kansas City Star	Kansas City	1,700
19.	AT&T Microelectronics	Lee's Summit	1,600
20.	MEMC Electronic Materials	St. Peters	1,500
21.	Rival Manufacturing	Kansas City	1,475
22.	Pulitzer Publishing	St. Louis	1,400
23.	Lee, H.D.	Lebanon	1,354
24.	Moog Automotive	St. Louis	1,350
25.	Procter & Gamble	Cape Girardeau	1,325

• Tied

Trends in Manufacturing Employment

Since 1972, total manufacturing employment in Missouri has remained relatively stable, declining only slightly. Major employment increases have occurred among manufacturers producing furniture and fixtures, lumber and wood products, electronic and electrical equipment, and printing and publishing; while major employment decreases have been recorded in stone, clay and glass products, primary metal industries, and fabricated metal products.

Photo courtesy of The Anheuser-Busch Brewery.

A tradition of excellence and company pride assures Anheuser-Busch a top spot as a leader in Missouri business. The brewing area is one part of this large company. The brew kettles have a capacity of approximately 650 barrels of beer. In these large kettles, a blend of imported and domestic hops are added to the wort. There, they are boiled vigorously, allowing the hops to impart their fragrance and delicate flavor.

QUICK FEATURES:

Stiff Reading –
The Faultless Starch Company was founded in 1887 in Kansas City, Mo., and is still in operation. The product's popularity was enhanced when salesman John Nesbitt took wagon loads of the Faultless Starch Books into Texas in the 1890s. He used rubber bands to attach the books to the boxes of starch. The books were designed as a supplement or substitute for school texts and primers, and 36 books were produced from the 1890s to 1930s. The titles included *Mother Goose Rhymes*, *The Owl and the Pussy Cat*, and the *ABC Book*.

Song and Dance –
Before radio and television, the Anheuser-Busch Co. in St. Louis used sheet music to advertise its brands. The company commissioned songs that contained references to the company or Budweiser in the title or lyrics. The song "Budweiser's a Friend of Mine" was introduced in the Ziegfeld Follies of 1907.

QUICK FACTS:

Buster Brown children's shoes were introduced at the 1904 Louisiana Purchase Centennial Exposition (World's Fair). The turnstile was also introduced then.

The first "Hallmark Hall of Fame" presentation was the world premiere of Gian Carlo Menotti's opera "Amahl and the Night Visitors" that aired on NBC-TV on Christmas Eve, 1951. In 1961 Hallmark received the first Emmy ever awarded a sponsor.

Source: County Business Patterns, 1988, U.S. Department of Commerce, Bureau of the Census.

High purity sand for industrial or silica sand use is mined from the St. Peter Sandstone in eastern Missouri.

In 1989, the retail establishments generating the most sales were automotive dealerships and food stores (grocery stores, etc.). The greatest total sales were generated in St. Louis and Kansas City, respectively.

Source: Sales and Marketing Management Magazine, 1989 Survey of Buying Power Data Service, Section 10.

Effects on the State's Economy

Wholesale and retail trade establishments provide more than 530,000 jobs and an annual payroll of over $7.7 billion.

WHOLESALE AND RETAIL TRADE COMPANIES: 1988		
	Establishments	Employees	Annual Payroll ($000)
ALL INDUSTRIES	**42,197**	**533,020**	**7,721,600**
WHOLESALE	**10,511**	**134,950**	**3,404,328**
Durable Goods	6,244	76,463	2,023,437
Nondurable Goods	4,134	50,607	1,136,862
RETAIL	**31,686**	**398,070**	**4,317,272**
Building Materials & Garden Supplies	1,735	15,740	234,637
General Merchandise Stores	785	45,484	448,297
Food Stores	3,458	53,693	565,283
Automotive Dealers & Service Stations	5,519	49,013	832,326
Apparel & Accessory Stores	2,812	21,670	179,286
Furniture & Home Furnishings Stores	2,232	13,962	197,645
Eating & Drinking Places	7,926	135,183	850,966
Miscellaneous Retail	6,862	44,301	518,431

Retail Activity Centers

There are a total of 34,069,784 retail establishments in Missouri. St. Louis has the most with 17,226,344 retail centers. Kansas City is second with 11,823,232 retail centers and Springfield is third largest with 2,039,980.

MISSOURI RETAIL SALES: 1989

DRUGS (2.8%)
BUILDING & HARDWARE (6.6%)
FOOD (20.4%)
GASOLINE STATIONS (9.5%)
EATING & DRINKING (10.6%)
AUTOMOTIVE (26.5%)
GENERAL MERCHANDISE (15.0%)
FURNITURE & APPLIANCE (4.1%)
APPAREL & ACCESSORIES (4.6%)

ESTABLISHMENTS, EMPLOYEES, AND PAYROLL OF SERVICE COMPANIES: 1988

	Establishments	Employees	Annual Payroll ($000)
ALL INDUSTRIES	40,294	544,572	9,192,025
Hotels & Other Lodging Places	1,102	26,130	245,406
Personal Services	4,246	26,349	275,781
Business Services	4,736	80,615	1,276,090
Auto Repair, Services & Garages	3,373	18,742	289,716
Miscellaneous Repair Services	1,366	7,435	136,970
Motion Pictures	671	5,832	65,306
Amusement & Recreation Services	1,526	16,888	269,217
Health Services	8,254	177,144	3,504,538
Legal Services	2,203	13,586	414,649
Educational Services	716	40,672	643,141
Social Services	2,336	37,149	322,216
Museums, Botanical, Zoological Gardens	53	1,114	13,037
Membership Organizations	5,563	47,952	483,136
Engineering & Management Services	3,451	38,007	1,063,395
Miscellaneous Services	514	1,787	33,390

QUICK FACTS:

Missouri is world headquarters to Southwestern Bell Corporation, which opened the advanced Technology Laboratory in St. Louis. The lab brings together telecommunications equipment from manufacturers around the world.

Source: County Business Patterns, 1988, U.S. Department of Commerce, Bureau of the Census.

Service Industries and the Economy

The most important service industries, both in terms of employees and establishments, are health services, business services, and membership organizations. These three service industries comprise more than 55% of the total employment and annual payroll in the services sector of the economy.

Retail sales in the Lake of the Ozark area are now estimated at close to $200 million per year.

Source: Fortune Magazine.

FORTUNE SERVICE 500 COMPANIES IN MISSOURI: 1989

Firm Name	Location	Industry Category	Rank Based On	1989 Rank	1988 Rank	Employees (000)
Boatmen's Bancshares	St. Louis	B	Assets	43	43	8.4
Commerce Bancshares	Kansas City	B	Assets	87	88	3.6
General American Life	St. Louis	C	Assets	37	40	7.8
Kansas City Southern Industries	Kansas City	E	Revenues	31	39	4.1
May Department Stores	St. Louis	D	Sales	9	9	115.0
Mercantile Bancorp.	St. Louis	B	Assets	76	76	4.3
Southwestern Bell	St. Louis	F	Assets	8	8	66.2
Unigroup	Fenton	E	Revenues	31	31	0.9
Union Electric	St. Louis	F	Assets	42	42	7.1
Wetterau	Hazelwood	A	Sales	18	15	14.3

Industry categories and number of firms ranked within each:
A-Diversified service companies; 100 ranked.
B-Commercial banking companies; 100 ranked.
C-Life insurance companies; 50 ranked.
D-Retailing companies; 50 ranked.
E-Transportation companies; 50 ranked.
F-Utilities; 50 ranked.

QUICK FACTS:

The St. Louis Car Company built the first electric streetcar and the first trolley-bus. It was the world's leading streetcar manufacturer at the turn of the century.

Missouri vehicle deaths in 1988: 1,082.

Employment in Transportation, Communications, and Utility Industries

Of the more than 130,000 Missourians employed in this sector, more than 32% work in trucking and warehousing, and 22% in communications. These two industries also account for more than two-thirds of the establishments in this economic sector and over 28% of the annual payroll generated in this economic sector.

ESTABLISHMENTS, EMPLOYEES, AND PAYROLL OF TRANSPORTATION, COMMUNICATIONS, AND UTILITY COMPANIES: 1988

	Establishments	Employees	Annual Payroll ($000)
ALL INDUSTRIES	5,350	136,676	3,696,404
Local & Interurban Passenger Transit	257	7,293	66,794
Trucking & Warehousing	2,826	44,332	998,176
Water Transportation	130	G	D
Transportation by Air	164	J	D
Pipe Lines, Except Natural Gas	19	C	D
Transportation Services	615	6,651	128,549
Communication	852	30,654	981,341
Electric, Gas & Sanitary Services	389	18,143	601,131

C - 100 to 249 employees   D - Withheld to avoid disclosure
G - 1,000 to 2,499 employees   J - 10,000 to 24,999 employees

Source: County Business Patterns, 1988, U.S. Bureau of the Census.

Since 1970, motor vehicle deaths have declined nearly 27% in Missouri.

The Jones Brother's Sale Barn in Warrensburg was the largest mule dealer in the United States during World War I. Some 6,500 mules and horses were shipped out from 1915-1916.

Number of Highway Miles

Missouri ranks second only to Illinois in total miles of urban roads among its neighboring states. The state has over 15,000 miles of urban highway and 104,200 miles of rural highway. Missouri has 7,018 total primary federal-aid highway miles and 1,177 miles of interstate.

Motor Vehicle Registrations

The number of vehicles registered in Missouri has increased by more than 1 million since 1970, and its share of total U.S. vehicle registrations has declined slightly. In 1989, there were 3,844,000 motor vehicles registered in Missouri, which was 2.05% of the total U.S. vehicle registrations.

Electric Energy

Over 80% of Missouri's electrical generation comes from coal, compared to about 57% nationwide. Electricity is generated by investor-owned utilities and rural electric cooperatives. The average residential electric bill for 1,000 kilowatt hours in 1988 was $73.30 in Missouri.

Natural Gas Energy

In 1988, there were 1,178,000 residential gas customers in Missouri. The recorded total sales were 225 trillion Btu. Total revenues in Missouri were $943 million.

Nuclear Power Plant

Missouri's only nuclear power plant is the Union Electric's Callaway Nuclear Plant near Fulton, Mo. The plant has a generating capacity of 1,150 megawatts (net). Power from the Callaway plant is used throughout the company's 24,000 square-mile service area in Missouri, Illinois, and Iowa. The plant went into service in December 1984.

NUCLEAR POWER PLANTS AND THEIR CAPACITIES IN MISSOURI AND NEIGHBORING STATES: 1988

	Number of Units	Net Summer Capacity (mil kW)	Net Generation (mil kWh)
U.S.	108	94.7	526,973
Arkansas	2	1.7	8,895
% of U.S.	1.85%	1.79%	1.69%
Illinois	13	12.6	69,166
% of U.S.	12.04%	13.32%	13.13%
Iowa	1	0.5	3,163
% of U.S.	0.93%	0.53%	0.60%
Kansas	1	1.1	6,650
% of U.S.	0.93%	1.19%	1.26%
MISSOURI	**1**	**1.1**	**8,935**
% of U.S.	**0.93%**	**1.18%**	**1.70%**
Nebraska	2	1.3	6,828
% of U.S.	1.85%	1.32%	1.30%

QUICK FACTS:

Natural gas is delivered through more than 22,000 miles of distribution mains and pipelines in the statewide network. Missouri ranks 18th among the 50 states in miles of natural gas pipeline.

Missouri exports substantial quantities of electrical energy to other states.

More than 100 cities in Missouri operate municipally-run power systems by purchasing or generating power for distribution.

In 1986, Missouri ranked 30th in petroleum consumption, using 240,000 barrels.

Missouri's only nuclear power plant provided a net power generation of almost 9 billion kilowatts in 1990. In a typical year, about one in every four kilowatt-hours of electricity which Union Electric customers use comes from the Callaway Nuclear Plant.

Source: U.S. Energy Information Administration, Electric Power Annual; Inventory of Power Plants in the United States, 1988.

QUICK FACTS:

Costs of Construction

In 1987, total Missouri construction receipts were over $10.1 billion, with over $7 billion from new construction. Industrial buildings and warehouses comprised the largest segment of the building activity, followed by office buildings, and single family residences.

MISSOURI CONSTRUCTION RECEIPTS: 1987
(THOUSANDS OF DOLLARS)

TYPE OF CONSTRUCTION	Total	New Construction	Maintenance & Repair
TOTAL CONSTRUCTION RECEIPTS	10,166,708	7,001,958	1,028,725
BUILDING CONSTRUCTION	8,315,892	5,781,799	756,073
Single Family Houses	2,281,804	1,727,313	227,184
Apartment Bldgs w/ Two or More Apts	368,117	266,757	34,974
Other Residential Buildings	357,478	199,999	22,514
Office & Bank Buildings	1,239,365	901,226	96,929
Farm Buildings	51,585	36,480	10,596
Industrial Buildings & Warehouses	1,563,155	1,027,283	162,116
Stores, Restaurants, Car Garages, etc.	1,062,840	700,959	95,834
Religious Buildings	106,350	52,990	15,168
Educational Buildings	315,869	178,627	34,080
Hospitals & Institutional Buildings	788,361	502,560	37,062
Amusement, Social, & Recreational Bldgs.	79,638	44,267	13,032
Other Nonresidential Buildings	70,076	43,338	6,584
OTHER CONSTRUCTION	1,850,816	1,220,159	272,652
Highways, Streets, & Related Facilities	688,642	421,914	82,609
Bridges, Tunnels, & Elevated Highways	152,813	109,073	13,976
Conservation & Development Construction	13,755	9,596	4,159
Power & Communication Lines, Towers, etc.	89,703	47,471	24,152
Sewers, Water Mains, & Related Projects	283,081	237,993	17,070
Pipeline, Other than Sewer or Water	36,319	(D)	(D)
Sewage & Water Treatment Plants	133,338	105,954	5,226
Mass Transit Construction	49,387	(D)	(D)
Heavy Industrial Facilities	124,677	62,811	31,980
Other Nonbuilding Construction	297,101	148,828	93,480
Construction Work, other	334,365	NA	NA

(D)-data withheld to avoid disclosure of individual firms.

Employment in Finance Sector

More than 128,000 Missourians are employed in the finance, insurance, and real estate sector of the economy. The banking industry is the largest employer. While banks account for 13% of the total number of establishments, they comprise 30% of the employment and nearly 39% of the payroll within this sector.

ESTABLISHMENTS, EMPLOYEES, AND PAYROLL OF FINANCE, INSURANCE, AND REAL ESTATE COMPANIES: 1988			
	Establishments	Employees	Annual Payroll ($000)
ALL INDUSTRIES	**10,353**	**128,712**	**2,972,070**
Depository Institutions	1,366	41,619	797,432
Nondepository Institutions	679	7,662	170,776
Security, Commodity Brokers and Services	413	9,569	367,489
Insurance Carriers	985	29,258	727,976
Insurance Agents, Brokers and Service	2,783	13,085	302,140
Real Estate	3,678	20,584	360,746
Holding and Other Investment Offices	419	4,635	167,263

Total Number of Banking Offices

There are 559 banks with 1,392 banking offices operating in Missouri, with total deposits of approximately $45.9 billion. Banking operations are highly concentrated in St. Louis and Kansas City, with 71.5% of the state's total bank deposits located in these two metropolitan areas.

INSURED BANKS AND DOMESTIC BRANCHES OF FOREIGN BANKS AND THEIR DEPOSITS: 1989			
Metropolitan Statistical Area	Number of Banks	Number of Banking Offices	Total Deposits ($000)
MISSOURI	**559**	**1,392**	**45,944,322**
Columbia	9	27	756,213
Joplin	16	41	833,819
Kansas City (1)	149	347	16,423,662
St. Joseph	6	20	822,132
St. Louis (2)	74	275	16,458,005
Springfield	23	60	1,790,423

(1) This MSA crosses state borders. Figures reflect total MSA.
(2) This MSA crosses state borders. Figures reflect state portion of MSA.

QUICK FACTS:

The average payroll of the more than 10,000 establishments in this economic sector represents an injection of almost $3 billion annually in the Missouri economy.

Among its neighboring states, Missouri leads in banking activity measured although it is only third in number of banks.

Source: 1988 County Business Patterns, U.S. Department of Commerce, Bureau of the Census.

Missouri is the only state with two Federal Reserve banks, which are located in Kansas City and St. Louis.

Missouri's gross state product (GSP) is an aggregate of all economic activity in the state. The GSP has risen from $33.09 billion in 1975 to $92.45 billion in 1988, with an average increase of 8.2% per year.

Source: Operating Banks and Branches Data Book, Federal Deposit Insurance Corporation, June 30, 1989.

Anheuser-Busch Companies, Inc., 1 Busch Place, St. Louis 63118-1852.
Branson/Lakes Area Chamber of Commerce, N. Hwy 75, P.O. Box 220, Branson 65616.
Cape Girardeau Chamber of Commerce, 601 N. Kingshighway, P.O. Box 98, Cape Girardeau 63701.
Chillicothe Industrial Development Corporation, 715 Washington St., P.O. Box 407, Chillicothe 64601.
Economic Development Corporation, 920 Main, Suite 214, Kansas City, MO 64105.
Faultless Starch/Bon Ami Co., 1025 W. 8th St., Kansas City, MO 64101-1207.
Grandview Area Chamber of Commerce, 12500 S. 71 Hwy., #100, Grandview 64030.
Greater Kansas City Chamber of Commerce, 920 Main St., #600, Kansas City, MO 64105.
H & R Block, Corporate Headquarters, 4410 Main St., Kansas City, MO 64111.
Hallmark Cards, Inc., P.O. Box 419580, Kansas City, MO 64141.
Harrisonville Area Chamber of Commerce, 400 E. Mechanic, Harrisonville 64701.
Independence Chamber of Commerce, 213 S. Main, P.O. Box 147, Independence 64052.
Industrial Development Authority of St. Charles County, Missouri, Mid Rivers Office Building, Suite 200, #1 Mid Rivers Drive, St. Peters 63376.
Joplin Chamber of Commerce, 320 E. 4th, P.O. Box 1178, Joplin 64802.
Kansas City Area Economic Development Council, 920 Main St., Suite 600, Kansas City, MO 64105.
Kirksville Area Chamber of Commerce, 209 S. Franklin, P.O. Box 251, Kirksville 63501.
Kirkwood Area Chamber of Commerce, 138 W. Madison, Kirkwood 63122.
Lee's Summit Chamber of Commerce, 610 291 Highway, Lee's Summit 64063.
Liberty Area Chamber of Commerce, 9 S. Leonard, Liberty 64068.
Maryville Chamber of Commerce, 115 E. 4th St., P.O. Box 518, Maryville 64468.
Mid-America Regional Council, 600 Broadway, Suite 300, Kansas City, MO 64105.
Missouri Department of Economic Development, Truman State Office Bldg., P.O. Box 1157, Jefferson City 65102.
Missouri Department of Labor and Industrial Relations, 421 E. Dunklin St., Jefferson City 65104.
Missouri Division of Insurance, P.O. Box 690, Jefferson City 65102.
Missouri Meerschaum Company, P.O. Box 226,Washington 63090.
Missouri State Chamber of Commerce, 428 E. Capitol Ave., P.O. Box 149, Jefferson City 65102.
Missouri State Historical Society, 1020 Lowry St., Jefferson City 65201.
Nevada Area Economic Development Commission, P.O. Box 807, Nevada 64772.
Northland Chamber of Commerce, 1860 Swift #207, North Kansas City, MO 64116.
Ralston Purina Company, Checkerboard Square, St. Louis 63164.
St. Louis County Economic Council, 121 S. Meramec Suite 412, St. Louis 63105.
St. Louis Regional Commerce Association, 100 S. 4th St. #500, St. Louis 63102.
Sedalia Area Chamber of Commerce, 113 E. Fourth St., P.O. Box 1625, Sedalia 65301.
South Kansas City Chamber of Commerce, 1820 W. 91st Place #301, Kansas City, MO 64114.
Springfield Area Chamber of Commerce, 320 N. Jefferson, P.O. Box 1687, Springfield 65801.
Stetson Hats Company, 4500 Stetson Trail, St. Joseph 64501.
Union Electric Company, P.O. Box 620, Fulton 65251.

CHAPTER 7
PLACES

Carthage Feature
Hermann Feature • Jamesport Feature
Ste. Genevieve Feature • Attractions

MISSOURI

PLACES

Photo courtesy of St. Louis Convention and Visitors Commission.

CHAPTER OPENER PHOTO: The spectacular Gateway Arch dominates the St. Louis skyline. The Arch was designed by the late Eero Saarinen and symbolizes St. Louis's role as "Gateway to the West." The Arch stands as high as a 62-story building, and some 5,119 tons of steel and 13,000 cubic yards of concrete have gone into the structure.

North, south, east or west, in every direction some unique place can be discovered in Missouri. One of the first things visitors notice about the state is the variety of landscapes. From the plains of central Missouri to the hills of the Ozarks, visitors and residents are often awestruck by the state's beauty. Beyond the physical beauty of the state there are many places to see. Unusual and sometimes inspiring attractions dot the entire state.

Most people are aware of the popular attractions such as the spectacular Gateway Arch in St. Louis or the Country Club Plaza in Kansas City, but many times it is the smaller towns that hold the key to discovering the real Missouri. Tucked away in the densely covered hillsides or on the open plains, interesting attractions cover Missouri. For visitors who enjoy the outdoors, Missouri offers parks, caves, and some of the most beautiful scenery in the country.

Missouri is widely known for its Ozark region, which is a popular destination for travelers from all over the Midwest. Boating, fishing, canoeing, and hiking are just a few of the recreation activities available in the area. Autumn is a spectacular time to visit the Ozarks, and guests are often treated to a brilliant display of fall foliage.

Missouri offers such a variety of attractions that visitors should never run out of places to see. From the modern attractions such as the St. Louis Science Center to the old time community of Amish at Jamesport and everything in between, Missouri has it.

For the wine connoisseur, Missouri offers some of the best wines in the nation as well as the world. In Hermann, the largest winery in the state is the Stone Hill Winery, which has won numerous gold medals in international competitions. The Bynum Winery in Lone Jack offers a range of wines from sweet to dry. After a hard day on the trail, pull into Weston where the McCormick Distillery offers samples of their products and tours of the buildings.

Theme parks offer activities for the entire family. The past comes alive with live craft demonstrations at Silver Dollar City in Branson. Worlds of Fun in Kansas City and Six Flags Over Mid-America in St. Louis feature roller coasters, water rides, and music shows.

Missouri has 50,000 miles of rivers and 900,000 acres of water, so it's no surprise that water recreation activities are a popular way to cool off during the hot summer months. The state has numerous water parks where family members can be daring and ride white water, shoot the flumes, or relax in the pool.

Anyone who simply wants quiet time to research or read can find an almost unending supply of materials in some of the state's libraries and archives. The Truman Library in Independence and the National Archives in Kansas City offer an abundant amount of materials.

Everything from high-technology to old-fashioned charm can be found in Missouri. All visitors need to do to discover the state's beauty and friendly people is to point in any direction and go. ❐

Jeepers Peepers

Clinton, Missouri, was known as the "The Baby Chick Capital of the World" during the 1930s and 1940s. The Henry County Museum and Cultural Arts Center houses an original incubator, trap nests, and a machine to make egg crates. World War I and II collections are housed there as well as an old loom.

Epitaph Times Three

Paris, Missouri, has a three-section tombstone that was for the three wives of Daniel Dulany. The one inscription at the base of the tombstone was for all three women. The tombstone was listed in Ripley's "Believe It or Not."

Some Like it Hot

St. Clair has two water towers, one marked "Hot" and the other marked "Cold."

The Original Grind

In 1886, Andy Cooper formed a partnership with Albert Jorndt and built the first rolled process flour mill, which was located in Dexter. This was the first mill of this kind in the country and people came from miles around to see it work.

Bloom Town

The lush, rolling land that attracted French farmers to the Florissant Valley in the 18th century inspired the name Florissant, which is taken from "fleurissant," meaning "the flowering or flourishing valley."

Little Sis

Kansas City has six sister cities: Xi'an, China; Kurashiki, Japan; Tainan City, Taiwan; Freetown, Sierra Leone; Seville, Spain; Morelia, Mexico.

Water Works

Mina Sauk Falls in Iron County are the highest waterfalls in Missouri. The main cascade has a drop of 105 feet.

Old Stories

Glasgow has one of the oldest functioning libraries. It was built in 1866.

French Accent

The Bequette-Ribault Farm House in Ste. Genevieve is an example of early French poteaux en terre construction.

Precious Moments

Just outside of Carthage, Missouri, nestled among the dogwood in the beautiful meadows of the Ozarks is the Precious Moments Chapel. A dream of nationally known artist Samuel J. Butcher, this chapel is his expression of love for the Lord and all of the people who appreciate Precious Moments. Sam Butcher moved to Carthage in 1984 and started work on his dream. Inspired by the awesome Sistine Chapel in Rome, Butcher began to painstakingly paint the interior of his chapel.

A delicate touch with the brush gives this chapel a feeling of light and inspiration unlike any in the country. Along the nave of the chapel, Butcher has re-created the Old Testament and the New Testament in square panels in his "Precious Moments" style. The chapel murals cover a total of 5,000 square feet. The painting is done in the deep, rich tones of the Renaissance and appear to glow from within much like the Sistine Chapel.

The ceiling spans 2,600 square feet and holds the largest mural of all: a breathtaking sky mural with angels. Along with the lovely paintings are 15 stained glass windows which are exquisite treasures in the chapel. Some windows have over 1,200 individual pieces of glass.

Photo courtesy of the Precious Moments Chapel.
The Precious Moments Chapel at Carthage.

Their intricate detailing makes them unique in the United States. The murals, stained glass, sculptures, and carvings are all done with a refreshing childlike view of God's word.

Visitors can enjoy a variety of attractions besides the chapel. Stroll through a European Village featuring storybook cottages, a moat and waterfall. There is even an enchanted forest. Butcher's preliminary drawings are displayed in a gallery located on the grounds. Figurines and collectibles are also on sale, and lucky visitors can have them signed by Butcher.

During the holiday season, visitors can enjoy a spectacular display of holiday lights where over 200,000 lights surround the Precious Moments Chapel. The non-denominational chapel is open to the public at no charge. Share in the inspiration of Precious Moments. *For more information call: Convention Center toll-free 1-800-543-7975.* ❑

A Bit of Germany Close to Home

Strategically placed on a hillside beside the mighty Missouri River is a German town with true Old World hospitality. The Germans who founded Hermann, Mo., carefully chose the location of their town site. This area had to remind them of their beloved home in the Rhine Valley. Those pioneers started building a town where authentic German culture could be maintained.

Today, Hermann is a bustling modern town, but the German heritage is still strong in the businesses and people of the area. From the tidy little homes and gardens to the exchange program with a sister city in Germany, Hermann has maintained its Old World values.

Visitors have an array of attractions and activities to choose from in Hermann. Some of the best wineries in the world are located in the rich valleys at Hermann. The wineries offer tours and taste testing. The beautiful historic district has authentic German architecture. For the craft and antique lover, Hermann offers a variety of shops. And the food, served in generous helpings, is an experience visitors have to discover for themselves.

Photo courtesy of Hermann Tourism Group.

The beautiful Stone Hill Winery in Hermann.

Hermann hosts a number of festivals throughout the year, and Octoberfest is perhaps the largest and best known. Take a horse drawn tour for a unique view of the town.

The largest winery in Missouri is Stone Hill Winery. Built in 1847, the winery sits atop a hill. The wine cellars are built into the hillside. There are 12 cellars, named after the 12 Apostles, and they are among the largest in the world. Before Prohibition, Stone Hill was the third largest winery in the world, producing over one million gallons of wine each year. Missouri wines are of such excellent quality that they began overshadowing the European wines at international competitions.

Stroll through the scenic town and let your imagination wander. For a moment, you may think you're in a village on the Rhine. *For more information contact: Visitor Information Center, 306 Market Street, Hermann, Mo. 65041. Phone: (314) 486-2744.* ❏

Step Back In Time

Many people talk about the good old days, but not too many people would give up modern conveniences to re-live those days. In Jamesport, Mo., there is an entire community that would have it no other way.

When coming into this Amish town, people truly feel as though they have traveled back 100 years. Horse and buggies travel the streets, people dress in traditional clothing, and very few modern conveniences are visible. This simple life suits Jamesport just fine. There is an atmosphere of ease and peace.

The Amish people came to the Jamesport area and settled in 1953. The Jamesport area has grown to be the largest settlement in Missouri. The Amish farms are located several miles south and east of Jamesport.

The lives of these Amish people are very similar to that of the farmers 100 years ago. Farming is the main occupation, but there are carpenters, blacksmiths, buggy makers, machinists, and shopkeepers. Most of the work is done in the traditional manner with either gasoline-powered or horse-drawn equipment.

Craft and antique shops offer the well-made works of the Amish. Visitors can take an Amish Country bus tour to get a glimpse of the Amish way of life.

For a time to remember, travel to Jamesport and step into the past to simple pleasures. And if you visit the Amish community, please remember that pictures of the Amish are not allowed as it is against their religious beliefs. *For more information call the Amish Exchange at (816) 684-6412 or City Hall at (816) 684-6111.* ❑

Photo by Carol Ellis, Jamesport Area Chamber of Commerce.
Horse and buggy hitches are a common site in Jamesport.

ste. genevieve

First Permanent Settlement West of the Mississippi

Located 60 miles south of St. Louis is a historic European town, the oldest permanent settlement west of the Mississippi. Ste. Genevieve, Mo., has a strong French influence that is reflected in the architecture and spirit of the community.

Established between 1725 and 1750, Ste. Genevieve has an excellent collection of historic homes and buildings. The original Ste. Genevieve was known by the name of Le Vieux Village or Old Town. It was located about three miles south of the present Ste. Genevieve in what is known as "Le Grand Champ" or Big Field, and was settled as early as 1725.

Some of the finest examples of French Colonial vertical log homes can be found here. These homes were built by the farmers and fur traders who crossed the river from another French town.

The history of Ste. Genevieve spans two centuries. This history can be seen in the homes and businesses in the area, and many are open for tours. The unique European atmosphere generates an excitement and romance for visitors. There are over 50 homes that are around 200 years old. Ste. Genevieve is the only authentic French Colonial town left in the United States.

There are numerous celebrations that run from February to December. One of the most well-known is the annual Jour de Fete in August with the largest craft displays in the area.

For visitors who wish to see life in authentic French flavor, a trip to historic Ste. Genevieve is a must. *For more information about historic Ste. Genevieve contact: Tourist Information Office, 66 S. Main, Ste. Genevieve, Mo., 63670. Phone: (314) 883-7097.* ❏

Sketch by Roscoe Misselhorn. Provided by the Ste. Genevieve Tourist Information Center.
The Gouibourd House, built in 1784, is one of the Ste. Genevieve's oldest homes.

PLACES

Alley Spring

Old Mill. The mill is maintained by the National Park Service as part of the Ozark National Scenic Riverways.

Augusta

Cedar Ridge Winery. The winery is surrounded by Augusta vineyards and the winery features wines ranging from dry European types to sweet dessert wines.
Montelle Winery at Osage Ridge. The scenery from Osage Ridge offers a scenic view of the Missouri River and area. The wine from the area is of excellent quality.
Mount Pleasant Wine Company. Guests can tour the old stone wine cellars, taste wine samples and enjoy homemade bread.

Ballwin

Castlewood State Park. The Meramec River flows through the park, and towering above the river are white limestone bluffs.

Belleview

Elephant Rocks State Park. Granite rocks one billion years old stand end-to-end in this state park.

Bigelow

Big Lake State Park. The 625-acre natural oxbow lake offers fishing and bird watching.

Bonne Terre

Bonne Terre Mine. Heralded as the largest man-made cavern in the world, this 1864 lead mine offers a unique scuba diving experience on weekends. Regular tours are also available.
St. Francois State Park. The park is rich in Civil War lore.

Branson

Shepherd of the Hills Trout Hatchery. The Visitors Center shows a 10-minute slide show about the hatchery. A 3,500 gallon aquarium holds lunker trout and two smaller aquariums contain native Ozark fish.

QUICK FEATURES:

German Town –
The German Settlement Society of Philadelphia was established in 1836 with the express purpose of establishing a colony that would be "characteristically German in every particular." George F. Bayer was sent to purchase land in Missouri for the Society. After choosing the name Hermann, the society drew up a street plan, naming many of the streets in honor of both American and German heroes. The main street of the town was named Market Street and was to be 10 feet wider than the Market Street in Philadelphia because the society believed that someday Hermann would be larger than Philadelphia.

Spanish Sister –
The Country Club Plaza in Kansas City is modeled after Seville, Spain, which is Kansas City's sister city. Two of the Plaza's unique elements, the Seville Light and Giralda Tower, are the exact duplicates of the originals in Seville. They symbolize the spirit of friendship and goodwill that unifies sister cities.

Shepherd of the Hills Homestead. Native Ozarkians re-enact the Ozarks' most famous story in its actual location.

Silver Dollar City. Theme park that re-enacts the late 1800s, including arts, food, and country music. Some of the best craftsmen in the country show their wares throughout the year.

Photo courtesy of Missouri Division of Tourism.
A blacksmith shows his skills at Silver Dollar City.

Stone Hill Winery. Guests can see a free movie on Missouri's wine industry and sample the wines.

Table Rock State Lake. The clear water makes it ideal for underwater scuba adventures.

Blue Springs

Spring Creek Winery. The winery is in a charming 1869 Victorian home that also includes antique shops and a gift shop.

Brighton

Snow Bluff Ski Area. The ski area offers eight slopes ranging from beginner's to advanced ski slopes.

Camdenton

Bridal Cave. Since it was opened to the public in 1948, the cave has been the site of nearly 1,000 weddings. Bridal Cave is noted for its large and naturally colorful onyx formation.

Ha Ha Tonka State Park.
The park is located in the Osage River hills and is a classic example of a topography known as karst, characterized by caves, sinkholes, underground streams, large springs, and natural bridges. The park overlooks the Niangua Arm of the Lake of the Ozarks.

Cameron

Wallace State Park. The park's wooded grounds and lake offer tourists a scenic camping area.

Cape Girardeau

All American Rose Test Garden. The garden, established in 1954, is located in Capaha Park. Approximately 180 different varieties are displayed.

Bollinger Mill. The four-story stone and brick structure is one of Missouri's few remaining grist mills. The 140-foot self-supporting Howe Truss covered bridge is one of four remaining covered bridges in Missouri.

Common Pleas Courthouse. The courthouse, built in 1854, served as the volunteer fire department and a farmer's market in the early days, and slave auctions were located there.

Trail of Tears State Park. The park's name is derived from the federal government's massive forced march of the Cherokee Indians from Georgia and the Carolinas. The park is believed to be where the Indians were forced to cross the Mississippi River during the harsh winter of 1838.

Carthage

Precious Moments Chapel. Murals and stained glass windows are done in the style of Precious Moments. Artist Sam Butcher laid on his back on a scaffold 35 feet in the air while painting the sanctuary ceiling mural.

Red Oak II. A rebuilt 1930s Missouri town is brought to life by artist Lowell Davis. Homes and businesses are refurbished and open to the public. Located outside of Carthage.

QUICK FACTS:

Legend has it the town of Clarksville was chosen to honor William Clark of "Lewis and Clark" fame.

With the completion of the Powersite Dam across White River in 1913, Lake Taneycomo was formed. At the time it was believed to be the largest impoundment of water in the country for the production of electric power. The dam is 1,300 feet in overall length. The spillway is 600 feet long and 50 feet high.

Florissant was originally called St. Ferdinand after a Spanish saint. The name of Florissant became official in 1939.

Burger's Smokehouse in California, Mo., is known nationwide for its exceptional smoked meats. By 1956, they were producing 5,000 hams a year, an amount unheard of for a small, family business.

The theme for Worlds of Fun amusement park in Kansas City is based on Jules Verne's book *Around the World in Eighty Days*.

PLACES
attractions

QUICK FEATURES:

Kingdom of Callaway – Residents of Callaway refer to their home county as "The Kingdom of Callaway." During the Civil War a thin band of local militia met an invading Union force with such guile that the Union commander agreed to a peace treaty. Having negotiated the truce with a representative of the U.S. government, residents proclaimed the sovereignty of "the Kingdom," and never officially rejoined the Union after the Civil War.

Sports Museum – Sports fans can see World Series movies, trophies, and displays on baseball, football, basketball, golf, soccer, Olympics, and hockey at the St. Louis Sports Hall of Fame located in Busch Stadium. Also included is a vast collection of awards presented to St. Louis's own Stan Musial.

Trail of Tears – As a group of weary Cherokee Indians were crossing at Moccasin Springs near Cape Girardeau on a bitter January day, legend says that Princess Otahki, daughter of a Cherokee leader, died following the crossing.

Cassville

Roaring River State Park. More than 20 million gallons of water gush forth daily from Roaring River Spring to form the headwaters of Roaring River. The park is well-known for its trout fishing and fish hatchery.

Chesterfield

Dr. Edmund A. Babler Memorial State Park. A wooded, 2,439-acre park located in the rugged Missouri River hills west of St. Louis.

Chestnutridge

Ozark Vineyard Winery. The winery nurtures the Labrusca grape, which is blended with other varieties to create 10 wines.

Clarksville

Lock and Dam No. 24. The Lock and Dam completed the channelization of the Mississippi River. The observation platform is a perfect place to watch the barge traffic maneuver through the locks or to see the Delta Queen pass through with its calliope playing.

Clinton

Harry S Truman Visitor Center. The Visitor Center is located at Kaysinger Bluff about 160 feet above the waters of Truman Lake. The exhibits commemorate the life of President Truman and document the Truman Reservoir project.

Columbia

Finger Lakes State Park. It is one of two state parks that allows off-road motorcycling.
Rock Bridge Memorial State Park. Devil's Icebox Cave, the natural rock bridge, and numerous sinkholes are part of the large limestone cave system.
University of Missouri. The University of Missouri in Columbia was founded in 1839 and became the first state university west of the Mississippi River. The university is well-known nationally for many of its programs, including the School of Journalism.

Conception

The Basilica of the Immaculate Conception. The Abbey Church building covers 47,504 square feet and features Romanesque style architecture. Construction of the church began in 1882 and ended in 1891.

Cuba

Mt. Pleasant Winery-Abbey Vineyard. Mt. Pleasant is situated on 14 acres and consists of several large buildings made from granite and redwood. Virtually all products sold at the winery are made by select artisans from Missouri.

Dadeville

Stockton State Park. The park offers many water activities and is popular with sailing enthusiasts.

Defiance

Boone County Winery. The winery is situated on a hill overlooking the Missouri River valley and is located in a turn-of-the-century home on property that was originally owned by the Daniel Boone family. The specialty is fruit-flavored wines. Visitors may sample and purchase wine in the tasting room while enjoying the view of the river valley from the deck and terrace.

DeSoto

Washington State Park. The area was once the ceremonial grounds for prehistoric Indians. The petroglyphs, rock carvings that are remnants of the Indian culture, are a unique attraction in the park.

Dutzow

Blumenhof Vineyards. Blumenhof, which translates from German as "Court of Flowers," takes its name from the Blumenberg family's ancestral farm in Germany. The special emphasis is on dry table wines produced from grapes grown in Blumenhof's Warren County vineyards.

QUICK FACTS:

The Judgment Tree that once stood on the property of Daniel Boone in Defiance was where Boone settled disputes between white men and Indians, using truth rather than man-made laws to arrive at just decisions.

Of the four bells originally installed in 1891 in the north tower of the Basilica of the Immaculate Conception, only the smallest remains. Two were replaced after the tornado of 1893 and another in 1940. The largest bell weighing 3800 pounds was acquired in 1940.

The "squirrel cage" in Gallatin was designed as a rotary jail. The idea of a circular jail traces back to an Englishman named Jeremy Bentham, whose panopticon prison was built in 1791. (A panapticon prison is built so that a centrally located guard can see all the prisoners.)

167

QUICK FACTS:

In the Spanish census of 1797 there were 40 people in Florissant; the census of 1950 counted 3,737.

Each month 80,000 rainbow trout are released into Lake Taneycomo. There are 15,000 to 20,000 brown trout released yearly there. In recent years 16-pound rainbow and brown trout have been caught in the lake, now considered to be one of the top trout lakes in the country.

At one time the Hall of Waters was the most ambitious public works administration project to take place in the state of Missouri at $1 million.

The Bonne Terre Mine in St. Francois County is the world's largest man-made cavern and is the only mine in the Ozarks open to visitors.

The first building at the Country Club Plaza in Kansas City was completed in March 1923. The Suydam Building was named after the first tenant. It was later changed to the Mill Creek Building.

East Prairie

Big Oak Tree State Park. The park got its name from giant trees, a number of which have been identified as the largest, or "champions," of their species.

Elvins

St. Joe State Park. Much of the nation's lead ore was extracted from deep shaft mines beneath the park for nearly half a century.

Excelsior Springs

The Elms Resort Hotel. The hotel has been a landmark in Missouri for more than 100 years and includes the famous spa and hot tubs. Many celebrities stayed at the hotel including Harry S Truman on the night he was elected as President of the United States.

Historical Hall of Waters. The Art Deco hall was built in 1937 and was the finest and most complete health resort structure in the United States. Excelsior Springs was the central dispersal site of various kinds of mineral water believed to have medicinal and curative properties.

Florida

Mark Twain Birthplace and State Historic Site. Samuel Clemens was born on Nov. 30, 1835, in a small two-room dwelling that is preserved inside a modern museum. The Mark Twain State Park was established in the 1920s. The main portion of the park, which has attracted visitors for more than 60 years, continues to provide a shady and scenic place for hiking, camping, picnicking, and nature study.

Forsyth

The Swan Creek Bridge. The bridge, near Shadow Rock Park, was placed on the National Register of Historic Places in 1984. It is one span of an original doublespan bridge and was constructed by the Canton Bridge Company, Canton, Ohio, in 1914. It represents a common type of early 20th century truss bridge.

Fulton

Church of St. Mary Aldermanbury. This church at Westminster College dates back to the 12th century in London. The church was dismantled and shipped from London to Fulton, where it was rebuilt as a memorial to Sir Winston Churchill.

Churchill Memorial. Sir Winston Churchill delivered his famous "Iron Curtain" speech on the campus of Westminster College in Fulton in 1976. The event is commemorated with a museum containing Churchill memorabilia and other exhibits.

Gallatin

Adam-Ondi-Ahman. The religious shrine is sacred ground to members of the Mormon church and its followers. According to Joseph Smith, founder of Mormonism, this spot was where Adam offered sacrifices to God after he and Eve had been driven from the Garden of Eden. The site is located just north of Gallatin.

The McDonald Tea Room. The nationally-acclaimed restaurant has continued its tradition of fine food. Virginia McDonald was the first person interviewed by Betty Crocker in a national radio series featuring the most interesting restaurants in the country.

Wooden Wheel. In 1989, a 150-year-old water turbine wheel was discovered accidentally during construction of a bridge near Gallatin. This well-preserved wooden wheel powered the Lewis Mill that was in operation during the Civil War.

Greentop

Western's Meat Market. The award-winning meat market is known for its smoked sausages and Missouri State Championship ring bologna, plus a variety of other fresh meat products.

Hamilton

Birthplace of J.C. Penney. Visitors can tour the birthplace of J.C. Penney, the department store entrepreneur. A museum is also on the grounds.

QUICK FEATURES:

First Steel Bridge – The world's first all-steel bridge was built in Glasgow, Missouri. Construction started in May 1878. The bridge was to have five 314-foot whipple truss spans, with 1,140 feet of approach spans, and 860 feet of wooden trestle. The cost of the bridge was $500,000. Many people believed that steel would not hold like iron and the bridge would collapse. The bridge served adequately for 20 years with no signs of weakness, but the weight and speed of the trains increased. In 1899, a new bridge was built beside the first, and the original was demolished. The 1899 bridge still stands.

Baldknobbers – In 1865, near Chadwick, a vigilante group known as the "Baldknobbers" was formed. Their goal was to make up for the insufficient law enforcement offered by officials in the area. The vigilante group eventually became violent and on May 10, 1889, three Baldknobbers were convicted and hung, attracting national attention.

QUICK FACTS:

Hannibal is still a riverboat town, and excursion trips are available on replica showboats.

Hermann has the only courthouse in the state of Missouri to be built by private funds. Charles D. Eitzen, a local philanthropist, donated $50,000 upon his death to build the Gasconade County Courthouse.

Hannibal

Garth Woodside Mansion. The mansion features one of the few remaining flying staircases which winds up three stories with no visible means of support and handcarved marble mantles.

Mississippi Riverboat Mark Twain. Cruises on the 400-passenger riverboat take guests on a sightseeing cruise complete with commentary about river history, legends, and sights.

Rockcliffe Mansion. When Mark Twain made his last visit to Hannibal in 1902, he was welcomed by The Hannibal Society in Rockcliffe's spacious reception hall. The rooms have been restored and are decorated in "art nouveau." National Historic Site.

Hermann

Bias Vineyards and Winery. The vineyards surrounding the Bias winery date back to 1843. Visitors can tour the vineyards in a golf cart and taste wine samples.

Photo courtesy of Hannibal Visitors and Convention Bureau.
The elegant Rockcliffe Mansion, built 1898-1900, can be seen in Hannibal.

Hermannhof Winery and Vineyards. The winery is a National Historic Site. Tours include visiting the stone and brick arched cellars and working "smokehaus," where authentic German sausage is made the Old World way.

Stone Hill Winery. Stone Hill began to make wine in 1847, and by the turn of the century it had grown to be the third largest winery in the world, producing 1,250,000 gallons a year. During Prohibition, Stone Hill survived by using the cellars to grow mushrooms. In 1965, Stone Hill began to make wine again. The main building is open for touring.

Imperial

Mastodon State Park. Mastodon State Park is one of North America's most important sites for Ice Age men and animals and is the site of an excavation of American Mastodon remains. Ancient specimens and artifacts from the park are on display at the visitor's center.

Independence

Harry S Truman Library. The Harry S Truman Library, which opened in 1957, is the second oldest presidential library in the National Archives and Records Administration. The library's archives contain more than 14 million pages of manuscript material, historical materials, books, photographs, and motion pictures and audio recordings relating to Truman's presidency.

Independence Square Courthouse. Today, the Square contains more than 150 shops and professional services. Harry S Truman began his political career as a Jackson County judge in the 1920s. A 30-minute presentation is available for viewing in the courthouse. The library's archives has papers dating back to the 1840s.

Jackson County Jail and Marshal's Home. The jail was built in 1859 and is the only restored jail in the Midwest. Frank James spent time in this jail while he was awaiting trial in Gallatin, Missouri.

QUICK FACTS:

Houston, Missouri, is the county seat of Texas County.

Hermann's Stone Hill Winery is the home of the mighty Catawba, the Vidal and Villard-Noir, the Norton and Chelois, and the delightful Missouri Riesling grapes. This variety of quality grapes makes wines of character and unique flavor.

The "mystery face" rock has become a growing attraction for people in the Truman Lake area. A boater spotted a large boulder with a mysterious "face" in it. No one knows the age of the face or how it got there.

Ha Ha Tonka is an old Osage Indian name meaning laughing water.

The Jefferson Hotel in Paris, Mo., has hosted several famous people. Harry Truman was a guest at the Jefferson Hotel when he was running for the United States Senate. Norman Rockwell stayed at the hotel for a week when he wrote and drew the "Life of a Country Editor."

QUICK FACTS:

The Mormon Visitor's Center, operated by the Church of Jesus Christ of Latter-day Saints in Independence, contains displays and artifacts of the church.

Jamesport grew to be the biggest shipping point between Kansas City and Chicago. Until 1925, up to 35 or 40 passenger and freight trains passed through Jamesport every day.

Hannibal got its name from Hannibal Creek, a name given to the present Bear Creek by Don Antonio Soulard, Spanish surveyor and general who mapped the area in 1800 for the Spanish government.

St. Louis is the country's second largest inland port, with barge connections to 29 U.S. metropolitan centers and the world via the Mississippi River and the Gulf of Mexico.

Ha Ha Tonka State Park covers approximately 2,440 acres.

The Governor's Mansion was first occupied by Gov. B. Gratz Brown and his family in 1872.

The Kemper Home. The home was built in 1881, and the exterior reflects Queen Anne styling of soft red brick and a slate roof. The house has the original stained glass windows and original wooden shutters hang in the first floor windows.

RLDS Church. The RLDS Auditorium, headquarters of the Reorganized Church of Jesus Christ of Latter-day Saints, is a landmark. The chamber has a 110-rank Aeolian-Skinner organ, one of the largest church organs in the United States.

Truman Depot. The depot figured prominently in the presidential career and 1949 "Whistle Stop" campaign of Harry S Truman. The station lobby has a display of the history about the Missouri Pacific Depot and its importance in Truman's career.

Jackson

Old McKendree Chapel. The chapel is the oldest Protestant church building standing west of the Mississippi River. The church was opened in 1819 and restored in 1970.

St. Louis Iron Mountain & Southern Railway. Passengers can ride the region's only steam passenger train and visit the working craft fair.

Trail of Tears State Park. The towering limestone bluffs above the Mississippi River and the rugged hills are characteristic of this park. A portion of the wilderness was once part of the route known as Trail of Tears.

Jamesport

Amish Community. Visitors can take a bus tour through the Amish community near Jamesport, which is the largest settlement in Missouri. Amish handcrafts and food items are available at shops.

Jefferson City

Governor's Residence. The residence now in use cost nearly $75,000 when it was built and furnished in 1871. The interior features a winding stairway and marble fireplaces.

Missouri Bear. The statue stands guard in front of the Jefferson State Office Building and is an example of the Missouri Bear, an important part of the state seal. Bernard Frazier took a year to chisel the bear from a 24-ton block of Indiana limestone.

Missouri Capitol. The Renaissance-style building covers three acres and includes some 500,000 square feet of floor space. A museum on the first floor contains exhibits on Missouri's history.

Joplin

Sky High Castle. The castle was built from 1927-1930 on the solid chert cliffs and includes a 40-foot turret and battlements along the roof. The native stone castle has nine rooms and a spiral staircase.

Kaiser

Lake of the Ozarks State Park. The 17,152 acre park is Missouri's largest state park and offers boating, camping, and hiking.

Kansas City

The Country Club Plaza. The Plaza occupies 55 acres and 14 square blocks. There are 187 retail and service establishments, over 30 restaurants, 4 financial institutions, and 8 movie theaters. Each Christmas the Plaza is decorated with thousands of lights.

Hallmark Visitors Center. A historical display features flowered postcards and two craftsmen show how Hallmark greeting cards are made.

Liberty Memorial. The Liberty Memorial honors the soldiers of the First World War. Kansas Citians raised $2 million in only 10 days to pay for construction of the Memorial.

National Archives. One of 11 field branches nationally, this archives includes genealogy data, diplomatic dispatches, and war documents.

Oceans of Fun. The water recreation park offers a giant water slide, a wave pool, and more than 35 water-related activities.

QUICK FACTS:

J.C. Nichols purchased the magnificent 300-year-old Seahorse Fountain in Venice, Italy, in 1925 to place in the Country Club Plaza in Kansas City.

After fire destroyed the old Missouri Capitol, a new Renaissance-style building was designed. A total of 721 train carloads of stone were used on the exterior and 44 in the interior of the building.

Worlds of Fun in Kansas City opened May 26, 1973. Since then over 23 million guests have enjoyed the park.

The Gateway Arch in St. Louis is the tallest of America's great monuments. The Arch is 630 feet tall whereas the Statue of Liberty is 305 feet tall, and the Washington Monument is 555 feet tall.

The American Royal in Kansas City is considered to be the nation's largest combined show, featuring a grand parade, western art show, and barbecue contest. The Saddle Horse Show is regarded as one of the nation's three top horse shows.

QUICK FACTS:

The town of Lexington, Missouri, was founded in 1822 by settlers from Lexington, Kentucky; hence the name.

Louisiana, Missouri, is touted by the State Department of Natural Resources as having "the most intact Victorian streetscape in the state of Missouri."

Sikeston has one of two London Fog Factory Stores in Missouri. The other is located at Osage Beach. London Fog offers the finest quality rainwear, jackets, outerwear, toppers and coats for men and women, and at the Factory Stores in Sikeston and Osage Beach these garments are offered at one-half retail price.

The sister city of Carthage is Tunisia, North Africa. The word Carthage is said to mean "new city."

Displayed on the main floor of the capitol building in Jefferson City is a model of the warship Missouri, launched in January 1944. The "Mighty Mo" was the site of the formal surrender of Japan on September 2, 1945.

Truman Sports Complex. The complex is the home of the Kansas City Royals major league baseball team and the Kansas City Chiefs NFL football team. Arrowhead Stadium is a 78,000-seat football facility.

Worlds of Fun. The theme park has 140 rides, shows, and attractions, including a wooden roller coaster, the Timber Wolf.

Photo courtesy of Worlds of Fun.
Cool off on the Fury of the Nile at Worlds of Fun.

Kirksville

Rainbow Basin Ski Area. The ski area has open hill and trail skiing on six slopes, five ski lifts, and ice skating.

Thousand Hills State Park. The park's green hills provide a scenic view.

Knob Noster

Bristle Ridge Vineyard and Winery. The winery offers a variety of wines ranging from a subtle dry white to a bright sweet red.

Knob Noster State Park. Native grasslands are managed to help preserve the landscape.

Laclede

Pershing State Park. The park is a memorial to General John J. Pershing. The park includes forested bottomlands and the wet prairie along Locust Creek.

LaGrange

Wakonda State Park. The park is a favorite among fishing enthusiasts.

Lake Ozark

Casino Pier. The pier is located south of Bagnell Dam, and visitors can take a river cruise on the Lake of the Ozarks.

Laurie

Mary, Mother of the Church Shrine. The shrine honors Mary and mothers everywhere and was created following the designation of Mary as "Mother of the Church" by Pope Paul VI. The open-air shrine is surrounded by landscaping and includes fountains and a waterfall.

Lawson

Watkins Mill State Park. The park is located adjacent to Watkins Woolen Mill, a state historic site. The mill is America's only 19th century textile factory with its original machinery still intact.

Leasburg

Onondaga Cave State Park. Onondaga Cave is well known for the quality and quantity of its formations.

Lebanon

Bennett Spring State Park. The park is centered around one of the Ozark's largest natural springs.

Lexington

Wentworth Military Academy. The Academy has grades 7-12 and a separate Junior College. All students participate in the ROTC program and are a part of a single Cadet Corps encompassing the entire student body.

Liberal

Prairie State Park. The park protects native prairie grasses and prairie animals, including prairie chickens and bison.

Pony Express – One of the most famous men in the overland trade west during the early days of Lexington, Missouri, was Alexander Majors, founder of the Pony Express. His parents brought him to Lafayette County in Missouri when Alexander was five, and he grew up there. In 1848 he began the freighting business with an outfit of six wagons and the necessary ox teams. In 1854, Alexander Majors and William H. Russell of Lexington formed a partnership. In 1857, William B. Waddell, also of Lexington, joined and the firm operated under the name of Russell, Majors and Waddell. The Russell, Majors and Waddell Pony Express Commemorative Plaque is located on the Courthouse lawn in Lexington.

QUICK FACTS:

Marionville is known for its unique white squirrel population.

Southwest Missouri has been under the jurisdiction of six flags: (1) the old flag of the French Bourbon Kings, 1719-1803; (2) the red and gold flag of Spain, 1763-1800; (3) the tri-color of the French Republic, 1800-1803; (4) the United States flag from 1803 on, except for the Civil War; (5) flag of Missouri for a time in 1861; and (6) the stars and bars of the southern Confederacy at several periods during the Civil War.

The first state capitol building in St. Charles housed both House and Senate rooms upstairs, and downstairs was a general store.

At the Battle of Lone Jack both Confederate and Union forces reported 110 casualties.

Crown Center is a $500 million redevelopment project in Kansas City. The complex features hotels, offices, restaurants, and shops with unique atmosphere and was developed by Hallmark Cards.

Liberty

Martha Lafite Thompson Nature Sanctuary. The hiking trails are open every day. Visitors can also tour the Nature Center.

Licking

Reis Winery. The estate winery is located atop the Ozark Plateau at an elevation of 1,350 feet. A 2,600-foot airstrip is available. Visitors can see a spectacular view from Reis, one of the highest vineyard locations in the state. Nearby Montauk State Park offers trout fishing, camping, and lodging.

Lone Jack

Bynum Winery. The Bynum's were among the earliest settlers to that part of the county, and the winery makes both sweet and dry wines.

Macon

Long Branch State Park. Long Branch Lake offers swimming, boating, and fishing on this 2,430-acre park.

Maryville

Nodaway County Courthouse. The courthouse was completed in February 1883. The tower resembles those found in Italy, and a pine cone structure symbolizing eternal life is atop the tower.

Miami

Van Meter State Park. The area was once home of prehistoric Indian tribes. The park is characterized by black walnut trees and wildflowers. Missouri Indians, for whom the state is named, were the last Indian culture to inhabit the area during the 17th and 18th centuries.

Middlebrook

Johnson's Shut-Ins State Park. Swift waters of the Black River flowing around some of the oldest exposed rocks in the nation have formed a series of canyonlike gorges or "shut-ins" in this park.

Montgomery City

Graham Cave State Park. Graham Cave is the principal feature of the state park. Radiocarbon dating has shown the cave was inhabited as long as 10,000 years ago.

Newburg

Onyx Mountain Cave. The cave has an underground river and large dripstone formations of white marble onyx. Some of the onyx was mined about 1890 and was used in public buildings in St. Louis.

Osage Beach

Indian Burial Cave. Attractions include boat rides on an underground river, plus visits to an archeological museum, and an underground waterfall. Guided tours available.

Paris

Union Covered Bridge. The bridge is the only "Burr-arch" covered bridge left in Missouri. The bridge, built in 1871, spans the Elk Fork of the Salt River. The 125-foot long, 17 1/2-foot-wide bridge was built by Joseph C. Elliot for $5,000. It is located five miles west of Paris on Highway 24, four miles south on County Route C and one-fourth mile west on an unmarked asphalt road. The bridge, which spans the South Fork of the Salt River, is closed to traffic but open for public viewing.

Patterson

Sam A. Baker State Park. The park encompasses 5,168 acres of St. Francois Mountain terrain.

Pittsburg

Pomme de Terre State Park. The park is located on the bank of the Pomme de Terre Reservoir. Visitors can fish for muskie.

Rocheport

Les Bourgeois Winery and Vineyards. The winery features Bordeaux-style table wines made from French hybrids and native blends.

QUICK FEATURES:

Longview Legacy – The Longview Farm in Lee's Summit originally had 12 small farms, containing 1,780 acres. The outstanding reputation of Longview Farm's saddle horses has stood through the years with champion stock. Here, R.A. Long, a lumber baron and philanthropist, supervised the construction of 51 buildings in 1914. Among them were a huge harness horse barn, saddle horse barn, half-mile track overlooked by a grandstand and clubhouse to seat 1,000 people, dairy barns, a hotel for unmarried male employees, a residence for the farm manager, homes for employees, blacksmith and carpenter shops, greenhouses, a garage, and a chapel. The mansion is designed with stucco walls and a red tile roof. The stables and other outbuildings at Longview Farm were designed to complement the mansion.

QUICK FACTS:

The Gateway Arch in St. Louis is 630 feet high. Its span is 630 feet. The wall thickness at the base is 3 feet. Its foundation is 45 feet deep, the exterior is made of one-quarter inch stainless steel and the interior is three eighths inch structural steel. The total weight of the arch is 43,000 tons.

Meramec Caverns near Stanton are estimated to be 70 million years old and were opened to the public in 1935. It is claimed that the Jesse James Gang used the caverns as a hideout during their outlaw days.

The notorious outlaw Jesse James was living under an alias of Tom Howard at 1318 Lafayette in St. Joseph when he was killed on April 3, 1882, by Bob Ford, one of his gang members.

The Sedalia stockyards, known as the end of the Rawhide Trail, once handled over 150,000 head of Texas Longhorn cattle enroute to St. Louis.

Rolla

Carver Wine Cellar. Located in the rolling hills of south central Missouri, the winery is known for it premium dry and semi-dry French hybrid wines.

University of Missouri-Rolla Stonehenge. Visitors can see the partial reconstruction of Stonehenge, the ancient megalith located on Salisbury Plain in England.

Rushville

Lewis and Clark State Park. The park is dedicated to Meriwether Lewis and William Clark, who visited this area. Many different birds can be seen in the area, as Lewis and Clark noted in their journal.

St. Charles

Winery of the Little Hills. Located on the cobblestone Main Street of historic St. Charles, the winery was founded in 1860 and overlooks the Missouri River.

St. James

Ferrigno Vineyards and Winery. Visitors can sample nine premium Ferrigno wines.

Heinrichshaus Vineyard and Winery. The winery specializes in producing dry wines and visitors are welcome year-round.

Rosati Winery. Italian immigrants found the lush region reminiscent of the vineyards they left in northern Italy. Rosati is known for its wide variety of sparkling champagnes.

St. James Winery. Sweet, semi-sweet, and dry wines are popular choices at St. James.

St. Joseph

First Street Trolley. Authentic reproductions of turn-of-the-century streetcars traverse the town with scheduled stops at local sites.

Robidoux Row. The houses were built by the city's founder Joseph Robidoux, circa 1850. The units were built as a temporary home for newcomers to St. Joseph.

Spirit of St. Joseph Riverboat. Visitors can take a cruise on the Missouri River.

St. Louis

Anheuser-Busch Brewery Tours. One of the largest breweries in the world, the Anheuser-Busch Brewery was started in 1857. Visitors can tour the brewery and witness the brewing and packing processes, plus see the famous Clydesdale draft horses in their stables. Most of the buildings on the grounds are National Historic Landmarks.

St. Louis Art Museum. The museum was the Fine Arts Palace of the 1904 World's Fair and today is considered among the top ten art museums in the country. The impressive building is guarded by a 47-foot statue of St. Louis the Crusader astride his horse.

Busch Stadium. Home of the National League St. Louis Cardinals. It was officially opened on May 12, 1966. The St. Louis Sports Hall of Fame is located within Busch Stadium.

Gateway Arch. The 630-foot Gateway Arch is the nation's tallest memorial. It commemorates the role St. Louis played during the Westward Expansion. Visitors who ride to the top of the arch are treated to a spectacular view of downtown St. Louis and the Mississippi River. The Museum of Westward Expansion is located under the Gateway Arch.

Grant's Farm. The land was once farmed by President Ulysses S. Grant. Visitors can ride a trackless train through the game preserve and see the restored cabin built by Grant in 1856. Grant called his farm "Hardscrabble" originally.

Missouri Botanical Garden. The botanical gardens were founded in 1859 by Henry Shaw and are now a National Historic Landmark. The gardens include The Climatron, the world's first geodesic domes greenhouses, which houses tropical plants.

Old Courthouse. The Dred Scott case began in the Old Courthouse. Visitors can tour five museum galleries and two restored courtrooms.

Purina Farms. The visitor complex features live pets and domestic animals, educational displays, videos, and live animal demonstrations.

QUICK FEATURES:

Gateway Arch Honors Pioneers – On Feb. 12, 1963, the first stainless steel section of the Gateway Arch in St. Louis was set in place. Nearly two and one-half years later, on Oct. 28, 1965, the last stainless steel section was fitted into place. The arch, symbolizing the "Gateway to the West," honors the pioneers who bravely traveled west in search of new lives.

Tribute to a Dog – Senator George Graham Vest delivered his famous eulogy to a dog at the Old Courthouse in Warrensburg. Senator Vest's "A Tribute to a Dog" was delivered during the *Burden v. Hornsby* court battle in 1870. That eulogy won the case for Charles Burden, whose favorite hound, Drum, was shot by a neighbor. A statue of Old Drum stands on the courthouse lawn in Warrensburg.

QUICK FACTS:

Originally Ste. Genevieve was known as "St. Joachim de Ste. Genevieve."

General Ulysses S. Grant built his home on Grant's Farm in St. Louis in 1856. The front gates of Grant's Farm are featured on Anheuser-Busch advertisements.

During the 1849 gold rush, St. Joseph served as the main outfitting point for wagon trains heading west. It was here that the Pony Express began in 1860. Many colorful characters added flavor to St. Joseph's history, including Jesse James and Eugene Field, whose famed poem "Lovers Lane St. Joe" immortalized the city.

On March 17th, thousands of letters are mailed from the St. Patrick, Mo., post office with their special cancellation.

The geode is a globular rock unattractive on the outside, but when opened it reveals unlimited beauty of crystals in all formations. At one time a geode mine sat among the hills of St. Francisville.

St. Louis Carousel. The carousel, which was hand carved by the Dentzel Co. of Philadelphia circa 1920, has been restored.

St. Louis Cathedral. The St. Louis Cathedral has the finest collection of mosaics in the Western world. Some 9,000 different shades of color and nearly 100 million pieces of stone and glass were used in the mosaics that portray scenes from the Old and New Testaments.

St. Louis Science Center-Forest Park. The Center features the McDonnell Star Theater, hands-on science exhibits, the Discovery Room, Science Showplace, and Science Park.

Six Flags Over Mid-America. The theme park includes rides, entertainment, and attractions for the entire family.

Zoological Park. The zoo is on 83 acres and has more than 2,800 animals living in naturalistic exhibits. Guests can also see the children's zoo and ride on the Zooline Railroad.

Ste. Genevieve

Hawn State Park. The state park is a superb example of the eastern Ozark sandstone country and contains native pines and hardwoods. The 10-mile backpacking trail, Whispering Pines Trail, is a special attraction to the park.

Ste. Genevieve Winery. The winery is in a turn-of-the-century mansion in the French Colonial town of Ste. Genevieve.

Salem

Montauk State Park. The headwaters of the Current River form where the 40 million gallons of water pouring daily from the Montauk Springs meet Pigeon Creek. The park is developed around the springs and the old grist mill, which served as a gathering spot for area settlers in the early 1900s.

Sedalia

Bothwell State Park. The stone Bothwell lodge was a country estate once owned by philanthropist John H. Bothwell and is located on a wooded bluff, now part of the state park.

Sikeston

Lambert's Cafe. The cafe is known for its "throwed rolls" and colorful, festive-like atmosphere.

Springfield

Bass Pro Shop. The 150,000 square feet sporting goods showroom is the world's largest sporting goods store and includes hunting and fishing departments, museum of fish and wildlife exhibits, restaurant, a four-story waterfall, and more.

Exotic Animal Paradise. Visitors travel through a 400 acre, 9-mile park featuring 3,000 exotic animals and rare birds from around the world.

Fantastic Caverns. It is the only cave known to be large enough to permit driving through. Visitors can view unusual rock formations while riding on a jeep-drawn train.

QUICK FEATURES:

A Show of Faith – The 27-foot shrine of Our Lady of the Rivers at Portage des Sioux, Mo., is a tribute to the faith of the townspeople. The monument in the Mississippi River is illuminated at night. The Blessing of the Fleet ceremony is performed at the statue each year. Boats on Alton Lake pass the statue in procession and receive blessings from a Catholic priest.

Photo courtesy of Fantastic Caverns.

Fantastic Caverns is the only all-riding cave tour in North America.

QUICK FACTS:

About 100,000 people visit Fantastic Caverns near Springfield annually.

Not only is Lake Taneycomo the first White River Lake developed but it is the oldest reservoir west of the Mississippi River.

The Bass Pro Shop in Springfield boasts to be the second largest attraction in Missouri following the St. Louis Arch. Known as the "Sportsman's Disney World," the Bass Pro Shop attracts over 3 million visitors annually.

Some of the onyx from the Onyx Mountain Caverns in Newburg was mined around 1890. Many of the public buildings in St. Louis used this onyx.

Stockton is known as the Bluegill Capital of Missouri.

The last Confederate veteran buried in the Confederate Cemetery in Springfield was laid to rest June 12, 1937. The last eligible person to be buried there was Martha Ann Hadden, widow of a Confederate cavalryman. She was buried on May 22, 1964.

Wilson's Creek National Battlefield. The battlefield was the site where Union and Confederate troops struggled to determine Missouri's fate. Visitors can drive through the historic park and each stop has maps and historical information about the battle.

Steelville

Peaceful Bend Vineyard. The wines Meramec, Courtios, and Huzzah are named after local streams that interlace the nearby popular resort area.

Stoutsville

Mark Twain State Park. The park overlooks the Mark Twain Lake.

Sullivan

Meramec State Park. The park's campground borders the spring-fed Meramec River, and hidden in the forest are several springs and more than 30 caves.

Thayer

Grand Gulf State Park. Grand Gulf was created when the ceiling of a giant cave collapsed, and some of the remaining roof forms one of the largest natural bridges in Missouri.

Trenton

Crowder State Park. The park includes an 18-acre stocked lake and several forest trails leading to Thompson River.

Troy

Cuivre River State Park. The park has more than 30 hiking and horseback trails.

Warsaw

Harry S Truman State Park. The park is surrounded by water on three sides and offers a marina, boat ramps, and campgrounds. **"Swinging Bridge."** Built in 1895 for just $2,100. Bridges of other designs were much more expensive to build ranging from $13,000 to $20,000. Each year the Swinging Bridge is decorated for Christmas.

Washburn

O'Vallon Winery. The winery specializes in dry and semi-dry wines.

Washington

Eckert's Sunny Slope Winery and Vineyards. The tasting room is operated from a two-story brick house dating back to the Civil War. The vineyards feature lush French hybrid grapes.

Weston

McCormick Distilling Company. Visitors can see the packaging operation and tour the large barrel houses. The whiskey "breathes" through the wood of the charred oak barrels and is allowed to age from three to ten years. It is the oldest continuously active distillery in the country, and was founded by Stagecoach King Ben Holladay in 1856.

Mission Creek Winery. The winery ferments, ages, and bottles several types of wine in a cellar under the tasting room.

Pirtle's Weston Vineyards. The vineyard operates from historic surroundings in an old church built in 1867. It is one of the few vintners to produce the ancient Mead wine made from a honey recipe.

Weston Bend State Park. The park is located along the Missouri River.

Williamsville

Lake Wappapello State Park. The park offers some of the best fishing in southeast Missouri as well as scenic Ozark terrain.

Wittenburg

Tower Rock. The natural scenic formation juts out of the Mississippi River. The rock was designated a National Landmark by President Ulysses S. Grant.

For more information about travel and tourism in Missouri, contact the Missouri Division of Tourism, Truman State Office Building, P.O. Box 1055, Jefferson City, Mo. 65102. Phone: (314) 751-4133.

QUICK FEATURES:

Tobacco Town – Weston is home to the largest tobacco warehouses west of the Mississippi and is the only town in Missouri where tobacco is grown. Approximately 3 million pounds of burley tobacco cross the New Deal Tobacco Warehouse's floor annually, generating nearly $5 million into the area's economy.

Ozarks Region – The Ozarks region covers about 50,000 square miles with 33,000 square miles being in Missouri, 13,000 in Arkansas, 3,000 in Oklahoma, and 1,000 in Illinois.

Taney County – The county was named in honor of Chief Justice Roger Brooke Taney, who assumed office in 1837 – the year the county was organized. This is the only county in the United States so named. Justice Taney was married to Anne P. Key, sister to Francis Scott Key who composed the national anthem, "The Star Spangled Banner."

Branson/Lakes Area Chamber of Commerce, P.O. Box 220, Branson 65616.
Camdenton Area Chamber of Commerce, Inc., P.O. Box 1375, Camdenton 65020.
Cape Girardeau Convention & Visitors Bureau, P.O. Box 98, Cape Girardeau 63702-0098.
Carthage Chamber of Commerce, 101 S. Madison, Carthage 64836.
Chamber of Commerce of Greater Kansas City, 600 Boatmen's Bank Center, 920 Main St. Kansas City, MO 64105.
City of Joplin, P.O. Box 1355, Joplin 64802-1355.
Clinton Area Chamber of Commerce, 200 S. Main, Clinton 64735.
Convention and Visitors Bureau of Greater Kansas City, 1100 Main, Suite 2550, Kansas City, MO 64105.
Daniel Boone Home, 1868 Highway F, Defiance 63341.
Excelsior Springs Chamber of Commerce, 101 E. Broadway, Excelsior Springs 64024.
Florissant Valley Chamber of Commerce, 1060 Rue St. Catherine, Florissant 63031.
Forsyth Chamber of Commerce, P.O. Box 777, Forsyth 65653.
Gallatin Publishing Co., P.O. Box 37, Gallatin 64640.
Grandview Area Chamber of Commerce, 12500 S. 71 Hwy., #100, Grandview 64030.
Greater Kansas City Chamber of Commerce, 920 Main St., #600, Kansas City, MO 64105.
Hagen, Harry M. **The Complete Missouri Travel Guide**. Missouri Publishing Co., 1984.
Hannibal Visitors Bureau, P.O. Box 624, Hannibal 63401.
Harrisonville Area Chamber of Commerce, 400 E. Mechanic, Harrisonville 64701.
Hermann Area Chamber of Commerce, 115 E. 3rd, Hermann 65041.
Independence Chamber of Commerce, P.O. Box 147, Independence 64051.
Jamesport Community Association, P.O. Box 215, Jamesport 64648.
Joplin Chamber of Commerce, P.O. Box 1178, Joplin 64802.
Kingdom of Callaway Chamber of Commerce, 409 Court St., Fulton 65251.
Kirksville Area Chamber of Commerce, P.O. Box 251, Kirksville 63501.
Lee's Summit Chamber of Commerce, 610 S. 291 Highway, Lee's Summit 64063.
Lee's Summit Journal, P.O. Box 387, Lee's Summit 64063.
Lexington Chamber of Commerce, 1127 Main St., Lexington 64067.
Liberty Area Chamber of Commerce, 9 S. Leonard, Liberty 64068.
Maryville Chamber of Commerce, P.O. Box 518, Maryville 64468.
Missouri Division of Tourism, Truman State Office Building, P.O. Box 1055, Jefferson City 65102.
Paris Area Chamber of Commerce, P.O. Box 75, Paris 65275.
The Plaza Merchant's Association, 4625 Wornall Rd., Kansas City, MO 64112.
Precious Moments Chapel, P.O. Box 802, Carthage 64836.
Rolla Area Chamber of Commerce, 102 W. 9th, Rolla 65401.
St. Charles Chamber of Commerce, 1816 Boonslick Rd., St. Charles 63301.
St. Joseph Area Chamber of Commerce, P.O. Box 1394, St. Joseph 64502.
St. Louis Convention & Visitors Bureau, 10 S. Broadway #300, St. Louis 63102.
Ste. Genevieve Tourist Information Office, 66 S. Main, Ste. Genevieve 63670.
Sedalia Area Chamber of Commerce, 113 E. 4th St., Sedalia 65301.
Springfield Convention & Visitors Bureau, 3315 E. Battlefield Rd., Springfield 65804-4048.
Trenton Area Chamber of Commerce, P.O. Box 84, Trenton 64683.
Warrensburg Chamber of Commerce, 116 N. Holden, Warrensburg 64093.
Warsaw Area Chamber of Commerce, P.O. Box 264, Warsaw 65355.
Weston Development Co., P.O. Box 53, Weston 64098.

CHAPTER 8

LAND

**Agriculture • Rock Formations
Geography • State Parks • Forests
Wildlife • Minerals & Mining
Water • Energy • Climate**

MISSOURI

LAND

Photo by Rob West. Courtesy of Silver Dollar City.

CHAPTER OPENER PHOTO: Beautiful Table Rock Lake winds through the Ozark Mountains near Kimberling City.

M issouri owns the claim to perhaps some of the most beautiful landscapes in the country. The state offers a vast collection of geographical wonders. Visitors and residents are consistently rewarded with breathtaking views. One of the most popular subject matters among artists and writers is the countryside of Missouri.

The state's unique landscape has helped tourism to blossom into a major industry. Throughout the state are many areas specifically designed for the interaction between nature and tourism. For example, Silver Dollar City, one of the most popular fun parks in the state, is nestled amid the Ozark Mountains. Visitors mingle through tree-covered paths to partake in activities. What makes the park so successful is the atmosphere of the peaceful, wooded countryside. This harmony between people and the land has become a vital part of the state's popularity.

Missouri offers some of the finest water recreation areas in the nation. The state has superb waterways and is known for the excellent fishing. For the professional or the amateur, Missouri has some of the best fishing in the world. Sportsmen and women travel from across the country to test Missouri's waters.

From the huge lakes to the peaceful streams of Missouri, visitors discover ever-changing boating and canoeing opportunities. Missouri streams are popular for their crystal clear waters and quality fishing. The major rivers in the state, the Mississippi and the Missouri, spawn the state's economic growth and offer recreational activities.

Missouri offers numerous camping areas with some of the most beautiful views around. The national and state parks contain historical and recreational areas to treat families. There are more parks in the state of Missouri than most of its surrounding states. Visitors who prefer to go off the beaten path can hike many miles through rough or mild terrain without seeing signs of civilization.

Caves are perhaps some of Missouri's finest assets. Missouri has recorded more than 5,000 caves. Missouri has more caves developed for touring than any other state. The striking features found in caves are an attraction for spelunkers of all ages.

Not only does the beautiful land of Missouri offer sensational recreation, but it has made the state a leader economically. The rich soil in the northern part of the state is ideal for farming and ranching. The rocky areas of the south are home of some of the largest deposits of minerals in the world. Today, Missouri's lead ore comes from the southeast part of the state which produces 82% of the nation's total lead production.

Missouri is a naturalist's dream. Anyone familiar with the state can testify that the land is a major attraction. From the smooth plains of the northern section to the rocky hills of the Ozarks, Missouri is a land of contrasts and pleasures for the eye to behold. ❐

Get The Lead Out Missouri is considered the most important producer of lead ore in the world. Total, all-time production is estimated at more than 17 million tons valued at nearly $5 billion.

Cave In There are 5,028 recorded caves scattered throughout 79 counties and the City of St. Louis.

Shore To Shore Lake of the Ozarks has 1,300 miles of shoreline, more than Lake Michigan and along the California coast, and 61,000 acres of water surface.

Bridge The Gap The Kimberling bridge across Table Rock Lake is 1,862 feet long with approaches measuring 1 1/2 miles.

Spring Into Action In Missouri, 15 of the major springs have average flows in excess of 24 million gallons per day, and four of these have average flows in excess of 100 million gallons per day.

Gum Shoe The south and east portions of Missouri have cypress and tupelo gum swamps. Visitors can see the swamp by walking the boardwalk at Mingo National Wildlife Refuge.

A Dirty Job The University of Missouri was the first university to have done research on soil erosion. That field is now on the Historical Register.

Deep Meaning At one time it was thought that caves were formed near the surface of the earth. However, today it is widely accepted that many caves were originally formed deep beneath the earth's surface, well below the water table, in what is called the phreatic zone. The numerous large springs in Missouri are active examples of deep phreatic cavern development.

The Forest Through The Trees The Bootheel area of Missouri was famous for its vast forests of virgin pine that gave rise to lumbering communities in the 1880s and 1890s.

Land Dedicated to Farm Use

As of 1987, nearly 30 million acres of the total Missouri land area was in farms, with more than 19 million acres of farmland as cropland. Total land in farms has decreased 20% since 1950, while cropland acres have risen slightly during the same period.

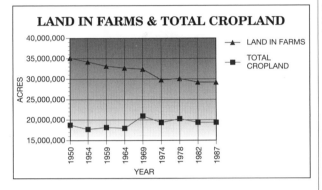

LAND IN FARMS & TOTAL CROPLAND

Size and Number of Missouri Farms

While the number of farms in Missouri has decreased by approximately 59% since 1920, the average size of farms has increased by approximately 43%. During this same time period, the total land acreage in farms has declined only 13%.

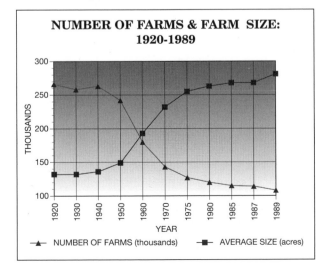

NUMBER OF FARMS & FARM SIZE: 1920-1989

QUICK FACTS:

The phrase "pomme de terre" is French for "apple of the earth," or potato. The Pomme de Terre River was probably named by early French trappers or fur traders for plants resembling potatoes that grew on its banks.

Source: 1982 and 1987 Census of Agriculture-State Data, Table 1, U.S. Department of Commerce, Bureau of the Census.

Ira P. Nash located and surveyed a claim in 1804 upon which Hardenan's Garden was located. Hardenan's Garden was a Botanical Garden and contained many rare plants.

Tomatoes grew exceptionally well in the Ozarks and became known as "Red Gold of the Ozarks."

Source: Missouri Farm Facts, 1971, 1976, 1979, 1982, 1987, 1988, 1990; Census of Agriculture, U.S. Department of Commerce, Bureau of the Census.

agriculture

QUICK FACTS:

In 1988-89, the Missouri crop with the greatest total production value was soybeans, followed by corn and hay.

In 1988, Missouri ranked second nationally in terms of the number of beef cows and cow crop, and among the top 10 states in the production of cattle, and hogs and pigs.

Source: "1990 Missouri Farm Facts," Missouri Department of Agriculture.

Farm Income and Expenses

In 1989, Missouri farms netted nearly $770 million in income. This resulted from over $4.6 billion in cash receipts from marketings and other income, less approximately $4 billion in farm production expenses.

Major Crops Produced in Missouri

The production of soybeans, corn and hay represent the major crop growing activities in Missouri. These three crops comprise 75% of total value of production and represent 63.2% of the total volume of farm production in the state. Also important is the production of cotton in southeast Missouri.

Value of Agricultural Products

In 1988-89, the total value of major Missouri farm products was nearly $2.3 billion. Soybeans accounted for more than 30% of the total, followed by corn, which represented nearly 23% of the total. Other crops that have significant value are hay and winter wheat.

VALUE OF MISSOURI CROP PRODUCTION: 1989

	Value ($000)	Production (000 units)	Price Per Unit ($)	Unit
Corn	516,624	219,840	$2.35	bu
Grain Sorghum	95,914	45,030	$2.13	bu
Soybeans	681,863	123,975	$5.50	bu
Winter Wheat	321,715	86,950	$3.70	bu
Oats	5,940	3,600	$1.65	bu
Rye	252	90	$2.80	bu
Rice	29,167	4,108	$7.10	cwt
Hay	503,918	6,764	$74.50	ton
Cotton	83,541	269	$0.65	lb.
Cottonseed	10,336	109	$95.00	ton
Tobacco	8,856	5,450	$1.62	lb
Apples	6,912	54,000	$0.13	lb
Peaches	1,215	4,500	$0.27	lb
Grapes	1,251	3.60	$347.50	ton
TOTAL	**2,267,504**			

National Ranking for Crop Production

In 1989, Missouri ranked second nationally in terms of production of non-alfalfa hay and all hay, and among the top 10 states in the production of corn for grain, soybeans for beans, sorghum for grain, general hay production, winter wheat, rice and concord grapes.

Highs and Lows in Crop Production

In the history of Missouri agriculture, 1985 through 1987 were bumper years for many crops, with record yield per ounce in sorghum for grain, corn, oats, soybeans, winter wheat, rice and cotton. Similarly, 1934 through 1936 was a low point, with record low production of sorghum, apples and soybeans, and low yields in sorghum, alfalfa hay, and soybeans.

Food Products Manufacturing

Of all food related manufacturing, meat products have historically created the biggest impact, both in terms of jobs and the value of product shipments. Overall, between 1967 and 1987, the greatest percentage gain in value of shipments has been in the dairy products industry.

Livestock Production and Value

More than 4.5 million cattle and 2.7 million hogs were on Missouri farms in 1989. Cash receipts from cattle and hog production was $927 million and $474 million respectively. Turkeys are the principal poultry raised in the state and more than $144 million were earned from their production in 1989.

QUICK FACTS:

Missouri had 108,000 farms in 1989. These farms produced $4 billion of farm marketings.

The average farm size in Missouri in 1989 was 281 acres.

The rolling hills of the Ozarks support substantial beef and dairy enterprises.

Platte County had 1,560 acres of tobacco with a yield of 2,190 pounds per acre in 1989.

Cotton and rice are produced on the delta lands in the southeast portion of the state.

Source: "1990 Missouri Farm Facts," Missouri Department of Agriculture.

TURKEYS: PRODUCTION AND VALUE IN MISSOURI: 1985-1989				
Year	Number Raised 1/ (000-hd)	Pounds Produced 2/ (000-lbs)	Price Per Pound 3/ cents	Value of Production ($000)
1985	12,500	242,500	44.0	106,700
1986	13,500	260,550	45.0	117,248
1987	15,500	310,000	35.0	108,500
1988	16,500	334,950	40.0	133,980
1989	17,250	351,900	41.0	144,279

1/ Based on turkeys placed Sept. 1 previous year through Aug. 31 current year. Excludes young turkeys lost. 2/ Includes home consumption. 3/ Live weight equivalent price.

rock formations

QUICK FACTS:

The "top" of the Missouri Ozarks is in the St. Francois Mountains, an area composed of the oldest rocks in the state.

In the Whispering Pine Wild Area, sandstone dominates the landscape. The Wild Area lies in the midst of the state's oldest and largest exposure of ancient Lamotte coarse-grained sandstone.

Sinkholes, such as the Devil's Ice Box located in Rock Bridge Memorial State Park, result when the roof of a cave collapses. Sometimes a portion of the cave roof will remain after the collapse of the surrounding cave, leaving behind a natural bridge, as in the case at Rock Bridge.

During the Ice Age about one-half million years ago, glaciers pushed down through northern Missouri and flattened the landscape. For the last one-half million years, streams have cut valleys into the hills to create the rugged terrain evident today.

Clifty Hollow Natural Bridge

Clifty Hollow Natural Bridge, located in Maries County northeast of Dixon, is a scenic location for photographers. The natural arch bridge has a span of 40 feet and is 13 feet high. The bridge was mentioned in geological reports of Missouri as early as 1857. The vertical bluffs nearby form a wet-weather waterfall from the top of the bluff. There is a one mile walk to the natural bridge.

Hootentown Natural Arch

The Hootentown Natural Arch stands 80 feet high from base to the crest, 60 feet from base to ceiling. It has a span of 80 feet and varies in width from 5 to 20 feet. Hootentown Natural Arch is one of the largest in Missouri. Trails lead to the top and the base of the Arch. It is located south of Springfield in Stone County.

Tower Rock

Tower Rock, near Wittenburg, is a large limestone rock that dominates the Mississippi River, about 150 feet from shore. Tower Rock is formed of limestone and is about 80 feet high at the normal river level. The sides are jagged due to erosion, but the summit supports a growth of grasses and shrubs. The rock was known to the Indians before the time of Columbus. In 1871, President U.S. Grant set aside Tower Rock for public purposes.

Elephant Rocks

Near Graniteville in Iron County rests numerous elephant sized igneous rocks properly called Elephant Rocks. The billion-year-old granite rocks stand end-to-end like a train of circus elephants. Tons of pink granite have weathered into spherical masses weighing around 160 pounds per cubic foot and standing 20 to 30 feet tall. "Dumbo," one of the largest, has been estimated as weighing 680 tons. It is nearly 27 feet tall, 35 feet long, and 17 feet wide. Just outside Elephant Rocks State Park is the state's oldest recorded granite quarry, which opened in 1869.

The Sinks

The natural bridge, or tunnel, is the only navigable one in Missouri. It is 200 feet long, 30 feet wide, and varies from 12 feet in height down to just a few feet. The natural bridge was formed by Sinking Creek eroding a wall of solid rock to its present level. The beautiful Ozark Mountains are along the bluffs and banks of Sinking Creek. The area has several springs and Lost Silver Cave, which has been linked with legends of buried treasure. The area is located north of Eminence.

Pickle Springs Natural Area

The rocks at Pickle Springs Natural Area, near Farmington, were formed nearly 500 million years ago. Since then, water, ice, rain, wind, and plants have worn away part of the hard sandstone, creating unusual rock formations and deep canyons. This type of sandstone, called Lamotte, outcrops in just a small portion of the St. Francois Mountains.

Visitors who walk the two mile trail through the natural area can see moundlike sandstone formations known as hoodoos or rock pillars. Hoodoos are eroded from jointed or fractured sandstone. The sandstone formations occur in varied and often unusual forms, such as a beehive or mushroom shape.

Johnson's Shut-Ins State Park

The swift waters of the Black River flowing around some of the oldest exposed rocks in the nation have formed a series of canyonlike gorges, called "shut-ins." The rhyolite rocks originated from volcanic eruptions more than one billion years ago. The hard, erosion-resistant rock began as hot molten liquid called magma. As the magma cooled, it became the hard ryholite and granite, which formed part of the earth's original crust. Today, the park is mostly wilderness, and contains more than 900 species of plants and wildflowers. The state park is located north of Lesterville in Reynolds County.

QUICK FEATURES:

Mountain Making – Mudlick Mountain is one of the most prominent exposed ancient domes that form the St. Francois Mountains. These domes began as a liquid called "magma." The St. Francois Mountains also possess unique geologic features known as "shut-ins," which consist of masses of hard, erosion-resistant igneous rocks that remained after softer sedimentary rock was washed away by a down-cutting stream. The result is a canyonlike gorge with solid rock ledges and large igneous boulders along the bottom. Shut-ins can be seen in both Big Creek and Mudlick Hollow.

Devil's Toll Gate – The Toll Gate is on Taum Sauk Mountain southwest of Arcadia in Iron County. The formation is a narrow defile 8 feet wide, 50 feet long, and 30 feet high. The road that passes through the gate was an old military road leading to the Southwest Territory. It is also a portion of the "Trail of Tears."

Source: Missouri Department of Natural Resources.

missouri caves

Caves Offer a World of Discovery

Caves in Missouri have a long tradition of history and folklore. Known informally as "The Cave State," Missouri is second only to Tennessee in the number of caves. In January 1990, the Missouri Department of Natural Resources announced that the 5,000th cave had been recorded in the state, and Governor John Ashcroft declared 1990 as "The Year of the Cave."

Caves are found most in the southern part of the state where there are thick limestone deposits. The caves range in size from more than 30 miles long to less than a foot long. Each cave is different and interesting. Marvel Cave, located within the Silver Dollar City theme park in Branson, is unique because visitors can go up and down the cave's chambers. More than 30 caves have been recorded so far in Meramec State Park. The caves in that area are known for their beautiful decorations. Graham Cave in Graham State Park near Minneola was the site of pre-historic and Indian habitations more than 8,000 years ago.

Photo courtesy of Hannibal Visitors & Convention Bureau.
Discovered in 1819, Mark Twain Cave was Missouri's first show cave. As a child, Mark Twain played in this cave in Hannibal.

While few caves are located in the northern portion of the state, the Mark Twain Cave near Hannibal is known for the extensive mazes that lead throughout the cave. Mark Twain made the cave popular by describing it in his book *The Adventures of Tom Sawyer*.

Ha Ha Tonka State Park is known for its complex of geologic features and formations. Geologically, Ha Ha Tonka is a classic example of "karst" topography, a landscape that is characterized by sinks, caves, underground streams, large springs, and natural bridges. This karst is best represented in the more than 5,000 caves that are known in the state. Eight caves have been recorded so far in Ha Ha Tonka park. The caves and the variety of other karst features make Ha Ha Tonka one of the nation's most important geologic sites.

According to Missouri Department of Natural Resources officials, an average of 140 caves are discovered each year and Missouri has maintained that average for the past 35 years.

For more information contact The Missouri Department of Natural Resources, P.O. Box 176, Jefferson City 65102. ◻

Highest Point of Elevation

The highest point of elevation in Missouri is the Tom Sauk Mountain, which is 1,772 feet high and is located in the St. Francois Mountain area.

Lowest Point of Elevation

The lowest point of elevation in Missouri is located in the "bootheel" on the St. Francis River and is 205 feet. It is the southernmost point in the state and is located where the river leaves the state of Missouri.

QUICK FACTS:

St. Louis is the geographic and population hub of the United States, at the confluence of the Mississippi and Missouri Rivers.

Source: Missouri Department of Natural Resources.

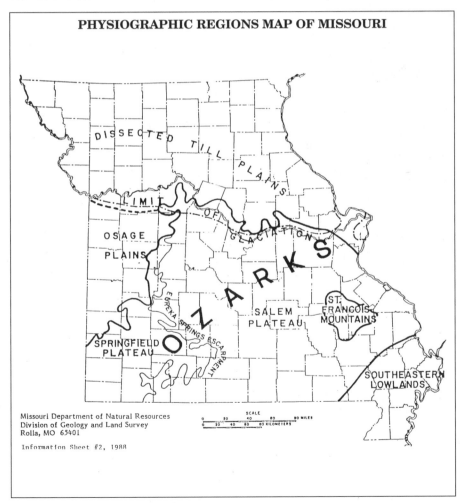

PHYSIOGRAPHIC REGIONS MAP OF MISSOURI

Missouri Department of Natural Resources
Division of Geology and Land Survey
Rolla, MO 65401

Information Sheet #2, 1988

QUICK FACTS:

Ha Ha Tonka State Park covers approximately 2,440 acres.

Lake of the Ozarks State Park is the largest in Missouri's state park system and covers more than 17,000 acres.

Most of Missouri's 5,000 known caves are in the Ozark region of the state.

Big Spring in Ha Ha Tonka State Park, provides 138,982,912 gallons of daily water flow.

The Lake of the Ozarks area boasts five caves: Ozark Caverns, Bridal Cave, Jacob's Cave, Indian Burial Cave, and Fantasy World Caverns.

Missouri has more "show" caves (those developed for touring) than any other state.

Number of state parks and historical sites in Missouri: 75.

Crowder State Park was named for Maj. Gen. Enoch H. Crowder, the Missourian who founded the Selective Service System in 1917.

Photo courtesy of Branson/Lakes Area Chamber of Commerce.

Ozark Mountain Country is paradise for the lover of water sports. Table Rock Lake, with 745 miles of shoreline, is among the cleanest lakes in the United States. It is delightful for skiing and sailing, plus it is one of the top five bass fishing lakes.

Missouri State Forests

There are over 285,000 acres of state forests in Missouri. These range from seven different forests with 160 acres each, to Indian Trail State Forest, with more than 13,000 acres. Lake of the Ozarks State Park is Missouri's largest state park and has more than 80 miles of lake frontage within the park. In addition, Missouri state parks offer approximately 320 miles of trails for backpackers, hikers, cross-country skiers, off-road-vehicle riders, horseback riders, and bike riders.

MISSOURI STATE PARKS

State Park	Town	Acres
Dr. Edmund A. Babler Memorial	Chesterfield	2,439
Sam A. Baker	Patterson	5,168
Bennett Spring	Lebanon	1,404
Big Lake	Bigelow	111
Big Oak Tree	East Prairie	1,004
Bothwell	Sedalia	184
Castlewood	Ballwin	1,780
Crowder	Trenton	673
Cuivre River	Troy	6,251
Elephant Rocks	Belleview	129
Finger Lakes	Columbia	1,123
Graham Cave	Montgomery City	357
Grand Gulf	Thayer	165
Ha Ha Tonka	Camdenton	2,507
Hawn	Ste. Genevieve	3,271
Johnson's Shut-Ins	Middlebrook	2,490
Knob Noster	Knob Noster	3,551
Lake of the Ozarks	Kaiser	17,152
Lake Wappapello	Williamsville	1,854
Lewis and Clark	Rushville	121
Long Branch	Macon	1,834
Mastodon	Imperial	425
Meramec	Sullivan	6,734
Montauk	Salem	1,353
Onondaga Cave	Leasburg	1,317
Pershing	Laclede	2,335
Pomme de Terre	Pittsburg	734
Prairie	Liberal	2,558
Roaring River	Cassville	3,354
Robertsville	Robertsville	1,099
Rock Bridge Memorial	Columbia	2,059
St. Francois	Bonne Terre	2,735
St. Joe	Elvins	8,263
Stockton	Dadeville	2,117
Table Rock	Branson	356
Thousand Hills	Kirksville	3,210
Trail of Tears	Jackson	3,306
Harry S. Truman	Warsaw	1,440
Mark Twain	Stoutsville	2,784
Van Meter	Miami	983
Wakonda	LaGrange	273
Wallace	Cameron	462
Washington	DeSoto	1,415
Watkins Mill	Lawson	1,442
Weston Bend	Weston	1,024

QUICK FACTS:

The Devil's Icebox, in Rock Bridge Memorial State Park near Columbia, is the habitat for the pink planarian, a small flatworm that is not found anywhere else in the world.

There are 151 caves more than one mile in length. Crevice Cave in Perry County is the longest with 28 miles of surveyed passage.

Perry County has the largest total of caves in Missouri: 629.

The seven clear, cold springs in Montauk State Park form the headwaters of the Current River. Regular stocking from a rainbow trout hatchery provides excellent fishing.

Van Meter State Park was once the home of prehistoric Indian tribes. The park is believed to have been inhabited by Indians as early as 10,000 B.C.

Source: Missouri Department of Natural Resources, Division of Parks, Recreation, and Historic Preservation.

QUICK FACTS:

Giant cane, a native grass species, is easily recognized by the bamboolike stem that can grow 25 feet high. Early travelers found they formed extensive and nearly impenetrable thickets or "canebrakes" with stems two to three inches in diameter. The stems were used for fishing rods, pipestems, and even musical flutes.

The pawpaw tree is common and forms groves. Heights can reach 25 to 30 feet. The sweet, fleshy fruits ripen in September. Known as "Missouri bananas," they are best to eat when soft and yellowish gray-green.

The Ozarks contained some of the finest white oak timber anywhere in the country. White Oak was in great demand for railroad ties.

The hilltops of Lake of the Ozarks State Park are the home for the yellow coneflowers that are found in the Missouri Ozarks, and according to recent records, nowhere else in the world.

National Forest System

Missouri has 12 million acres of forest land, of which 1.4 million acres are within the National Forest System. Among neighboring states, only Arkansas has more land within the National Forest System.

NATIONAL FOREST SYSTEM & LANDS* AND OTHER LANDS WITHIN UNIT BOUNDARIES, IN MISSOURI & NEIGHBORING STATES: 1988

	Gross Area Within Boundaries (000 Acres)	National Forest System Lands (000 acres)	Other Lands Within Unit Boundaries (000 acres)	Total Forest Land (000 acres)
U.S.	230,206	190,613	39,593	731,377
Arkansas	3,502	2,485	1,017	16,987
Illinois	840	263	576	4,265
Iowa	0	0	0	1,562
Kansas	116	108	8	1,358
MISSOURI	**3,082**	**1,473**	**1,608**	**12,523**
Nebraska	442	352	90	722

* National Forest System Lands-a nationally significant system of Federally owned units of forest, range, and related land consisting of national forests, purchase units, national grassland, and other lands, waters, and interest in lands which are administrated by the Forest Service or designated for administration through the Forest Service. National Forests-units formally established and permanently set aside and reserved for national forests purpose.

Source: 1990 Statistical Abstract.

Timber/Wood Product Manufacturing

As of 1987, lumber and wood product manufacturing accounted for only about 9,600 employees statewide, producing shipments of slightly more than $602 million. While employment has risen only about 30% since 1967, the value of shipments has more than quadrupled. The largest industries within this sector in terms of both employment and shipments are the sawmills and planing mills, followed by the millwork industry.

Photo courtesy of Branson / Lakes Area Chamber of Commerce.
Ozark Mountain Country has a rich forest life.
Thick groves of trees line the lakes in the area.

Forest Cover

More than 76% of all the forest cover in Missouri is composed of oak-hickory stands. The next largest tree group, oak-pine, comprises only about 4%.

FOREST COVER TYPES IN MISSOURI: 1989	
Tree Type	**(000 acres)**
Shortleaf pine	239.2
Eastern redcedar	237.3
Eastern redcedar - hardwood	587.0
Shortleaf pine - mixed oak	378.0
Oak - hickory	45.7
Post or black oak	2,669.0
White oak - red oak - hickory	5,024.1
White oak	2,988.5
Oak - gum - cypress	114.2
Elm - ash - cottonwood	612.6
Cottonwood	29.3
Hard maple - birch	995.7
Understocked forest land	49.2
TOTAL	**13,969.8**

QUICK FEATURES:

Champion Tree – The enormous black oak in the front yard of the Hanley House in Clayton is a State Champion Tree, accredited by the Missouri Department of Conservation as the largest black oak in Missouri. The tree measures 15 feet in circumference and is estimated to be 300 years old.

Thong Trees – Early Indians marked trails, springs, or caves by means of tree markings. Indians wanting to note a cave or spring would find a sapling about thumb width, usually a white oak. They would take a green-forked limb (called a thong) from another tree and force it into the ground. The sapling would be bent through the fork at right angles. Lower down the trunk the Indians would use another forked limb and invert it in the ground to hold the tree in place. The tree would be bent horizontally to the ground. Thong trees can still be found throughout the Lake of the Ozarks area.

Source: Missouri Department of Conservation.

Missouri Known for Excellent Hunting and Fishing

There are over 3,000 recreational areas in the state of Missouri, and most are small, having less than 10 acres. As a whole there are over 2.8 million acres devoted to recreation. Hunting and fishing are among the most popular outdoor activities.

For the hunter, a wide range of game is available due to Missouri's rich lands. White-tailed deer, turkey, squirrel, rabbit, quail, and duck are favorites among sportsmen. Missouri's bird populations have been increasing; therefore, allowing better hunting. The season for quail in Missouri is November 1 to January 15 with a daily limit of eight and a possession limit of 16. The quail population in Missouri has steadily increased since 1984-1985. For pheasant, the season runs from November 1 to January 15 in the northwestern part of the state with a limit of four males. In the southeastern part of Missouri the season runs from December 1 to December 12 with a limit of one male. The number of turkeys harvested in 1988 was approximately one-third the number of permits issued.

Missouri's quail population has steadily increased since 1984-1985.

For hunters, white-tailed deer is a challenge. In 1987, during firearms season, a total of 132,500 deer were harvested. The length of season and other regulations usually is announced in July. For resident firearms a deer permit will cost $10, and resident archer deer and turkey permits cost $12. For nonresident firearms a deer permit will cost $100, and for nonresident archers a permit is $75.

Missouri is famous for its fishing, and an abundance of fish is available in the state. Lakes provide large quantities of bass, crappie, walleye, muskellunge, catfish, and more. Streams have been stocked with record trout and sportsmen travel nationwide to fish Missouri streams. A resident season fishing permit costs $8 and for an additional $6 residents can purchase a trout stamp and enjoy some of the finest trout fishing in the country.

The Missouri Department of Conservation is helping supplement the existing fish population in Missouri by continuously stocking area lakes and streams with new fish. Fish hatcheries such as Roaring River Hatchery raise quality fish to stock the state's waterways and continue the tradition of great Missouri fishing.

Visitors from around the world find Missouri to be one of the richest areas for hunting and fishing. The balance of a healthy environment and careful management will ensure good fishing and hunting opportunities for years to come. With the collective efforts of individuals and groups such as the Missouri Department of Conservation, wildlife will continue to thrive in the state – and provide a challenge for outdoor enthusiasts of all ages. ❏

MISSOURI ENDANGERED AND RARE SPECIES

FISH
Southern brook
  lamprey (R)
American brook
  lamprey (R)
Lake sturgeon (E)
Pallid sturgeon (E)
Alabama shad (R)
Central mudminnow (E)
Alligator gar (R)
Northern Pike (R)
Cypress minnow (E)
Sturgeon chub (R)
Sicklefin chub (R)
Blacknose shiner (R)
Taillight shiner (E)
Sabine shiner (E)
Eastern slim minnow (R)
Brassy minnow (R)
Lake chubsucker (R)
Highfin carpsucker (R)
Ozark cavefish (E)
Spring cavefish (E)
Brown bullhead (R)
Mountain madtom (E)
Neosho madtom (E)
Mooneye (R)
Plains killifish (R)
Bantam sunfish (R)
Trout-perch (R)
Arkansas darter (R)
Crystal darter (E)
Swamp darter (E)
Harlequin darter (E)
Niangua darter (R)
Goldstripe darter (E)
Redfin darter (E)

Bluestripe darter (R)
Longnose darter (E)
Stargazing darter (R)

AMPHIBIANS
Oklahoma salamander (R)
Four-toed salamander (R)
Mole salamander (R)
Illinois chorus frog (R)
Northern leopard frog (R)
Wood frog (R)
Eastern spadefoot (R)

REPTILES
Alligator snapping
  turtle (R)
Yellow mud turtle (E)
Illinois mud turtle (E)
Western chicken turtle (E)
Blanding's turtle (E)
Great Plains skink (R)
Texas horned lizard (R)
Northern scarlet
  snake (R)
Western fox snake (E)
Dusty hognose snake (R)
Plains hognose snake (R)
Western smooth green
  snake (E)
Eastern massasauga (E)
Western massasauga (E)

BIRDS
American bittern (E)
Little blue heron (R)
Snowy egret (E)
Black-crowned night-
  heron (R)
Cooper's hawk (R)

Sharp-shinned hawk (R)
Swainson's hawk (E)
Northern harrier (E)
Mississippi kite (R)
Bald eagle (E)
Greater prairie-
  chicken (R)
Pied-billed grebe (R)
King rail (E)
Interior least tern (E)
Barn-owl (R)
Short-eared owl (E)
Bachman's sparrow (E)
Henslow's sparrow (R)
Common moorhen (R)
Swainson's warbler (E)
Yellow-headed
  blackbird (R)

MAMMALS
Plains harvest mouse (R)
Eastern spotted skunk (E)
Gray bat (E)
Small-footed bat (R)
Indiana bat (E)
Black-tailed jackrabbit (E)
Swamp rabbit (R)
Black bear (R)
Long-tailed weasel (R)

(R) = Rare; present in small
  numbers in Missouri.
(E) = Endangered; indicates
  survival in Missouri is in
  immediate jeopardy.

*Source: "Checklist of Rare
and Endangered Species of
Missouri," 1991, Missouri
Department of Conservation.*

Endangered Species

The Missouri Department of Conservation lists 88 species of wildlife that are rare or endangered. Of this number, 38 species are classified as endangered and 50 species are rare and present only in small numbers in Missouri. The 38 endangered species encompass vertebrates, birds, reptiles, mammals, and amphibians.

Pomme de Terre Lake is the only lake with a muskie stocking program in progress. The muskellunge, or muskies, are a member of the pike family.

QUICK FACTS:

The total value of non-fuel mineral production in Missouri in 1988 was nearly $968 million. Portland cement, crushed stone, and lead represent nearly 68% of the total value.

Source: "Minerals Yearbook," Vol. II, Area Reports-Domestic; Years 1988, 1986, 1980, 1975, 1970, U.S. Department of the Interior, Bureau of Mines.

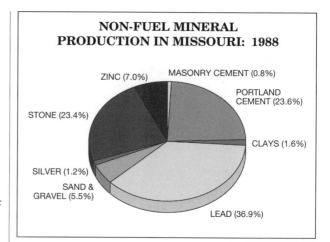

NON-FUEL MINERAL PRODUCTION IN MISSOURI: 1988

ZINC (7.0%)
MASONRY CEMENT (0.8%)
PORTLAND CEMENT (23.6%)
STONE (23.4%)
CLAYS (1.6%)
SILVER (1.2%)
SAND & GRAVEL (5.5%)
LEAD (36.9%)

Today, all of Missouri's lead production comes from the Viburnum Trend district, a very narrow, 35-mile-long ore district in southeast Missouri. In 1989, eight Missouri mines in the region produced a total of 407,000 tons of lead (82% of the U. S. total) valued at more than $326 million.

Source: County Business Patterns, 1988, U.S. Department of Commerce, Bureau of the Census.

Non-fuel Minerals Production

The principal non-fuel mineral products in Missouri in 1988 were Portland cement, crushed stone, and lead. While these have remained the primary products during the past 20 years, the value of Portland cement and crushed stone has increased significantly. Among neighboring states, Missouri leads in total value of mineral production and is ranked twelfth nationally.

Mining Industries and the Economy

Mining industries account for more than 5,428 jobs in Missouri, and provide an annual payroll of more than $179 million. The nonmetallic minerals industries comprise 52% of the employment and 42% of the payroll of total mining industries.

MINING ACTIVITY IN MISSOURI: 1988

	Establishments	Employees	Annual Payroll ($000)
ALL MINING INDUSTRIES	323	5,428	179,5111
Metal Mining	15	948	35,196
Coal Mining	10	(F)	(D)
Oil & Gas Extraction	47	(E)	(D)
Nonmetallic Minerals, Except Fuels	238	2,806	76,253
Other	13		

(E) 250-499 employees (F) 500-999 employees (D) Withheld to avoid disclosure of individual firms

Water Consumption

Missouri's per capita water consumption totals about 1,210 gallons per day. Compared to neighboring states, only Iowa uses less water per day than Missouri on a per capita basis. Most of Missouri's water use comes from surface water sources, and most is used for thermo-electric generation.

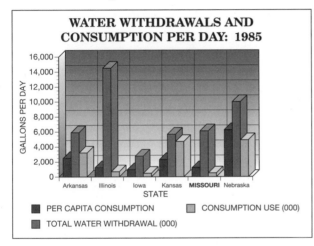

WATER WITHDRAWALS AND CONSUMPTION PER DAY: 1985

GALLONS PER DAY

STATE: Arkansas, Illinois, Iowa, Kansas, **MISSOURI**, Nebraska

- PER CAPITA CONSUMPTION
- CONSUMPTION USE (000)
- TOTAL WATER WITHDRAWAL (000)

Water Use

The principal use of Missouri's water resources is for power generation, coming primarily from surface water resources. The heaviest use of ground water is for irrigation. Ground water resources account for only about 10% of all water use in Missouri.

WATER USE IN MISSOURI
(MILLIONS OF GALLONS, ESTIMATED, 1985)

	Total Use
Agricultural	14,892
Self-Supplied Domestic	19,360
Self-Supplied Commercial	6,231
Self-Supplied Industrial	32,266
Irrigation	111,690
Mining	10,074
Power	1,799,450
Public Water Supply	235,425
TOTAL	**2,229,388**

LAND
energy

QUICK FACTS:

Bagnell Dam generates enough electricity to meet the household needs of 225,000 persons.

Missouri has an estimated 50 billion tons of coal lying beneath the surface.

In 1988, Missouri produced 4,057,957 tons of coal.

Source: Missouri Department of Natural Resources, Division of Geology and Land Survey; Energy Information Administration; Department of the Army Corps of Engineers, Kansas City District.

Missouri exports substantial quantities of electrical energy to other states.

Missouri's energy needs are supplied predominantly by petroleum. Missouri has the second highest energy consumption per capita among its neighboring states.

Source: Statistical Abstract of the United States, U.S. Department of Commerce, Bureau of the Census, Table 943.

Energy Sources

Since 1950, Missouri has recorded an increase in all types of energy production. Coal production has increased 35% during the 1950-1988 period. Crude oil production has doubled since 1978, and hydroelectric energy produced in 1988 is more than four times what it was in 1974.

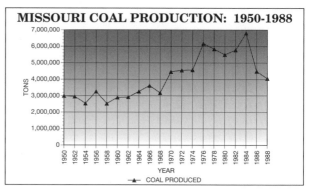

MISSOURI COAL PRODUCTION: 1950-1988

Crude Oil Production

Unlike most of its neighboring states, Missouri produces almost no crude oil, and only shows production after 1978.

Natural Gas Production

Unlike most of its neighboring states, Missouri produces almost no natural gas, and only records production figures after 1984.

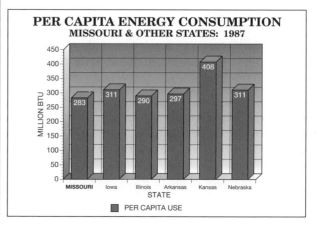

PER CAPITA ENERGY CONSUMPTION
MISSOURI & OTHER STATES: 1987

Tornadoes

On average, there are 27 tornadoes each year in Missouri, resulting in 2 deaths and 51 injuries. Since 1959, the most severe tornado year occurred in 1973, with 79 separate tornadoes. However, the 70 tornadoes in 1967 were more damaging, resulting in 8 deaths and more than 300 injuries.

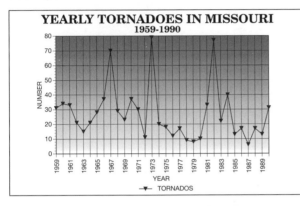

YEARLY TORNADOES IN MISSOURI
1959-1990

Temperatures and Precipitation

Of the nine reporting stations listed for which there is complete data, yearly precipitation in 1988 was lowest in Kansas City, with slightly more than 24 inches, and was highest in Popular Bluff, with almost 51 inches. St. Louis had the high average temperature for the year, with 82.7 degrees Fahrenheit in August, while Maryville had the low average temperature, with 21.9 degrees in January.

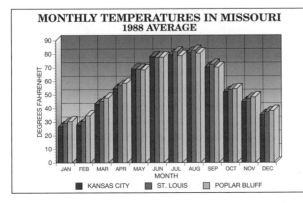

MONTHLY TEMPERATURES IN MISSOURI
1988 AVERAGE

QUICK FACTS:

Eleven miles southwest of Joplin, near the Tri-State marker where Oklahoma, Kansas, and Missouri meet, a "spirit" is said to appear nightly. Called the Hornet Ghost Light or Spook Light, the phenomenon has appeared every evening for the past 70 or more years. The light has been described as "a bobbing lantern," "a bouncing light on the road," and "white light which changes colors or splits into two or three lights."

Source: National Severe Storm Forecasting Center.

On Dec. 16, 1811, the inhabitants of New Madrid, Missouri, were startled by the first of a series of violent earthquakes. During the quakes many swamps and lakes were pushed upward and almost dried up, and the site of New Madrid settled 15 feet.

The coldest month in Missouri is January, with an average high temperature of 27 degrees Fahrenheit.

Source: U.S. Department of Commerce, National Oceanic and Atmospheric Administration, Environmental Data and Information Service.

Bolivar Area Chamber of Commerce, P.O. Box 202, Bolivar 65613.

Camdenton Area Chamber of Commerce, P.O. Box 1375, Camdenton 65020.

Excelsior Springs Chamber of Commerce, 101 E. Broadway, Excelsior Springs 64024.

Joplin Convention & Visitors Bureau, P.O. Box 1355, Joplin 64801.

Lake of the Ozarks Association, P.O. Box 98, Lake Ozark 65049.

Lake of the Ozarks West Chamber of Commerce, P.O. Box 555, Sunrise Beach 65079.

Missouri Crop and Livestock Reporting Service, P.O. Box L, Columbia 65205.

Missouri Department of Agriculture, P.O. Box 630, Jefferson City 65102.

Missouri Department of Conservation, 2901 W. Truman Blvd., P.O. Box 180, Jefferson City 65101.

Missouri Department of Economic Development, P.O. Box 1157, Jefferson City 65101.

Missouri Department of Natural Resources, Division of Geology and Land Survey, P.O. Box 250, Rolla 65401.

Missouri Department of Natural Resources, P.O. Box 176, Jefferson City 65102.

"Missouri State Parks and Historic Sites," Missouri Department of Natural Resources, Division of Parks, Recreation, and Historic Preservation, P.O. Box 176, Jefferson City 65102.

Paris Area Chamber of Commerce, P.O. Box 75, Paris 65275.

Piedmont Chamber of Commerce, P.O. Box 101, Piedmont 63957.

"A Profile of Missouri Agriculture, 1988," Missouri Agricultural Statistics Office, P.O. Box L, Columbia 65205.

Ripley Area Chamber of Commerce, P.O. Box 368, Doniphan 63935.

Sikeston Chamber of Commerce, P.O. Box 99, Sikeston 63801.

Silver Dollar City, Branson 65616.

Table Rock/Kimberling City Area Chamber of Commerce, P.O. Box 485, Kimberling City 65686.

Van Buren Chamber of Commerce, P.O. Box 356, Van Buren 63965.

"Wildlife Code of Missouri Rules of the Conservation Commission, January 1, 1991," Missouri Department of Conservation, P.O. Box 180, Jefferson City 65102.

index